COLLECTED POEMS

COLLECTED POEMS

PETER PORTER

Oxford New York Melbourne

OXFORD UNIVERSITY PRESS

1983

821
POR
POR

Oxford University Press, Walton Street, Oxford OX2 6DP

London Glasgow New York Toronto
Delhi Bombay Calcutta Madras Karachi
Kuala Lumpur Singapore Hong Kong Tokyo
Nairobi Dar es Salaam Cape Town
Melbourne Auckland

and associates in
Beirut Berlin Ibadan Mexico City Nicosia

Oxford is a trade mark of Oxford University Press

British Library Cataloguing in Publication Data

Porter, Peter
Collected poems.
I. Title
821'.914
ISBN 0-19-211948-6

Printed in Great Britain
by Butler and Tanner Ltd.,
Frome, Somerset

284040

Preface

This book includes the great majority of poems I have published over a period of twenty years, beginning with my first book, *Once Bitten, Twice Bitten* in 1961, up until *English Subtitles* (1981). I have done very little selecting or rewriting, confining myself to the exclusion of pieces which strike me now as overstepping even the most relaxed bounds of proprietary tolerance, or which have proved to contain mistakes or untruths. In this I have been guided by Louis MacNeice's exemplary recommendation, that the poet faced with collecting his past utterance is well advised to 'leave even not-so-well alone'. Reading through the many pages of this book, I have often been visited by feelings of disapproval of my gauche or cocky past self, but I do not want to act the prig to the man who wrote these poems.

The poems are grouped chronologically under the titles of the eight books in which they originally appeared. Between the first two books I have reprinted some of the poems that made up my representation in *Penguin Modern Poets No. 2* (1962), and also 'Eat Early Earthapples' which appeared in *A Group Anthology* (1963); three other poems, previously uncollected but printed in magazines, are added at the end of sections at the appropriate date.

The versions from the Latin, *After Martial* (1972), are taken out of the order of original publication and, being translations, placed at the end.

I am grateful to Scorpion Press, publishers of my first three books, both for giving me the right to reprint my early work, and for having taken me on in the first place; and to Oxford University Press for persisting with me as far as this present omnibus undertaking.

P.P.

Contents

ix

English Subtitles (1981)

For my daughters, Katherine and Jane

COLLECTED POEMS

ONCE BITTEN, TWICE BITTEN

A Giant Refreshed

The market gardeners of my home town,
Good Chinese, by the creek grew lettuce
In the sun and left on their own,
As the water ran by and the tadpoles swam,
Just worked to live or with a gun
And saltpetre fired at trespassers.
I do not often think of them but I dread
Such sober judges of me when I am dead.

I think now of your prescribed joy
That from a suburban home came –
(The arrogant freckled girl kissed her boy
At the gate by the juiceless garden) –
You are the praised portrait of trust in men,
Swimming in all those brown and blue eyes, warm
With this love which the syringes try.
In all our home courtesies, we learned the lie.

Forefathers' View of Failure

Men with religion as their best technique,
Who built bush churches six days a week,
Stencilled failure's index on their brains.
Whisky laced the mucous of their heads,
Flushed their pores, narrow-bored their veins,
But they were building still on their death-beds
Having no life but the marking-time of work,
Sleeping collapsed outside despair and talk.

These ancestors might pity or despise
Free will, willing despair into lives.
They used sin as a weather-telling limb,
Climbed to bed with a bottle, took

3

Days on a bender but never had a whim
Like protest or millenium from a book –
These narrow fates had a viciousness
They drank for, but no vicariousness.

It would seem failure to them to have
Knowledge a Scottish textbook never gave
Or to fear regular love on an iron bedstead
With children lying awake a wall away.
Their sophistication was only to be dead
After drinking the sun down into the bay.
Their gulps shake out time, their health
Is in country roses, a hard red wealth.

The weatherboard churches bleached white
As the calcimined crosses round them invite,
Like the War Memorial with ten names,
Eyes up to plain Heaven. It is hard to see
Past good intentions – on any visitor the same
Wind trespasses ashore from a wailing sea.
In this new land the transplanted grasses root,
Waving as sulkily as through old falling soot.

Once Bitten, Twice Bitten;
Once Shy, Twice Shy

The trap setter in a steel dawn
Picks up his dead rabbits and goes home
Whistling: his tune lies over the wet fields
In the shrinking morning shadows.
The gift of morning life brings
Five broken backs for the rabbits
Dangling in his hessian wrap.
In his own house an old mother
Wastes herself for a busy cancer,
She has always sacrificed flesh and time
For others – a thin heart hates a fat man
In the same room of waiting,
And outside, two children chase
A cockerel from a hen; their sister,
In love with a school teacher,

Pushes back the sex in her measuring blouse.
Now the house basks in bridal sun
Brimming with doves. This is where
The dead rabbits come, giving life
To the fat dog and his mange and the tired wife
Dried by the recurring sun of her kitchen.
Now it is electric eleven o'clock – the stewing meat
Smells savoury past the pruned back roses
And wafts on the street's spindly limits,
The only fragrance of defence and love.

Mr Roberts

He was the great Consul and his teacher's gown
Out-toga'd the forum of his Latin Class.
His eyes translated what they rested on:
Boys of the pudding world, unstoical faces,
Ears beyond the ablative, all thickened glass.
Staring into them he might have drowned
In such transparency – A Roll Call of some spaces –
They wore their fear to match his moral frown.

This pedagogue pushed: he owned them for four years.
A Rugby field was the Republic's mould
Which that soft thing the self so rightly feared.
The gravel rash, the sweaty jersey kept
Faith with the Silver Age, The Men of Old;
Your father stepping from an otiose car,
In the school's shadow as the Speech Day sun crept
Up, felt an ancient fright, a gladiator's jar.

Headmasters dwindle but contrive to last.
Thicker bodies fray than stood the cane.
Later a man shot himself, a man went mad – ask
The secret smoker in the bike shed what
Sour light stood on the school's weather vane,
What Tartarus vented in the boiling Bell Tower
But no revolution came: that comic spot,
The Old School waits and presages each unshining hour.

A Christmas Recalled

The water pushed at its thin scud of oil
And knocked the musseled rocks, the opal broke,
Its skin of lights went out – the prawns were small
A foot down in the water jerking at
My glass bottle – from the dock cranes smoke
Stood straight up, the gulls and cicadas noisily sat
On our huge summer: even the air was fat.

Summer was December and the water sounds
Of the presiding Harbour. Ferries named
For Governors' Ladies wallowed round
The river bends, past one haunted house, by
A thousand boatsheds, past the water games
Of Spartan Girls Schools, regatta crowded bays,
Resting heavily at barnacled, bituminous quays.

In this time I heard my uncle calling my mother:
'Marion, I've made a new one, give it a try.'
I saw my face stretched in his cocktail shaker
When I wiped the condensation off. We were
A drinking family and I would quietly lie
Eight years old drinking Schweppes in bed, their
Noise a secure lullaby, drinking up my fear.

But after eating too much one bloated day
When I broke three toys wantonly and clumsily
My uncle started to talk of the war, not the way
Men talk of the Last War but as prophets do
Of retribution – 'We've got about two or three
Years before the Japs come' – and I ran to
The garden to cry – wars were not new

To any innocence – I thought of them
As I sat crying under the pepperina tree.
I thought too of death which was a word like 'when'
And not a thing like cat, so as they called
Me in for washing-up I looked to see
If they had painted what their talk foresaw
On their Christmas faces, the picture of a war.

6

Sick-room at Home

Your stomach, darling, is upset.
Your head runs its cold, yet
From your bed you smile on the room
For love of love; your head assumes
A bright sickness and your eyes
Flavour our dry temerity.
Our quiet is the spoken words of fear,
Yours the waxy entering ear
That takes your sick-room pulsing in
Through the wireless anodyne;
Ours too this waiting, healthy on chairs,
For further lovers down the stairs.
We do not know whose kiss has bled
The pale lips on the vivid bed
But wait still as the coughing comes
For your eyes, some sick-bed crumbs.

All Other Time is Peace

What is locked in a book
Of a Civil War, of a king
Watching over the unwalled marshes,
Of disease in the Long Walls awaiting
A hot day, of panic and cold night marches
To cities on heavy plains
Is history which once was done
Congregationally in the sun
For the living who will remain.

While the city burned to the water
And the merchants sailed away,
Murder, the child's friend, wept
The four-sided dead: where are they,
Foul and alone, the well-kept
Of time? Asleep, which is death
And cannot be slept out,
Where they lie mouth to mouth,
Apart, not kept together by breath.

Main peace is worn down
To fear and the glamorous war:
Friend for his friend gives away
That life, his Sanitary Law
He knows he still must obey.
All time is war and all men
Live in the picture of death;
The Heaven and Hell they bequeath
Is old time, old peace again.

Syrup of Figs will Cast Out Fear

The crafty baby surrounded by his cot
Sweats under the weight of love and blankets.
In summer he screams because he is hot,
In winter because he's kicked off the clothes to his ankles.
You can't kid him he is what he is not.

He is a love sucking up to much.
Mother is the nearest, dearest fountain.
The world goes by his house and such
Visits will never again bring Mahomet to the mountain.
Chafing and talcum are Hell and Heaven in the crutch.

But perhaps this is just our looking back –
An overestimation of the bowels.
Growing up is the great amnesiac,
And innocence is corrupted with the vowels.
The light of birth extols both white and black.

I know from my Father I was a sullen child
Scolding my indulgent parents' love.
Today in bed, the hegemony of smiles
Raises the prison cot bars – I might prove
Lucky in the future dark, but not reconciled.

The Picture of Nobody

Dear, the people I count on
Are not here nor swim upon the sound
(A helpless music) of London nor,
Locked up in my witness, ask
Which way to incorporate death
In memory – not even from the past,
Not the stuffed body in its glass
Where by the waters it strolls on.
Wholly incautious, I want
Two chairs facing and the eyes aground,
Two specious trusts giving vent
To voices coming in, with accents then
Close and sweet, parochial as honey.

Private mythology perhaps,
Private abounds in verities.
I found my ruin when the garden fell
To executive birds and aphis at
The work of beauty. In an elegant lapse
The lizard from the dead cow's side
Posed as a black stone – no less than death
Crawling away he seemed, up rose
His frilled hackles and the bloodshot hills
Stood out behind him: world enough
Among the merely merciless
To set the eye bending, let it dilate
Inwards for both the cancer and the rose.

Magical, unmentioned, die
Also for us the tragic disciplined –
Such heroes unlackadaisical
Hoarding a hard sunburned imagery –
Let us honour our unlucky Hectors,
Who before right trespass was defined
Served the pleasure of an Imperial hour,
The tall defenders of commercial Troy,
But for us entombed cupidity
In death: when to our music
Their great world dances, we shall see
Their plain and clever faces looking out
Upon a plain and irritated earth.

Conventions of Death

We live under the stately mushroom shadow –
A cliché to walk with going up Bond Street.
The dead parked in the Triumph dealer's window
Arc this year's models, require no upkeep.

Isolated by what I want, calling it love,
I do not feel them dead, I think them pretty.
No loving goose-flesh on the skin they're made of,
Their sane madness built and skinned the city.

What I want is a particular body,
The further particulars being obscene
By definition. The obscenity is really me,
Mad, wanting mad possession: what else can mad mean?

Mad can be put upon a bed and watched,
Do tests, get ECT, pile blocks,
Get cured; its snake of brain is scotched
But waits in faces, phone calls, letters, clocks.

Love winces once and then the mad lie low.
Skulking in frail beer joys then
I try to make a lying philosophy go:
We are all doomed, all men and women.

So give up thinking, work hard, buy a car,
Get married, keep a garden, bring up kids –
Answers to all the problems that there are,
Except the love that kills, the death that lives.

Metamorphosis

This new Daks suit, greeny-brown,
Oyster-coloured buttons, single vent, tapered
Trousers, no waistcoat, hairy tweed – my own:
A suit to show responsibility, to show
Return to life – easily got for two pounds down
Paid off in six months – the first stage in the change.
I am only the image I can force upon the town.

The town will have me: I stalk in glass,
A thin reflection in the windows, best
In jewellers' velvet backgrounds – I don't pass,
I stop, elect to look at wedding rings –
My figure filled with clothes, my putty mask,
A face fragrant with arrogance, stuffed
With recognition – I am myself at last.

I wait in the pub with my Worthington.
Then you come in – how many days did love have,
How can they be catalogued again?
We talk of how we miss each other – I tell
Some truth – you, cruel stories built of men:
'It wasn't good at first but he's improving.'
More talk about his car, his drinks, his friends.

I look to the wild mirror at the bar –
A beautiful girl smiles beside me – she's real
And her regret is real. If only I had a car,
If only – my stately self cringes, renders down;
As in a werewolf film I'm horrible, far
Below the collar – my fingers crack, my tyrant suit
Chokes me as it hugs me in its fire.

Death's Morning Shadows

It's light, here's thumping in the pipes – spit
Sounds in the wall, a tap's settled sob.
Water in my eyes – I have some sleep left – in it
I can watch my Father. They'll have a job
To kill him but they're going to – a minute
From now he'll be dragged off by the mob.

Caught by a bellied tear I come awake.
Espresso sugar pricks an eyeball.
I press sleep back into my eyes – a lake
Of grinning water holds no splash – slow crawl
(I'm a stylish sleep swimmer), then the ache
Of overarm, the sound of waterfall.

I'll gear the dream to sex. That sharp face
Is with me now – it will not let me use

11

Its landlocked body. I try to kiss a place
Where I have been. It scolds, its words refuse
My tongueing. I am naked, in disgace
With love, skulking under its high-heeled shoes.

Quick change to the toothache dream. I'm in pain
But know I am only a man and tooth in bed.
The pain in me hunts my flesh – my name
Locked in the alarm clock bursts my head.
The lit room rings with morning and again
I hear the sore pipes singing for the dead.

Beast and the Beauty

His fear never loud in daylight, risen to a night whisper
Of a dead mother in the weatherboard house,
He had this great piece of luck: a girl
In Paris clothes, ex-school monitor, chose
Him for her lover. Twenty-one and experienced,
She showed his hands the presentiment of clothes
And first at a party kissed him, then took
Him home where they did what he'd always supposed.

Her sophistication was his great delight:
Her mother and father drinking, throwing things,
The unhappy marriage, the tradespeople on Christian
Name terms – all the democractic sexiness – mornings
With the Pick of the Pops and the Daily Express
And yet the sudden itching despair, the wonder in King's
College Chapel, the depth that lived in her soul
Of which this raciness was only the worldly covering.

But the sophistication chose to kill – the itch
Was on the inside of the skin. Her family of drunks
Were shrewd, wine-wise young barristers and gentlemen-
Farmers fought for her hand. In the loft there waited trunks
Of heirlooms to be taken seriously. He found himself
Ditched, his calls unanswered, his world shrunk
To eating in Lyons', waiting outside her house at midnight,
Her serious tears to haunt him, boiling on his bunk.

So he sits alone in Libraries, hideous and hairy of soul,
A beast again, waiting for a lustful kiss to bring
Back his human smell, the taste of woman on his tongue.

12

Walking Home on St Cecilia's Day

It is sublime adjustment: now
The only home for a deep sunk spine
Raising blood cordial, the plain wine
Of the bored. They can never tresspass enough

Against us, who use their surly right
Of making the world hateful. The rose
Foot is in the clay and the catgut clothes
The notes of ink. On our backs the freight

Is never less and the pack sores rub,
But these are scabs of scarab, Atlas' welts
Where the whole world has hung or else
No single blade of grass could stand up.

The packed authority is in one glance.
The injustice of delight! All that is made
Makes this ventriloquist's serenade –
Words to sing, beautiful impermanence.

And feeling my death in me, I walk home,
Rehearsing wrongly Mozart's own congruity.
Thus I say to the gatepost, see
I could be drunk and not fall to this huge drone.

It is the maker's gift, mechanic sound,
Which they say can analyse to God.
But here is hunger where we would feel greed;
We can learn it, a miracle on the ground.

But it still won't make tomorrow other than
Another day of chafing, shaving, sitting still:
Nodules on noses grow, pet cats get killed,
The lush and smooth upstage the scrag and thin.

But I know now as I charge my battered heart
With thirty years' unhappiness on end,
There is a practice of music which befriends
The ear – useless, impartial as rain on desert –

And conjures the listener for a time to be happy,
Making from this love of limits what he can,
Saddled with Eden's gift, living in the reins
Of music's huge light irresponsibility.

Reflection on my own Name

P eter – a name I share with many others –
E very day someone says it – no brothers
T o share my surname with, no sisters
E ither; few young boys were kissed as
R arely as I was. Peter was afraid of girls.

P eter is now an irritant for pearls.
O f all the things I'd like to be, a Casanova,
R andy, vulgar, would be best. A lover
T raining the South Ken. girls in his two-seater,
E gged on by Hickey, Tanfield, sexy in a sweater,
R aping the honest, loveless, childhood Peter.

Changes Wrung

With the white blouse almost starched,
Drip-dried, mercerised, we start
Undoing the clothes she stands in.

We forget in the imaginary marches of the groin
A voice honeying trivia to the last grain,
The near neatness kept by a safety-pin.

We watch eyes like shutters, deep
As bogy-holes, moist as lettuce, as peep
Bo-peep plays the sympathetic feminine.

But as metaphysical stilts go
Those legs are calipers on the globe.
The warm freighter keeps its mild regimen.

Her body calm with science waits
Untouched. She reads: Is purity out of date?
Only where to start is her confusion.

Only indeed will masculine props support
This flowering trunk, these matching parts.
The smile is outside: inside, the discipline.

Seduction is not only dirty but a bore.
Hands grip, clumsy lips push and no more.
Her factitious love stays a brutal virgin.

Tunes for the Fortunate

With a narrow strip of garden and a hedge
For his cat to prowl along by night,
A pram under the line of washing, two veg.
And meat each night, wine weekends,
One man accumulates God. He is right
To look through his flowers at his friends –
His eyes make nature of his privilege.

The singular unfairness lasts – a person is
The velvet which the kissing lip smears.
There is a God in the inviting of the kiss,
Only rogation in the sweats of love.
The world of road signs offers brandished fears
To timidity at breakfast. We improve
In selfish loving, sore analysis.

Two suns of misfortune and grace
Blaze in one ball on the precipitant sky
Flushing the blood vehicular in the face.
One ear of love waits for the gate to click,
A Hell of hate simmers under one eye
And a fat world's pictures circumscribe the sick.
Humid history populates each space.

We fix our minds on grinning girls and boys
Whose senses stir immaculate deceit.
Theirs is the touch which mends our broken toys;
Now they use breasts and armpits, grown-up kit,
Making a rodent summer with their heat.
Theirs is all gold – only for them we sit,
Screaming to the walls, imprisoned noise.

Lament for a Proprietor

This was the end of a man but also died
Ten suits, twenty shirts, Clare College ties
And scarves, a radiogram, one hundred dance discs
And Vivaldi's Seasons, shells picked up
On Sark and Ibiza, Phaidon and Skira books
Coverless and crooked – twenty invitations

15

To Balls and Bottle Parties, some still to be held,
Gin, Whisky, Cointreau, Kirsch, Drambuie,
And an unopened letter from his Mother,
An unfinished letter to a Rowing Coach.
As his Granny was still alive the pots of cash
He would inherit did not die, but who
Could breathe life back into his possessions,
Put Humpty Dumpty safe on the high sea wall?
They died for him since he had lived for them.
In death they share a room – nobody knows
He was alive now all his things are dead.

What a Lying Lot the Writers Are

To put it all down now I take my pencil up
And a bilge of hate can be sluiced up top.
I have no time in a bored lifetime
To love a body in its sour confines
Because the love is a meeting place
Of impossible pictures on a disputed face.

But people make metaphysics out of this
And play among bodies with a such or thus.
Their eyes picture a world but they call
What they cannot see, Heaven or Hell.
To be above the tearing fingers of the ruck
You need good teeth, a good income, good luck.

This then is the lie: we write and perform
Great solemnities in the mind's frame.
The lovely are loved, the victims rail,
Beds hold the sick and the hale free-wheel,
Great events are remembered as history,
Science understands us, we are free.

Books tell us stories of friendship and love,
Animals and plants help us stay alive.
Talking until the last minimum of death
We praise God or opportunity or both
But we die in the first room we see,
The bright locked world, the captivity.

John Marston Advises Anger

All the boys are howling to take the girls to bed.
Our betters say it's a seedy world. The critics say
Think of them as an Elizabethan Chelsea set.
Then they've never listened to our lot – no talk
Could be less like – but the bodies are the same:
Those jeans and bums and sweaters of the King's Road
Would fit Marston's stage. What's in a name,
If Cheapside and the Marshalsea mean Eng. Lit.
And the Fantasie, Sa Tortuga, Grisbi, Bongi-Bo
Mean life? A cliché? What hurts dies on paper,
Fades to classic pain. Love goes as the MG goes.
The colonel's daughter in black stockings, hair
Like sash cords, face iced white, studies art,
Goes home once a month. She won't marry the men
She sleeps with, she'll revert to type – it's part
Of the side-show: Mummy and Daddy in the wings,
The bongos fading on the road to Haslemere
Where the inheritors are inheriting still.
Marston's Malheureux found his whore too dear;
Today some Jazz Club girl on the social make
Would put him through his paces, the aphrodisiac cruel.
His friends would be the smoothies of our Elizabethan age –
The Rally Men, Grantchester Breakfast Men, Public School
Personal Assistants and the fragrant PROs,
Cavalry-twilled tame publishers praising Logue,
Classics Honours Men promoting Jazzetry,
Market Researchers married into Vogue.
It's a Condé Nast world and so Marston's was.
His had a real gibbet – our death's out of sight.
The same thin richness of these worlds remains –
The flesh-packed jeans, the car-stung appetite
Volley on his stage, the cage of discontent.

Sick Man's Jewel

Number and movement mock the sultry citizen
Upon his bed, unending Number One,
Who loves nothing Number Two deploys,
At Home, away: enjoins, denies, enjoys.

This is equality a sadness can compel –
The stratas do not matter in this Hell.
An absence does not need a space to live;
It has a face to follow, gift to give,
Touches the railings of the locked-in world,
Shakes flowers, slurps tea, watches little girls.
This is a sick man you say and watch him go
Out of your life who entered only now –
This morbid one done licking at his sores
Drops symptom bundles at social workers' doors;
For his statistics becomes lovable
And for his eyes is asked to speak of Hell –
Have they not been there and can speak of it
A thousand lyric gestures of defeat.
Play him a record then to spin out the dark
(Instrumental music leaves no mark).
The saturated silence holds the sound
In his true co-ordinates of up and down,
Where the bright nerves have colours to commend,
Deaths for pictures, hatreds to befriend.
No one is here, the therapy will say,
The world is dead, the world has gone away,
All other states are stars, the world is here
Unwinding in the workshop of the ear.
Unwilling to be dead, again he'll be
An embarrassment sucking his saucered tea
In Lyons' when you come to quickly snatch
A meal before the theatre or before you catch
A train to a countryside of weekend calm,
Steepled trees, tan cows and model farm.

Made in Heaven

From Heals and Harrods come her lovely bridegrooms
(One cheque alone furnished two bedrooms),

From a pantechnicon in the dog-paraded street
Under the orange plane leaves, on workmen's feet

Crunching over autumn, the fruits of marriage brought
Craftsman-felt wood, Swedish dressers, a court

Stool tastefully imitated and the wide bed –
(The girl who married money kept her maiden head).

As things were ticked off the Harrods list, there grew
A middle-class maze to pick your way through –

The labour-saving kitchen to match the labour-saving thing
She'd fitted before marriage (O Love, with this ring

I thee wed) – lastly the stereophonic radiogram
And her Aunt's sly letter promising a pram.

Settled in now, the Italian honeymoon over,
As the relatives said, she was living in clover.

The discontented drinking of a few weeks stopped,
She woke up one morning to her husband's alarm clock,

Saw the shining faces of the wedding gifts from the bed,
Foresaw the cosy routine of the massive years ahead.

As she watched her husband knot his tie for the City,
She thought: I wanted to be a dancer once – it's a pity

I've done none of the things I thought I wanted to,
Found nothing more exacting than my own looks, got through

Half a dozen lovers whose faces I can't quite remember
(I can still start the Rose Adagio, one foot on the fender)

But at least I'm safe from everything but cancer –
The apotheosis of the young wife and mediocre dancer.

Apophthegms Come to the Party

The rain is sick on to the ground outside,
Inside red wine spills on a drunken dress.
Here where the cornucopias are wide
Vomit comes up in gentleness.

Patting and stroking: the puritan knees
Swing open for the gargoyle face of love.
Any words off the close breath will please,
Words across lips are filtered enough.

But lucky moon drinks up the rain,
Time eats the savoury lechery,
The party pops – dead in the drain,
Bottles are haunted, the sleepers go free.

By dawn when the waxy words have died
In the entering ear, comes the wet
Responsible kiss: it is not party pride
Makes this love but party etiquette.

A Moral Tale has a Moral End

Death is immaculate: we must not write of it,
Living in the scenery of its sick wit.
Words will not cancel, time cannot condone
Pemmican flesh on cantilever bone,
Their sounds decorate only the meshed hands
To show more reasonably where sorrow stands.
Hauntings out there are obtrusive here:
This death in the sticky side of the year –
An old woman from a wide top room,
Mourned by gas-ring, biscuit tin and broom,
Whose plants nobody wants; they will die
Above the child staring into the bomb-bright sky
And their roots will go with her frail rot,
An historical dust in a verandah pot.
On the next balcony two girls entertain
With Bev and ginger-nuts; their blouses stained
Under the arms drip on a rubber-plant, they take
An hour undressing and lie an hour awake.
The salute to the dead we commonly give her
(Thinking of ourselves with a warm shiver)
Will be a remark made at large
On her unwatered geraniums or a guess at her age.
Let others suffer for us, we are soon dead,
Orthodox, masonic in a darkened bed,
Tugging a minute's life from a grudged breath
In the equality of unequal death.

South of the Duodenum

Not everybody wants to live. When they carted away
Old Terrestrial to hospital, he had been
Eighty years an inmate of his smoky house
And he went up blue to Heaven asking why.
The answer was endemic to the voice.
Eighty years dead, at last death quits the brain.

Keeping alive in jealous pools of eyes, astir
At windowings of Vogue or such
A conniving click of a car door, this innocence
Is life's. Come up like the moon upon the stars
The great wash of death makes no pretence;
A perfect scansion drops at this approach.

O the cancer atolls, growing by writing light
In money's time – you are the machines
Of hate and love. Here nothing trusts itself
But in your proof: early to live, the late
Body blooms in your garrulous health –
At your death-bed both killer and victim shine.

Death in the Pergola Tea-Rooms

Snakes are hissing behind the misted glass.
Inside, there are tea urns of rubicund copper, chromium pipes
Pissing steam, a hot rattle of cups, British
Institutional Thickness. Under a covering of yellowing glass
Or old celluloid, cress-and-tomato, tongue-and-ham
Sandwiches shine complacently, skewered
By 1/6 a round. The wind spitefully lays the door shut
On a slow customer – ten pairs of eyes track
To his fairisle jersey; for a few seconds voices drop
Lower than the skirmishing of steam.
Outside by the river bank, the local doctor
Gets out of his '47 Vauxhall, sucking today's
Twentieth cigarette. He stops and throws it
Down in the mud of the howling orchard.
The orchard's crouching, half-back trees take the wind
On a pass from the poplars of the other bank,
Under the scooping wind, a conveyor-belt of wrinkles,
The buckled river cuts the cramping fields.

Just out of rattle reach and sound of cup clang,
The old rationalist is dying in the Pergola.
Two Labour Party friends and the doctor
Rearrange his woven rugs. The blood is roaring
In his head, the carcinoma commune, the fronde
Of pain rule in his brain – the barricades have broken
In his bowels – it is the rule of spasm, the terror sits.
He knows he is dying, he has a business of wills,
Must make a scaffolding for his wife with words,
Fit the flames in his head into the agenda.
Making up his mind now, he knows it is right
To take the body through committee meetings and
                                          campaign rooms
To wear it and patch it like a good tweed; to come to
The fraying ends of its time, have to get the doctor
To staple up its seams just to keep the fingers
Pulling blankets up, stroking comfort on other fingers,
Patting the warm patch where the cat has been.
There is no God. It is winter, the windows sing
And stealthy sippers linger with their tea.
Now rushing a bare branch, the wind tips up
The baleful embroidery of cold drops
On a spider's web. Inside the old man's body
The draught is from an open furnace door – outside the room,
Ignoring the doctor's mild professional face,
The carnival winter like the careful God
Lays on sap-cold rose trees and sour flower beds
The cruel confusion of its disregard.

Suicide Unmasked

The longest image of a private truth:
With a shilling borrowed from his landlady,
He looks out on the slate and sliding roofs
And sees the world a murderer already.

He still must pay for sentiment at large.
Pitied at home, his eye is everywhere.
Under his hand, flies on the window's edge,
Ugly and free of pity take the air.

Whatever he blesses undoes him again.
The sun's mild pilgrimage in the dirt
Here makes a white world of the window-pane –
It's one world only and it cannot hurt

Creatures of stagestruck innocence abroad,
Walking the sticky streets, bored and real.
The introspection then must be the fraud –
He happens upon himself who wants to feel.

A shilling's worth of gas floats in the room.
Despair not being wordy gets things done.
All the paraphernalia of gloom
Belongs to death and must be left someone.

Small and secure the thing we so despise
Being alive, we welcome being dead.
Palpably on the dead these living eyes
Fix the same empty picture in their heads.

Away, Musgrave, Away

This engineering of the flesh, this once
Tall and now dead frame of decay,
After the pictures of the sweetness of fronts,
Is best in marble or right out of the way
Beyond the fire – lest a headstone hunts
Down its juicy self and ghosts come out to play.

All about dying is to be known beforehand –
All that affects knuckles, eyeballs, teeth.
Under the ugly face old age has planned
Sour compensation for the hour of death:
This philosopher's skull which time has trepanned
Was yesterday the lover underneath.

Forever the obsessional staring out
As today with its isinglass eyes;
Looking in the other world of glass they hurt
A self of corroding vanities,
Which seconds measure and fears flout
Puffing the live skin from its death's face.

Jack and Jill

Like brother and sister wish
(Fly on the fruit, fruit in the dish)
Peril is permit and is
The one glow she loves and his
One fraud: thus in the saline kiss
Like an Indian God, arms
At a clockface, potency swarms.

So she says: as water in colander
I cannot contain you; under
The last stand winter will
Show his husband flanks filled
With a gentle swelling of the wild
And Jack gone from me, you will go
Under as the crocus and the lilac know.

This is the authentic history
Of his impotence: new misery
From his sister whom he loves,
His archaic incest paired like gloves
He writes only at midnight – loaves,
Fishes and the real world are with her,
His wilful tease but only avatar.

The Smell on the Landing

Where the decay begins, the sun
Through barred windows
Falls to its knees. We turn
The key two floors below
And walk towards the smell:
It is not the smell of death
Or of violence or even of Hell;
It is the odour of having no hope,
Of lying late, of being itself alone.

Trapped on the landing, a sea
Of cabbage air is pushed
To furrows with the turning key.
The tower collapses, rushed

Past the falling flower and its sound;
We retch involuntarily,
For our stomachs have found
The common taste of filth,
We are the thinking flesh left on its own.

One family lives in the one room
Whose door is never open,
But the wireless and children quietly boom
Alive behind its walls; when
Armageddon on the stairs
Muffles the company and steals
A winding whisper through its ears,
Then can all the eaten meals
And dirty clothes come into their own.

On the street it is flag day – a flag
For a coin is conscious charity,
But here where charity begins,
A Home is home enough to be
Our street of Victorian fronts,
Our refuge from the acid rain,
So we may hurry from the yellow fog
To the dead life on our stairs once
More ourselves in ourselves alone.

Party Line

The bottles redly close an unborn sound.
Here come the liberators who will set
Free actions which were tightly bound.
Aggressors in jeans and evening dress, the brash
Music of these fitted marmosets,
Brimming in clothes, brings the bated crash:
This is splendid value for a pound.

One girl undressed because she thought it right;
Another, trained in truth, watched what she did
Loving her mirrored love, her second sight.
A judge of conduct gasped to see the fun,
A valued impotence safe in his head –
A private creature staring out the sun
Not warmed by it is seeing by its light.

Oh this is arrogant the dancers say.
The conjured revellers are just in touch,
Which witness moves them dancing as they sway.
Wallflowers at School Balls and pimply men,
Wanting love and made to want too much,
May not be saved; ceremonious haters then,
Their world rebels where first it would obey.

All coats lie fallen on the party floor
Where an angry guest threw them one by one.
The permutations of love are finished for
One evening. Here we go home, out
Of reach of drunken communion,
Secular saints who do without
Power, a pleasure left behind the door.

But to these aspirations everything belongs.
Here is the bed's silence, the parcel of
A dream wrapped in dirty songs
Pillow-rehearsed: it is five o'clock
When nobody is making love –
The body floats in the mind, a shock
Of sleep comes, steeped in party wrongs.

Euphoria Dies

Your light attracts the moth: the Sibyls move.

You are the figure to whom the lights allude,
Your charming grace, such standard turpitude.

Come into the room and with your coming eyes
Glancing kingdoms enter, the glasses glow,
The rattle of wit and understanding dies.

Dry Martini deserts spread away beyond
Figures like fruit bowls, hostages moving there –
Up assembly halls, the carpets, the drumming stairs,
Catharsis chases the fine erectile blonde.

I knew a man and that was scarcely once;
I knew before the growing; such legs, such locks;
Wet easy doors on willing hinges where I've sunk.
At holes for freedom plant I steady stocks,
But see on one hand the moon comes skidding, drunk.

But, Sir, the talk has always been like this.
Up notches in my wisdom all ascend,
Your face is calibrated from my looking end;
Your witty voice, your utterly violent charm
Sustain the evening – in your eyes I kiss
Myself to keep myself from harm.

My hostess is a woman of great tact.
You saw her silting slowly on her back?
Well, today, the recusant cadences are flat
And drink like swimming moonlight percolates
Our cartilege-clad city: the gold is at
The mathematics of our several hates
And these sweet things are destined for the rack.

Good-night, Good-night, my bold two feet, Good-night.
Switch skipping out and grabbing put the light.
Are you incommodiously desperate? I'll say
Not more than a little living left, although
Here where the carpet seems to be, my toe
Is cordoned off from my friends who move away.
Charming I'll time it to, so brutally say
Thanks for the loan and darkness where I go.

For John Clare from London

The lean October night is only outside
My window which the dark cannot hide
And the swinging curtain flaps and goes
At the scouting wind on its tiptoes.
Under my eye the streets sting and crack –
A murderous pinch of the whole pack –
So bolting home through the wafer light
Papering pavements with its thin sight
I open the newspaper page after page
And warm myself at its vicarious rage.

27

Rise then tomorrow to the vain alarm clock
And clean the teeth against a shock
Of decay, while from the pleated eyes
Stir the crusts of sleep an unseeing clockwise,
Put on socks, shoes and in the mirror's rind
Watch the washed face, the ikon of the mind.
Brimming with its torpor, step out and resent
A weak tea sun on brick and cement,
But stifle resentment again for the sake
Of the passionate cough and proud headache.

A Vicious Vignette

In the trees around the small summerhouse
The birds still raggedly call
In uneven entries, high and shrill and sour.
The custodian in a grey uniform
Shows visitors the room where the great
Symphonies were written; here for hours
While his wife wrote letters and made cakes
The composer put man and nature in a cage
Of furious sound – they raged for him, the powers
Of sickness and life. Critics of our day have shown
His Pantheism in the birdsong in his scores,
More feeling than painting, they say, this
His great mother, Nature, and her song.
The Biographer who came here in winter knows
(Padding about the wind-walled cottage
His grant spent on rococo Austrian treasures and rich food)
That, rising from his desk in the bright house,
The Composer took his gun and broke the Summer,
Shot at the birds calling in the leaves,
Went in then to compose to a silence
Of clangorous birds in his head
Music of his guilty childhood's peace.

All, All of a Piece Throughout

Derived from Babylon, this nymph
Warms her buttocks on a plinth
Of our new city and her mouth runs
Ice-cream from a hundred cones
Over her breasts; her treacle eyes,
(Blood-shot Eleusinian mysteries)
Dance the postures upside down,
A brutal, cataleptic dawn.

The shoe shops sparkle her regard,
The faceless traffic, people, ward
Off flies from café garbage, this
Slavish light shines in a dress
A snarling model drops by the bed;
She stands for love that in a raid
On merely selfish people wills
A walking Hell in their four walls.

But lick on lick the summer sweet
Heat melts asphalt underneath,
Collars in grime richly stick,
Pathetic fallacy the neurotic
Wit turns on itself a force
Like widowed incest its own face;
The sum immense in a sky of glue
Is our moon: we only glow.

Minatory now, our nymph is bored
By brutal elegance and breakfast food.
The cut-glass edge of early air
On this maimed province wired
For sound brings back austerity
To the tough city of dismay;
Latter-day nymphs upon the grass
Hedge in the violence of dead Greece.

We live on static history:
Wars we win to make war by,
There is no guard from our diligence
Or refuge from our bland science,
Economic man is one
More creature on his own,
Transvestist till his love can turn,
His life is murder in the town.

The Historians Call Up Pain

When his father died still apostate,
The new Emperor took his grandfather's name
(The eighth to be so called) and appointed
The most zealous Inquisitor
History has yet recorded. In the subject lands,
The Eastern Pale, the prosperous Low Countries,
And even in his own great hinterland,
Ten thousand heretics were burnt to death
In one year. Men dreamed of Millennium
The more; martyrs died soundlessly at the stake,
Their eyes hotter than the flames. The Emperor
Caused his father's grave to be opened
And sent the Pope his bones packed in the ashes
Of a thousand Adamites. This, of course, was
Six centuries ago: today this persecution
Is a best bet Honours question
In the History Tripos; it has also provided
Several specious parallels for Marxists
Praising Thomas Muntzer and American Scholars
Screening for chiliasm. Yet if we keep
Our minds on the four last things
And join the historians on their frieze of pain
We may forget our world of milk gone stale,
Cancer touches in the afternoon, girls in Jensens,
Gramophone records scratched and warped,
Managers fattening tumours of ambition.
We cannot know what John of Leyden felt
Under the Bishop's tongs – we can only
Walk in temperate London, our educated city,
Wishing to cry as freely as they did who died
In the Age of Faith. We have our loneliness
And our regret with which to build an eschatology.

Annotations of Auschwitz

1

When the burnt flesh is finally at rest,
The fires in the asylum grates will come up
And wicks turn down to darkness in the madman's eyes.

2

My suit is hairy, my carpet smells of death,
My toothbrush handle grows a cuticle.
I have six million foulnesses of breath.
Am I mad? The doctor holds my testicles
While the room fills with the zyklon B I cough.

3

On Piccadilly underground I fall asleep –
I shuffle with the naked to the steel door,
Now I am only ten from the front – I wake up –
We are past Gloucester Rd, I am not a Jew,
But scratches web the ceiling of the train.

4

Around staring buildings the pale flowers grow;
The frenetic butterfly, the bee made free by work,
Rouse and rape the pollen pads, the nectar stoops.
The rusting railway ends here. The blind end in Europe's gut.
Touch one piece of unstrung barbed wire –
Let it taste blood: let one man scream in pain,
Death's Botanical Gardens can flower again.

5

A man eating his dressing in the hospital
Is lied to by his stomach. It's a final feast to him
Of beef, blood pudding and black bread.
The orderly can't bear to see this mimic face
With its prim accusing picture after death.
On the stiff square a thousand bodies
Dig up useless ground – he hates them all,
These lives ignoble as ungoverned glands.
They fatten in statistics everywhere
And with their sick, unkillable fear of death
They crowd out peace from executioners' sleep.

6

Forty thousand bald men drowning in a stream –
The like of light on all those bobbing skulls
Has never been seen before. Such death, says the painter,
Is worthwhile – it makes a colour never known.
It makes a sight that's unimagined, says the poet.
It's nothing to do with me, says the man who hates
The poet and the painter. Six million deaths can hardly
Occur at once. What do they make? Perhaps
An idiot's normalcy. I need never feel afraid
When I salt the puny snail – cruelty's grown up
And waits for time and men to bring into its hands
The snail's adagio and all the taunting life
Which has not cared about or guessed its tortured scope.

7

London is full of chickens on electric spits,
    Cooking in windows where the public pass.
This, say the chickens, is their Auschwitz,
    And all poultry eaters are psychopaths.

Who Gets the Pope's Nose?

It is so tiring having to look after the works of God.
    The sea will run away
    From martyrs' feet, gay
Dissipated Florentines kiss tumours out of a man's head,
Scheduled liquefactions renew saints' blood,

In Andean villages starved Inca girls
    Develop the stigmata,
    Dying dogs pronounce the Pater
Noster on the vivisection table, the World
Press report trachoma'd eyes that drip wide pearls.

All investigated, all authenticated, all
    Miracles beyond doubt.
    Yet messengers go in and out,
The Vatican fills up with paper. The faithful
Work for a Merchant God who deals in souls.

Was there ever a man in Nazareth who was King of Kings?
>   There is a fat man in Rome
>   To guide his people home.
Bring back the rack and set the bones straining,
For faith needs pain to help with its explaining.

Fill a glass with water and gaze into it.
>   There is the perfect rule
>   Which no God can repeal.
Having to cope with death, the extraordinary visit,
Ordinary man swills in a holy sweat.

And high above Rome in a room with wireless
>   The Pope also waits to die.
>   God is the heat in July
And the iron band of pus tightening in the chest.
Of all God's miracles, death is the greatest.

The Conservation of Energy

With scaly soft fire and salted wounds
It has been seen before. Because we wait
In town or country, taking our milk in,
Sending off to school, waiting for the balloon
To go up, we wait for fire. It is part of the state,
A rigour for slack times, something to believe in.

Number One in our Anthology of Technics. Gets rid of
Morals – the atom's structure passes judgement.
We have a concordat now: The Course of History –
And millions still bothered by their chance of love.
In the laboratory, not Bauhaus – just brick and cement –
Universal like the arquebus, the H Bomb comes to seed.

Who now would torture the besieged of Münster?
This new fire will smother the whole plate of earth
And we eaters will cry for tears – our own eyes.
Golf course switch control, President's advisers, no monster
Raving on mankind's sins – merely the birth
Of light without shadow, world without size.

33

To have caught God up is something. He said
His patience would thin out. We have more tact
And grow more tolerant every day. But in nature
Comes the irony: the will to crush a lark's head,
The force to break its wing, makes a terrible fact:
We can lower the sun on to a million local creatures.

We only need the means, the will to good or evil
Does not matter. The means have always been there –
Death has waited years in 'First Year Physics',
The innocent Chem. Lab. poses as the Devil.
The way we see chemistry is by rules. Despair
Is energy too. For fire you rub together two dead sticks.

Too Worn to Wear

Dear Lie, between the trusting chair
And bashful fire, a world enough
(Though schizophrenic air
    Divides its real to worn and rare)
Purports to watch; the red cough
Pastilles know the need they share
With mucous, a rage of stuff
Wasted upon a shift of air.

Old-fashioned issue done in pleats –
Desire compels again to shock
(Barbarous islands in the heat
    Bake fetishes but don't grow wheat);
This image is made by decanter and lock –
Such a spine for poison's seat
Her continuum is, oceans knock
The dead fish at her wading feet.

By severed cages outer eyes
Choose bars to hang; in pots
(Once in an Age of Black Surmise
    Virgins bled but had no sighs)
A way of life paid in through slots
Just grows to grow, not otherwise.
So trespass passes, here who rots
Comes strangely back to health crabwise.

Mild danger and yet in mild
Contempt love is quite lost.
(The model railway plays the child
Home out of the felt and wild)
But now unable to bear the cost
Carnival whim, the depthless smile
Vamps on private Pentecost
The history of a green exile.

Nature Comes to Stay

Striped reality for the cat
Is the cut-up sun falling in the room;
It is not hot but winter warm,
Rare from the garden of green seats
Comes at breakfast time to be
The slide of dust's complacency.

A retail murder of degree
Is this huge light underground.
The room is fed since light is free
Lifting the dust on golden grounds
After bare feet have passed its way
Their sockless, knuckled holiday.

The cloying silent satrapy
Of eyes has this laminated world.
The fire uncurls; the cat is curled
Before the fire it feels and sees,
It shuts its eyes; on its black lids broods
The lit and fizzing neighbourhood.

Phar Lap in the Melbourne Museum

A masterpiece of the taxidermist's art,
Australia's top patrician stares
Gravely ahead at crowded emptiness.
As if alive, the lustre of dead hairs,
Lozenged liquid eyes, black nostrils
Gently flared, otter-satin coat declares
That death cannot visit in this thin perfection.

The democratic hero full of guile,
Noble, handsome, gentle Houyhnhnm
(In both Paddock and St Leger difference is
Lost in the welter of money) – to see him win
Men sold farms, rode miles in floods,
Stole money, locked up wives, somehow got in:
First away, he led the field and easily won.

It was his simple excellence to be best.
Tough men owned him, their minds beset
By stakes, bookies' doubles, crooked jocks.
He soon became a byword, public asset,
A horse with a nation's soul upon his back –
Australia's Ark of the Covenant, set
Before the people, perfect, loved like God.

And like God to be betrayed by friends.
Sent to America, he died of poisoned food.
In Australia children cried to hear the news
(This Prince of Orange knew no bad or good).
It was, as people knew, a plot of life:
To live in strength, to excel and die too soon,
So they drained his body and they stuffed his skin.

Twenty years later on Sunday afternoons
You still can't see him for the rubbing crowds.
He shares with Bradman and Ned Kelly some
Of the dirty jokes you still can't say out loud.
It is Australian innocence to love
The naturally excessive and be proud
Of a thoroughbred bay gelding who ran fast.

Tobias and the Angel

When I play the sad music my conscience urges,
I hear through the great summary of our loss
My father praising the long cataract before his eyes
Where on the retina he starves for light.
We are an unlucky family and we have faith
For which we praise our oppressors and our God.

This has been a long journey; my dog is tired,
My companion is a holy dandy, his clothes are praise.
The fish leap from the river, short verbs hold time
For me in a haul – I have an inventory of praise
And do not tire of the simple entering in,
Like my father closing his Day Book on his trade.

There is no justice: love relies on luxury,
Faith on habit, health on chemistry,
But praise sits with persistence. Today
There is a sun pestering the water, tomorrow
A water falling from the sun and always
The pilgrim cursing the falling water and performing sun.

I shall get home one day or if I die instead
An Insurance Angel will tell my waiting wife
His grave is furnished by his good upbringing,
His habits were proper, his doubt all to the good;
From his warm orthodoxy melancholy shrinks,
He did what he was told, obedient and sane.

So when the miracle strikes from the open door,
The scales fall from my father's eyes and light goes in,
I shall be eating a traveller's heavy meal
Made much of by the kitchen staff. Our house
Is not a tabernacle, miracles are forgotten
In usefulness, the weight and irony of love.

Your Attention Please

The Polar DEW has just warned that
A nuclear rocket strike of
At least one thousand megatons
Has been launched by the enemy
Directly at our major cities.
This announcement will take
Two and a quarter minutes to make,
You therefore have a further
Eight and a quarter minutes
To comply with the shelter
Requirements published in the Civil
Defence Code – section Atomic Attack.
A specially shortened Mass
Will be broadcast at the end
Of this announcement –
Protestant and Jewish services
Will begin simultaneously –
Select your wavelength immediately
According to instructions
In the Defence Code. Do not
Take well-loved pets (including birds)
Into your shelter – they will consume
Fresh air. Leave the old and bed-
ridden, you can do nothing for them.
Remember to press the sealing
Switch when everyone is in
The shelter. Set the radiation
Aerial, turn on the geiger barometer.
Turn off your television now.
Turn off your radio immediately
The Services end. At the same time
Secure explosion plugs in the ears
Of each member of your family. Take
Down your plasma flasks. Give your children
The pills marked one and two
In the C.D. green container, then put
Them to bed. Do not break
The inside airlock seals until
The radiation All Clear shows
(Watch for the cuckoo in your
perspex panel), or your District

Touring Doctor rings your bell.
If before this, your air becomes
Exhausted or if any of your family
Is critically injured, administer
The capsules marked 'Valley Forge'
(Red pocket in No. 1 Survival Kit)
For painless death. (Catholics
Will have been instructed by their priests
What to do in this eventuality.)
This announcement is ending. Our President
Has already given orders for
Massive retaliation – it will be
Decisive. Some of us may die.
Remember, statistically
It is not likely to be you.
All flags are flying fully dressed
On Government buildings – the sun is shining.
Death is the least we have to fear.
We are all in the hands of God,
Whatever happens happens by His Will.
Now go quickly to your shelters.

Legend

We walk home past
    Silver and salted fish
As the first rain strikes
    The five-storeyed town
To be marooned with tea
    In a room and waspish
Waiting for music
    Walk up and down.

And when it comes
    The tea tray shakes,
The pinned-up prints
    With curled edges fold;
Sitting on the bed
    And holding hands makes
The green rain in the trees
    Violent and cold.

Keep me close dear,
   We listen by heart
To caravans of music
   From Sheba and Ophir.
Comforted by pain
   In the red desert, they start
With jewels of murder
   For each quarter of the year.

From Ophir with gold
   And indulgent spice
Into green lands of light
   Yellow sands blowing
One way, it brings tribute
   To our precious avarice
Of touching; it unskeins
   The skin of journeying.

Somme and Flanders

Who am I to speak up for the long dead?
Three uncles I never knew say I'm right.
Their tongues are speaking in my head
I'm related to their flesh by fright.

Their world was made of nerves and mud.
Reading about it now shocks me – Haig
Gets transfusions of their blood,
Plum-and-apple feeds them for the plague.

Those Harmsworth books have sepia'd
Their peasants' fields sown with barbed-wire.
In Nineteen-Nineteen, crops of crosses appeared
Seeded by bodies ripened in shell-fire.

One image haunts us who have read of death
In Auschwitz in our time – it is just light,
Shivering men breathing rum crouch beneath
The sandbag parapet – left to right

The line goes up and over the top,
Serious in gas masks, bayonets fixed,
Slowly forward – the swearing shells have stopped –
Somewhere ahead of them death's stop-watch ticks.

40

Soliloquy at Potsdam

There are always the poor –
Getting themselves born in crowded houses,
Feeding on the parish, losing their teeth early
And learning to dodge blows, getting
Strong bodies – cases for the warped nut of the mind.
The masterful cat-o'-nine-tails, the merciful
Discipline of the hours of drill – better
Than being poor in crowded Europe, the swan-swept
Waters where the faces dredge for bread
And the soggy dead are robbed on their way to the grave.
I can hear it from this window, the musket-drill
On the barrack square. Later today I'll visit
The punishment block. Who else in Europe
Could take these verminous, clutching creatures
And break them into men? What of the shredded back
And the broken pelvis, when the side-drum sounds,
When the uniformed wave tilts and overwhelms
The cheese-trading burghers' world, the aldermanic
Principalities. The reformers sit at my table,
They talk well but they've never seen a battle
Or watched the formed brain in the flogged body
Marching to death on a bellyful of soup and orders.
There has to be misery so there can be discipline.
People will have to die because I cannot bear
Their clinging to life. Why are the best trumpeters
Always French? Watch the west, the watershed
Of revolution. Now back to Quantz. I like to think
That in an afternoon of three sonatas
A hundred regiments have marched more miles
Than lie between here and Vienna and not once
Has a man broken step. Who would be loved
If he could be feared and hated, yet still
Enjoy his lust, eat well and play the flute?

Nine o'Clock Thoughts on the 73 Bus

Client meeting at twelve, that lot of layabouts
Will have to be spoken up for, must tell Ann
To get a new ivy for the office, louts
I saw trying to touch her up, lovely bum
Though. Everyone tries to get as much sex as he can,
The copywriter is flushed by the client's sun.

Ghosts

1

A large woman in a kimono, her flesh
Already sweating in the poulticing heat
Of afternoon – just from her bath, she stands,
Propping her foot on a chair of faded pink,
Preparing to cut her corns. The sun
Simmers through the pimply glass – as if
Inside a light bulb, the room is lit with heat.
The window is the sun's lens, its dusty slice
Of light falls on the woman's foot. The woman
Is my Mother – the clicking of her scissors
Fascinates the little feminine boy
In striped shirt, Tootal tie, thick woollen socks,
His garters down. Memory insists the boy is me.
The house still stands where we stood then.
The inheritance I had, her only child,
Was her party melancholy and a body
Thickening like hers, the wide-pored flesh
Death broke into twenty years ago.

2

The red wind carrying dust on to my Sunday shoes
Reddens also my nostrils and my mouth.
I stand by the school's venerable, fifty-years-old,
Washed cement veranda, waiting for my Father.
The Bunya pines along the straggling drive
Drop chunky cones on gravel – windswept bees
Slog across the Masters' Garden to lemon flowers;
Boys shout, dogs bark, no second is quite silent.

42

My Father with the Headmaster comes to me.
It is Sunday, Parents' Visiting Day. The drive
Is churned by cars. When we go down town,
Despite milk shakes and a demure high tea
In the Canberra Temperance Hotel, I only sulk.
I have kept this priggishness, Father;
The smart world laps you round. Your fear of this
Small child is now my fear – my boarding-school
World of rules rules me – my ghost
Has caught me up to sit and judge
The nightmares that I have, memories of love.

3

My Mother married all that there was left
Of an Old Colonial Family. The money gone,
The family house remained, surrounded by the dogs
He'd buried, forty years a bachelor –
We came there every Sunday in a silver tram
For tennis, when my Mother was alive.
Sometimes I try to find my face in theirs:
My Father in the Lacrosse team, my Mother
Nursing in the War – they tell no story
In family photographs. Their city is changed;
Coca-cola bottles bounce upon their lawn,
No one grows flowers, picnics are no fun,
Their aviaries are full of shop-bought birds.
Who goes for weekends down the Bay
In thirty footers to St Helena, Peel and Jumpin' Pin?
No yachts stand off the Old People's Home,
Out past the crab-pot buoys and floating mangrove fruit.

I was born late in a late marriage. Psychiatrists
Say it makes no difference – but now I think
Of what was never said in a tropical house
Of five miscarriages. If the words were said
They'd start the deaths up that I left for dead.

Eat Early Earthapples

There were boys at my Prep. School my own age
And three stone heavier, who made fifty pounds
Over the holidays selling kangaroo hides
They'd skinned and pegged out themselves
On their fathers' stations. Many shaved, several
Slept with the maids – one I remember
Running his hand up the Irish maid's leg
At breakfast not ten feet away
From the Headmaster's enormous armature of head.
Then there were those marathon journeys home
In the train for the holidays, without sleepers,
And the carriages full of Glennie and Fairholme
Girls sitting up all night – some crying
In the lavatory, some sipping sweet sherry
From dark label-less bottles passed them in the dark,
Some knowing what to do and spattered
By Queensland Railways' coal dust trying
To do it on the floor, their black lisle
Stockings changed for wartime rayon. There were
So many ways of losing a troublesome innocence
But so many ways of keeping it too. Being troubled,
I found a sophistication which drove me mad
Sitting out dances, a viewed humiliation,
Walking through waltzes on boracic'd floors,
(Chopped horsehair rising, said to make girls sexy).
The girls were nicer than I needed, the Headmaster
Led the Jolly Miller, the knowing athletes
Waited for the Gypsy Tap, their stories next day
Full of what they'd managed on the dark verandah.
My schooldays when I was so eagerly unhappy
Have me back among them when I sleep
Freely associating with those baffled fears.
The lascivious miler, the confident three-quarter
Are thick men now with kids and problems.
There is no way back into their wormy Eden,
Ripe with girls, esplanaded with sex,
To stuff myself to sickness and forget
(Taking their chances, my old wounds averted)
The boy with something wrong reading a book
While the smut-skeined train goes homeward
Carrying the practised to the sensual city.

Reading MND in Form 4B

Miss Manning rules us middle-class children
Whose fathers can't afford the better schools
With blue, small, crow-tracked, cruel eyes.
Philomel with melody – a refrain
Summoning the nightingale, the brown bird
Which bruits the Northern Hemisphere with bells –
It could not live a summer in this heat.

Queen Titania, unaware of Oberon,
Is sleeping on a bank. Her fairy watch
Sings over her a lullaby,
The warm snakes hatch out in her dream.
Miss Manning is too fat for love,
We cannot imagine her like Miss Holden
Booking for weekends at the seaside
With officers on leave. This is not Athens
Or the woods of Warwickshire,
Lordly the democratic sun
Rides the gross and southerly glass.
Miss Manning sets the homework. Thirty boys
Leave the bard to tire on his morning wing;
Out on their asphalt the teams for Saturday
Wait, annunciations in purple ink,
Torments in locker rooms, nothing to hope for
But sleep, the reasonable view of magic.
We do not understand Shakespearean objects
Who must work and play: that gold stems from the sky:
It poisons 1942. To be young is to be in Hell,
Miss Manning will insulate us from this genius,
Rock the ground whereon these sleepers be.

Elsewhere there is war, here
It is early in an old morning, there is pollen
In the air, eucalyptus slipping past
The chalk and dusters – new feelings
In the oldest continent, a northern race
Living in the south. It is late indeed:
Jack shall have Jill, all shall be well,
Long past long standing eternity,
Eastern Standard Time.

POEMS ANCIENT & MODERN

The Unicorn's Horn

That which may be tamed
Is the server of cities,
That which serves on maps
Takes its name from the dead:
Warmed by our money
Great larches and wise labradors
Sweep envied land;
Blood ages in 625 veins;
When the gifts are used and we
Sail the black soil plains
Of death, what shall we do
But sing? Raise your voice,
You are a protestant of love
And before the drum strikes
You are judged by music:
Cry in the world, mythical beast,
Dip your horn in the freshet of death,
The circle you make will never die.

Septimius Severus at the Vienna Gate

Eastwards it is all plain with saw ice
On the grass stalks; the cricket tinks.
Fly butterfly, tell Rome
The Man with the Nose is coming,
He can smell pride as surely
As a butcher's dog can sniff out a slaughtering.
Tell Rome she stands on a southern sea,
The winds from Africa bring her no good,
They waft her an Emperor who speaks Punic.
He will multiply religions
Till they are as many
As the ways men die; he will make

47

Gods like starfish, stranded
Prayer-wheels that point no way.
Here by the Danube he swears
He will fill the moon with death:
The Emperor Semite
Needs blood for the purple, let Rome take
Peace from his hands: he has murdered war.

A Minor Lear

That big piece I've left for the sparrows,
Back you starlings, you've had your share.
That square of neat pink icing
Is for my calm dove – a threepenny cake
Doesn't go far among my courtiers.

I divided my substance. Yes, once
I kept exchequer of my crumbs,
I budgeted. The air was blurred with wings
When my subjects beat to my hand
To take their patrimony: I gave and I withheld.

Now my plants won't live. All's mutinous and new,
The city simmers, listen to the sun.
My youngest daughter runs an estate car.
The cost of living! A packet of cut bread
Used to feed a generation of such sneaks.

Down Pride – a man's not a king because
He's followed by his pensioners
To the top of the world. I go down in the lift
And am polite to Mr Morgan in his box.
The sky's got into my head: it's raining quails and death.

Stepping from a flat-bottomed boat,
You break the sun's face in the water,
Bury the pick ten yards up the beach
And sprawl on the immediate gold edge
Of the blood-soaked continent. Prize
Your long nails and flense a mangrove leaf.
The air between you and a stranded
Beer bottle is a frame of mica. Flies
Surround the festering kelp, tiny
Bladders pop in the heat, the sun sits still.
A nervous system is not too high a price
To pay for Copernican advantages.

Vienna

This Imperial city
Needs no Empire: turks, saints, huge nineteenth-
  Century geniuses,

  Poets with the tic, the spade
Bearded patriarch who raised to the nth.
  The power of love, these came

  Here like spokes to their axle.
Europe needed a capital – tenth
  Sons needed to be Civil

  Servants: such imagined strength
Focused on a style. The statued squares
  Don't know that wet Hungary

  Isn't theirs. Their birds can fly
To Balaton. The attic's story
  Is that Haydn was beaten

  There. An old lady who liked
Hitler's voice says Schubert's family
  Lived fourteen to a room. Now

  The tall Minnesotan will
Tell his wife 'we wash too much, you can't be
  A genius in America'.

At Whitsun cars and buses
Carry large dragonflies, God can fly
In this architecture. Dreams

Adorned like cream cakes fatten
The citizens; they wake to abuses
That need icing. Smiling men

Arrive at work at seven
a.m. and a tourist confesses
To his unknown neighbour he

Was unfaithful on the boat.
Grapes grow up to the tram terminuses,
Nature is one of the boasts

Of lost prestige. History
Which puts the pop singer and the iron-
haired conductor in the same

Plane crash has kept this city
To vindicate its geniuses.
The trivial is immortal.

Sydney Cove, 1788

The Governor loves to go mapping – round and round
The inlets of the Harbour in his pinnace.
He fingers a tree-fern, sniffs the ground

And hymns it with a unison of feet –
We march to church and executions. No one,
Even Banks, could match the flora of our fleet.

Grog from Madeira reminds us most of home,
More than the pork and British weevils do.
On a diet of flour, your hair comes out in your comb.

A seaman who tried to lie with a native girl
Ran off when he smelt her fatty hide.
Some say these oysters are the sort for pearls.

Green shoots of the Governor's wheat have browned.
A box of bibles was washed up today,
The chaplain gave them to two Methodists. Ross found

A convict selling a baby for a jug of rum.
Those black hills which wrestle with
The rain are called Blue Mountains. Come

Genocide or Jesus we can't work this land.
The sun has framed it for our moralists
To dry the bones of forgers in the sand.

We wake in the oven of its cloudless sky,
Already the blood-encircled sun is up.
Mad sharks swim in the convenient sea.

The Governor says we mustn't land a man
Or woman with gonorrhoea. Sound felons only
May leave their bodies in a hangman's land.

Where all is novel, the only rule's explore.
Amelia Levy and Elizabeth Fowles spent the night
With Corporal Plowman and Corporal Winxstead for

A shirt apiece. These are our home concerns.
The cantor curlew sings the surf asleep.
The moon inducts the lovers in the ferns.

Madame de Merteuil on
'The Loss of an Eye'

No letters. What's to become of an
Epistolary style it was no
Vanity to pride oneself on: chess
With a stupid curé, giving bad
Advice about abortions to girls
With long chins whom no vice could ruin
Nor uxoriousness ever spoil.
Delphine has two kittens – how can I
Wheedle the cook's son to set his humpbacked
Tom on them? The tom is almost blind. We're two
Cerberus surveyors of the dark.

A young man called today. I recognized
The smell of boredom, the trap closing
In his eyes, a provincial appetite
For fame – the foxy diarist of love
Just waiting for old age to wax the world's
Ears with sententious aphorisms.
Sitting before a moral dish of nectarines,
I am pregnant again with self-love.
Crippled, sun stickying the socket
Of my dead eye, I choose *work*.
I can still plot the overthrow
Of a seminarist (a cut-price
Pascal with warts), plan the humbling of
A local Sévigné, wait calmly
For death to pay the courtesy of a call,
An old woman smelling lilac while her
Functionaries do evil in the sun.

A Huddle of IQ's

Béla Bartók is
Out, Schönberg is in: Hi-Fi
Sales remain the same.

PUNCH picks a new joke:
A layer of dust settles
Over the whole world.

Jack Cotton dreams Hyde
Park is flats: he wakes – trees are
Growing on money.

Bored fashion writers
Take up their pens – brassières
Hang their heads in shame.

The tea girl isn't
Wearing pants: the draughtsman oils
His tight calipers.

Motor bikes go
To church on Sunday: people stay
Home to wash the car.

A million girls
Look for Mr Right: the one who
Finds him is Miss Wrong.

The World of Simon Raven

Rooks are raging where great elms were felled,
Family silver's been lent for the Fête,
Nanny's facing Nigel with stained sheets,
Telegrams announce James is expelled,
Mrs Diamond from Sea View Estate
Tempts a team in training with boiled sweets.

Meanwhile sturgeon from Odessa packed
For Black's and Tan's, renowned St James's Clubs,
Laced with spanish fly, cause randy scenes
At Ascot, a Bishop's face is smacked;
Debs and guardsmen break up Chelsea pubs,
Blackmailers send snaps to dons at Queen's.

Unpaid Mess Bills get a Blue cashiered,
Boys from Balham pelt a First in Greats
With Latin Grammars, Israeli agents
Put pubic lice in Prince Muhammad's beard,
Doctor Boyce cuts off his cousin Kate's
Clitoris – the favourite fails the fence,

Bookies' reminders frighten Adjutants,
Crockford's man is found with a marked deck.
Somewhere beyond Maidenhead an old
Lady rings her bank for an advance
On her pension, sends her son a cheque,
Watches with the cat as it gets cold.

The Frankenstein Report

Put those amps through these membranous wires. I will
Lick your bright toes, sing Alleluia, point to
A banana on a chart, show my Free Will
In many ways pleasing to you.

I'll make rough clapping sounds and then you'll say
It's the monster's music, make chalk strokes my art
(Like phalluses of course) and I'll quietly play
With myself when you play me Mozart.

The asylums are full of my brothers. I
Implore them – Unhappy Brothers, follow me, you
Have nothing to lose but your brains but they cry
We have lost our brains already and do

Not know where to find them. The materials
Are in deep freeze. An electrified copper rod
Sets the cells firing: a scientist watches dials.
We are writing the consumer's report on God.

The Sins of the Fathers

In a street of plane trees and white
Freehold houses was a notice board
Set in a privet hedge – on it a polite
Address to Londoners who could afford

A cheque or banker's order: Help to stop
Vivisection, trapping, horse-meat
From Ireland, myxomatosis, shop-
Windowed pets, martyrdoms on four feet.

A few faded snapshots, the sun so bright
It made you squint; one, overexposed,
A world bleached blind; the white
Is snow; a patch of shade shows

Teeth of a trapped bear dancing on
Nothing. Elegantly extended,
His paw shakes hands with a trap. He's wrong
To grin, his eyes can't follow. It ended

A long time ago among tacit conifers
This dance from the bite of the trap's
Teeth. Somewhere every second occurs
Some unswervable agony. Perhaps

Only my mind's trite safety
Needs excusing. I walk in the sun
And welcome guilt. In the thirteenth century
As his idea of forensic fun

Hulagu Khan forced a satrap to eat
Himself to death. The bits of meat
Hacked off and cooked, he never caught
Up, though he devoured his two feet.

Which of my extremities will I be robbed of?
I pay out my ungrudged money
And long attritions of my love
To raise a daughter. In her pram, she

Looks up at the plane trees. Daddy owes
Her his flesh like a fattened steer.
The happy love-transfusion grows
More palpable. She subtracts him year

By year until the world is cold
And he is fit only for eating plants.
His meaty sins on her, the old
Trap of his body bites and he must dance.

Requiem for Mrs Hammelswang

Let us lament her now, this lady with
The fat-stained apron and the dazzling dropsy,
Her voice a kindness to the sniffing dogs
Who all her life could never speak no English
But only morse her thoughts with banging forks.
She kept a billy goat and shared its smell.
They all slept in one room. While we snored
Her family was Transylvania in the dark.
We were the democrats our parents were
And gave our seats up in a crowded tram –
'I've warmed it for you Mrs Hammelswang'.

Her daughter Elsie, born not more than
Ninety miles from Freud, got pains –
They eased her with the drugs of '35.
No good, they took her to the primrose
Hospital that got our Lord Mayor knighted,
And gave her lumbar punctures – she
Never winced nor ever smiled again.
With calm and sweet determination
She sorted chocolate cards right through
The stock of hundreds till she found
The one you wanted. Her headaches filled

Europe's body till it stank upon the map.
Their Rumania was made of mullet eyes
Spat at by hours of burning fat.
The fish they sold was rich with Danube mud;
Cheap white metal canisters shook out
Saline persecution, dandruff salt.
The White Australians in the next-door store
Took away her custom and she died. Elsie took
To wearing odd stockings. Gum trees shone
Like gun barrels, wattle smelled of dust,
A new tram stop was painted, trade revived.

Two Merits of Sunshine

'When you were about seven you were playing
Among the fallen fleshy palmnuts
On the pink cement path running through buffalo grass.
It was four o'clock in the afternoon,
Your mother had been shopping – you saw her come past
The paling fence and click the stiff clickety latch.
She was powdered in a talc of sweat
And smiled a brown and gold mouthful
Of smile, a donation of her stones
Of sunburned fat. She gave you a wind-up toy,
Pillar-box red with a registration number,
And you broke the spring by overwinding it
A minute afterwards. That was what the friends
And neighbours meant: you had broken your mother's heart.
In the kitchen, among the blue-ringed jugs,
Your mother was under a spinnaker of laughter

56

And all the time she was bellying out to death.
Having defined love you never needed it again,
Or its fat victim in a flowered dress,
Or a garden to tease perfection in.'

'I don't remember anything about it.
I recall only fireworks, basket bombs,
Burning letter boxes, jumping jacks,
The long-bonnetted cars of relations,
The two green snakes dangling by their tails
From a branch of the umbrella tree
And always the great antiphlogestine sun
Packing my chest with smells, the grass fires
Burning in my eye, the sulky afternoon
Drifting slowly down the cloudless sky.
As for love, I smell sex drying,
A fish box on a quay, a tin of mullet gut,
The gleam of slime that comes upon
The silver sleep of her adjacence.
I now read fashion magazines and
Deplore Mother's Day. There are no
Lovable fat women in Heaven, nothing crooked
Is made straight and no rough places plain.'

The View from Misfortune's Back

May God who is good make the porridge
Have more sugar today. Also as
Privilege let me sit next to Kleinschmidt,
And if I whisper don't let the patrol
Monitor hear me. I put water
On my hair, I washed my face, I owned
Up when the chess set disappeared.
Please let me get down town this week to
Cleaver's bookshop. I know that you, like
R. M. Ballantyne, can reveal
Our faults to us – like last week when
I wouldn't put my hand down the bowl
Of the lavatory to save my mother's
Picture, or when I joined in when they
Went for Armitage. I thought then of
Peterkin and the spider and those

Long hard swims to the wreck. Or do I
Mean the Swiss Family Robinson
Whom God tucked up in a cosy island
And showed the natural way to live.
I am a castaway in a world
Ruled my Matron – she is the right hand
That makes my world left-handed – I dredge
My hate of her to understand her.
Her brain is sick with health, mine with fear.
She secretly knows why it is some
Boys' collars stay stiff but mine goes limp,
Their shoes keep a shine, mine don't, why when
Clothes are left in the locker room they're
Always mine. And why the monitors
Who win trophies don't want me in their
Dormitories. I am on misfortune's back.
Here comes Kunkel from organ practice –
Let him like me, don't let me wince when
He asks for the syrup in his high
Girl's voice, or leave him when it's roll-call
And I want to be with James's Lot. Love
Lives outside our granite, we are kept
From people's sight. When all our sharp faces
Go into the world, I want to love
The softness of people, the sheer chance
Which makes them lovable. I'll lose at
Draughts tonight to show you I mean it.
It takes sacrifice to make the world
Worthwhile – meanwhile, there's Reithmuller who
Pissed in my locker, him and his
Acne. To forgive him I sit up
Straight while grace is said and pass him the
Dripping he always gets done out of.
If we go to the Baths today, let
Me and Sorrenson stay late and swim
Without our togs. Let me dream about
My Mother and the airedale as I used to.
I have only this black orphanage
And the map of the world with all its red
To make me real. We have to die, so
There must be Someone Else who says
This man shall be happy and this one
Have a long one and this a good swimmer
And this someone everyone likes, or

58

Else we'd be responsible for ourselves
And having seen Dickinson how could
This be so? Prayers are over, birds raise
Their voices in the licey eaves and
Plain daylight hovers everywhere.
Someday it'll all be measured, but
Misfortune leaves its bite mark and you
Are never free of anything you did.

An Anthropologist's Confession

A few miles above here the stifling water
   Bursts from its intransigent confines,
Scouring milk quartz and couch grass, then falls shorter
   Tiring on this plain, and soon resigns
Itself to a crystal cantering at three and a quarter

Knots. Sheep that stumble in can wade out again;
   There are three fords in a mile, a frightened
Bird is confident enough to nest (a hen
   Bird widowed by crack slingers) on lightened
Twigs over the paltry rapids – local men

Say they can spit higher than the rising spray.
   Very likely. But it is terrible
Here. I quote from my diary. Late in the day
   I came to this spot full of the smell
Of wild honeysuckle. I knelt in white clay

To scoop water from the vague stream. Then I saw
   On the other bank a naked girl,
Beautiful as pearl, wade from the shelving shore
   Till waves tapped her vagina. She curled
Her hair up high and splashed her body. Before

My eyes she cleansed herself with water and a leaf,
   Two naked girls stood behind her. Then,
Roaring upstream, a goatherd, miserly thief
   Of his own flock for the grim woven
Cloth he wore, splashed to her side, his bulging beef

Fuming with lust. He spreadeagled her and laid
    Her on the milky clay. I watched from
Across the mild water, my ears and eyes sprayed
    By yells and splashes. I felt the thong
Of his lust whipping her, his short sword invade,

His tongue in my own lips like a strap of fire.
    Fill her with blood I heard myself say.
He left her and cooled his face in the river;
    Her maids propped her on the hard grass. Day
Turned over to night, the tight moon climbed higher

Than the fence of hills – I left the place purged in
    Conscience by this rape as though my own
Semen had uncurdled. I knew myself virgin
    And my shame fell on me like a stone.
I went to the village headman, my urgent

Need banking a headache. I promised him
    Two Mausers he coveted – a smile
And a touch of his death's hand and a cold whim
    Was fact – they dragged that goatman a mile
On his head and set the village dogs on him.

I was conducted to the body, the throat
    A jungle of cables, the face gone
Utterly. I am determined to devote
    My life's work to their legends, the dawn
Of life is still alive here. I intend to quote

His death in my 'Myths and their Parallels'.
    I visited the old men in their
Council, gave them aspirin to combat spells
    From goat bleats, paid ten pounds to repair
Their totem, drank from their malarial well.

A man must never flinch beneath the hard rod
    Of his purpose. I went without sleep
All night priming their bard, a gummy Hesiod
    With Bright's disease. The fixed stars run deep
As dreams. I too am made in the image of God.

Homage to Gaetano Donizetti

There was a sugar farmer's son (hyperthyroid)
I knew who was just like Nemorino,
And a girl in the Everest Milk Bar
Whose tits rubbed the cold of the ice-cream churn
As she reached down with her cheating scoop –
You saw more if you asked for strawberry –
She had a cold Christ hung over that defile
Crucified in silver, his apotheosis
In dry ice fumes. She was just like bel'Adina,
All the magic in the world wouldn't get
Your hand down her front unless she'd heard
Your rich uncle had just died.
Transistors behind her played Pat Boone,
But only to make a money music
In the till. Dear Master, what they say
About your big guitar is academic prejudice.
The truth is Dr Dulcamara's got
The Times Music Critic's job; the rustici
Are cooking on Sicilian gas, Venetian composers
Are setting Goethe to gongs and spiels and phones,
Teutons still come south to add a little
Cantilena to their klangschönheit
(Not to mention the boys of Naples), and those apostles,
The Twelve Notes, are at work on their Acts
To beautify our arrogance. Why should you care
That your audience are stuffed shirts if you know
That half at least have paid up for their seats.

Happening at Sordid Creek

I chose the blonde from the chemist's, thirty-six,
Twenty-three, thirty-seven. I was Midas,
We had a lifetime's touching to get through.
The triple-jointed animals ran to our hands
To be made gold. I put her on my island
With the things saved from the wreck, the stove
We made, the palm-leaf bra, the dog

That howled outside whenever we made love.
I showed her the ribbed rubber print left
By the Master-Sergeant. I undertook the naming
Of nascent things; the empty frame of the enormous
World excited me until it became just
Like death: it stopped when I said stop,
Although we still had to take a reading

Of the sun and our goats were sore with milk.
Here they come then, my rescuers. Bang, bang,
But they don't fall down. It draws the juice
Out of your spine and you go mad. The world's
A hospital, we won't get well. I was a sieve
That held water: I rejoice I thought of you.
One day I'll sit in an eau-de-nil office
And ask Miss Palethorpe the time, then go
Down to folded white napkins, the set lunch
And my first stroke at about half past one.

The Great Poet Comes Here in Winter

Frau Antonia is a cabbage:
If I were a grub I'd eat a hole in her.
Here they deliver the milk up a private path
Slippery as spit – her goddess' hands
Turn it to milk puddings. Blow, little wind,
Steer in off this cardboard sea,
You are acclimatized like these vines
Warring on an inch of topsoil
You are agent of the Golden Republic,
So still blow for me – our flowers look one way,
If I were a good poet I would walk on the sea.

The sea is actually made of eyes.
Whether of drowned fishermen or of peasants
Accustomed to the hard bargains of the saints
I cannot say. Whether there will be
Any mail from Paris or even broccoli
For dinner is in doubt. My hat blew off the planet,
I knelt by the infinite sand of the stars
And prayed for all men. Being German, I have a lot of soul.
Nevertheless, why am I crying in this garden?
I refuse to die till fashion comes back to spats.

From this turret the Adriatic
Burns down the galley lanes to starved Ragusa,
How strange it can wash up condoms.
The world is coming unstitched at the seams.
All yesterday the weather was a taste
In my mouth, I saw the notes of Beethoven
Lying on the ground, from the horn
Of a gramophone I heard Crivelli's cucumbers
Crying out for paint. In the eyes of a stray bitch
Ribbed with hunger, heavy with young,
I saw the peneplain of all imagined
Misery, horizontal and wider than the world.
I gave her my unwrapped sugar. We said Mass
Together, she licking my fingers and me
Knowing how she would die, not glad to have lived.
She took her need away, I thought her selfish
But stronger than God and more beautiful company.

How to Get a Girl Friend

1

Be concealed among the lower bushes
Under a mixture of shadows
Cast by the teasing sun,
Have the parts of a God straining to move,
Know the ways nymphs take through the woods,
Be even more knowing,
Have read the scholiasts and their heirs
The New Scholars,
Be finally knowing,
Have trained your nose away from familiar scents
To this difficult virgin undertaking.
Here she comes at the proper pubescence,
Step out and say: I am your fate.
Then the rest is parting of hairs.
Tuning her cries to the old scale,
Washing the country face in its own tears
And if found out a minor constellation
Or perhaps two old parents on a pension till death.

63

Be tubercular in a city
Where there have been two pogroms
Since the last census: be baptised
By old and doting parents, have been patted
On the head by the senile Emperor
On his morning walk across the park,
Have just spent too much on a minor example
Of rococo the same evening your avant-garde
Story is being read to the Literary Society,
Be snug in the knowledge
Of the great Diaries timed to explode
In at least three capitals when your lungs
Give out: then, at last, approach
That thin girl with the Missal
In the open-air café where the Hungarian Band plays,
Show her the entries for June 5th and August 9th
And while the lovely tubercule tunnels
Get beyond the Mimi stage, arrive at
The calm of many quarrels till
Surrounded by friends your unnecessary affair
Achieves its apotheosis and the Gods
Hang Heaven black with emblems for you.

When your girl dies they'll turn your summerhouse
Into a tram shelter where men write
I want it tonight and nylon knickers give off sparks
And birds find nothing new whoever shelters there.

Be man enough to end those pointless weekends,
Bitching in her tiny kitchen, talking Zen,
Sneaking down the dark steps mined with bottles –
Take a new room across town, don't open her letters.

Put oriental wisdom and cryptic sense
Under your foot – dress well, get drunk once a week,
Build up debts: somebody has to take
Responsibility of all these girls.

Be exposed to mirrors and start to burn.
Then to work. That girl you're looking at
Who seemed to be with that appalling type
Is looking back : bring your leg across.

She's talking about the different tastes
Of oysters: she can't mean it. Now
Puff up those small feathers, they may dazzle.
You can grow wings flying to the sun.

4

Be coaxed from parsing love's fine language,
Be the right man in the right place for once.
Suck the straw she passes you,
Lick the grass stain off her skinny knees –
The air of afternoon is hairy,
The ground thick in dismembered bees.
Soon enough, thundering in the distance,
She turns her Breughel landscape round
To trap the late sugar of the sun.
Say to her, Darling, kiss my hot ears,
Touch my eyes with your tongue,
Cure me of the plainness in my mind.
You are the great Atlas of my childhood,
All your names are furry caterpillars
Crawling to me across the tall Carpathians.
You have come so far to see me
I will sleep when you have gone. The outer
Suburbs are selling lime drinks though
The sun is now low down, the clang
Of iron gates carries like glockenspiels
Across the valley, the old quarry
Is filled with light, tadpole fishers
Are ready to hear their mothers' shouts.
It can never have been so beautiful
Or worth so many lics: I am at home here
In my nest of doubts. Open your eyes love,
The sun adorns us with its happenings.

Story from a Time of Disturbance

The forest is on fire. The red sun's doing
  That, going down. If you put your hand
Over your face and look at the light, your fing-
  ers glow. I know how things work, understand
More than just hiding. I can sneak close and sing

To deceive the prophet bird and the stock dove.
    I know how to pray and dance – I can give
Eine feste Burg ist Unser Gott loud above
    A hailstorm. The black eagle can't live
If it breaks a wing; I walk on bogs, I shove

The bear from his hole in the tree. You won't find
    Me fretted by ants or eyeless from
Crow pecks. But I have a fault, I'm colour-blind
    From seeing blood. I'm on the high Dom
At Ulm and the blood's rising; there's a red rind

On the world. You'd think rain was green if it had
    Colour, not being sticky or hot,
But it's red as the froth on a stuck sow. Dad
    Used to say the world was a lung of God
And we were the blood. The hermit who went mad

Saw angels propping a ladder on the sky
    Like a barn ladder leading to Heaven –
Up it go the soldiers and the girls while I
    Hide in the turnip bin, count seven
And open my eyes. They're making peasant pie –

Two soldiers with a girl for filling. And here
    They've shoved an iron funnel down Dad's throat:
They're good at priming pumps – cold Swedish punch, beer
    From the cess pit. He's a paper boat
Losing shape as death rides him over the weir.

They flood him to flatness. I was humming with fear,
    I thought they'd hear me. For seven days
Like a sleeping top I sang in the same air
    Among the ripening dead. I took sprays
Of green oats from the field and stood in despair

Under the forest roof. I'm looking for God
    Now, but the blood keeps following me.
When they drain men down to their souls, to the bod-
    ies of nest-shaken wrens, then will we
Be saved, gold at last before the God of blood.

Nine Points of the Law

1

I am not put off by the gold filling
Beating in your tidal mouth,
Your orange sign will never change to GO.
Your orange sign will never change to GO.
I wish I were a nylon thread
Meshed against your thigh: we stand
Together and cannot move our arms
Or prick desire out of this frozen flail.
Up close a 15 denier smoothness is
Vector of all intolerable strains.

2

When you haven't been too careful
Making up your mask,
When the duty you owe your vanity
Has been skimped for other vanities,
Looking at your face reminds me of these things –
A landlady's chocolate cake for
The oldest guest's birthday, a picture
Of Aunty Helen in costume as Yum Yum,
An author's smile on a remaindered book,
A lizard with a broken tail, a fruit-tray
From the coronation of George VI,
Half a page of record reviewer's prose.

3

A few minutes after you said No,
I saw him come down Smiler's Alley,
The Moral Re-Armament Man, throwing
The sun over his shoulder to daunt
The clouds, heaving largesse of his good
Digestion on the fuming air, clutching
A record of Matt Monro in one hand
And acknowledging the world's greeting with the other.

4

With your hop, hop, hop, flickering
At topics, you have just intentionally
Killed an innocent hour. You slay me, you say.
Just then I saw you where the sea piled up its dead,
Head down through woodsmoke tallying
The heroes, and in the clatter of that sea
I heard the sound of a world's breaking:
This and the Emperor's night music
Keeps the stars off, mollifies the slain.

5

Leave a bit early on Friday and come down
On the Director's train. Change at Ufton,
Get the old blue bus at the terminus.
Mrs Scraggs's shop is now second last
In the street – look for the new school,
All glass and Finnish timber. I've put
Some beer in the 'frig. I'm afraid there won't be
Any roses, my pruning was a flop.
The cow parsley's high now as the house,
Twelve delphiniums are flowering
On the south side, I've counted them
Topping the rack and ruin of the grass.
Beat by beat we'll get our summer back,
Go upstream where the crow's corpse hangs,
Your old guide to a good place to make love;
There in the fiction of a moment
We'll set the poor history of our nerves;
Rein in to the nearness of the sun.

6

Now said the machine I speak your want,
Words are what I use,
Labels on that ten square feet of skin,
Your friend, my friend, old tabby, your grin
Running the wrong way – I give you
These old symbols, unequal letters which
You put in hand – itch/bitch/kitsch –
Problems from the cradle, you're still bandy
And I can't ride a bike. The oracle speaks.
Two tickets to the Dunciad on Ice,

Kierkegaard was a commuter too, can I come and smell you,
I am a graduate in English from Madras?
A bored funicular of books crosses
The barbarous centuries to us, a Paradise
Open seven days a week where you needn't
Take the missus or the kids. Kein musik
Ist ja nicht auf erden, die unsrer
Verglichen kann werden. Can you afford
Such holy architecture? As V.I. Lenin
Said to L.D. Trotsky, if you can't
Join them, beat them. Now touch
Those printed words with sugar tongs,
They're bloody. He read them, went to Spain
To a city of ten thousand whores
And a budget for swamp drainage. He wrote back
Words are for what you cannot do.
Sleepy men watch him writing in a ruled
Exercise book – three parrots watch. The heat
He said, is full of *instant* pain,
Just now I'm glad at least of
Dr Donne, firm crab meat, my mosquito net.
Outside my cot the words of malice jump,
They turn into people looking out for gin,
Now they'll have rights and wrongs and promises,
Preferences known to Privy Councillors,
Ways of being unkind to the three parrots.
I hate the world beautifully, indifferently,
And your glands and your heart not more than any.
That's right for sound, that's syntax if you like,
That's what I'm pursuing down your throat,
You word I want, flesh from the beginning.

7

That over-sexed actor Manicius
Dark as Mauretanian molasses
Has been run in for beating up a tart
Who'd been sharing a hammock with one
Of Domitian's generals. There's been
A defeat somewhere cold: the informers
Turned on Sulpicius, Police Chief Galba's
Before the Senate now. There's no doubt
Old city families hate big buck pushers
From North Africa, Sardinian goat-feet,

Depilated little grubs from Gades.
Old Cato made his one joke – I don't like
Chocolate éclair. Well, they've had to let
Manicius go, because the tart was lying.
As for me, I'm off to Baiea
Before the informers get warmed up,
Even though it's the holiday season
And there's a drunk up every tree.
I saw that little thistlehead, Martial,
At the bookshop, pollinating opinions,
Sparing some time from dining out
To push his poems. I tried him on a riddle.
'If the golden bowl be broken, the silver cord
Unloosed, the seven sleepers stirred
In their pot of dreams, how does Hippo-
Campus keep his tail curled, whose civil farts
Fan the long face of middle ocean?'
I left him in the tangle of his tongue,
His host's silver cheese stirring in his throat
A pair of borrowed sandals to his itch.

8

What belongs here is hard houses
Flayed to their stucco, the veins
Of plumbing frozen, to which come
Men in gloves for the soldering winter
Sworn to set free stuffiness again.
These lupins are owned by looks – let them dance!
Spring-heeled crocus needs no green fingers
Of young married to come erect.
These houses stand against Doomsday,
They ruin the parkland of my mind.
But there's always one focus of pardon,
The ancestral chestnut, its roots underpinning
Every jostling outhouse, that and a voice
Following the black lashing of the phone.
The Estate Agent's car scatters gravel,
Suede shoes usurp the velvet of old grass.
To make me native of his gingerly ground
You must welcome me with secrets
And family names for roses: I could grow
Into hope here, walking with the dogs
Piloting acres in their iron round.

Managed as they say about such men
To get his foot on the ladder; owed
His success to his first wife and his second
Wife to his success. Took that car
All the way to Smyrna, argued in Turkish,
Powers that helped him swing a boardroom.
Used nicknames in the pits and nobody
Winced, carved thin like a seaside
Landlady and everyone called it eccentric,
Mended his own fuses. Was seen once
Crying on a northern station, his book
On coarse fishing dropped and the tan boxer
Licking his hand with unforced love.
We do not mind if our city is known for him,
That the unnamed scavengers of fact
Catch him asleep, this ambitious planner
Who had no imagination and did well.
Call him suzerain of green – it will destroy him.

To Start a Controversy

Despite its late exhibition at the
Biennale, I hold it in fact
To be really archaeological
Evidence of my controversial
Claim – that claim, gentlemen, in defence
Of which I stand before you – that it
Is definitely none other than
A perfect example of what
The ancients called LOVE. I can see from
Your expressions you are incredulous;
No one ever found more than a hint
Of love before, how can I dare claim
I have identified it. Well, gentlemen,
Let me describe it. It was formed
Through the action of volcanic dust
Settling on the bodies of two humans,
Then slowly replacing their flesh and
Bone in a process of chemical
Substitution, while preserving their
Outlines as in a sculptor's mould.

We find the resulting image very
Beautiful. The woman is on
Her back, her legs are arched up beside
Her trunk so as to permit access
To the fork between them. One of her
Hands is under her own posterior
As if to jack it up. The man is
Lying on her, his own legs pretty
Straight but bent just enough to give his
Toes purchase – otherwise he's stretched
On top of her, his face on her face,
His body along hers. Where they fulcrum
Is merged and can't be identified
Certainly. It would seem the ancients
Were impelled somehow to go through this
Act for reasons we do not understand.
With one hand, for instance, he's squeezing
Her chest, the other is behind her back,
And reappears up over her neck
Clutching her breast bone. Why are they in
This uncomfortable position?
The act this larva-mould portrays
Is, I am sure, that act of love the
Ancients wrote of, of which we have so few
And such very tantalising records.
Unfortunately, I acknowledge
Most of these talk of souls, loss, tears, dreams,
Separation, painful absence, star-
Crossings, hopeless interviews, etc.
Professor Wedekind insists that
To the ancients love was the same as
Copulation, a procreative act
About which we possess even less real
Information. I suggest that what
We have here proves him correct. Experts
On art speak of this relic's sense of form,
Its golden mean of beauty, balance
Of opposites, cantilever poise.
It is undeniably very
Beautiful, but if love as we think
Was the mainspring of ancient life, then
Wasn't it beautiful and didn't
Art adopt its forms? We cannot know
What made this man and woman

Perform this act whose record we admire
Such centuries later – it is enough
To have identified it. Looking,
We see that time has left nothing on their faces.
I pause on the springboard of my real
Discovery. Gentlemen, are we
Not also in the actual presence
Of DEATH; now we may unveil their whole
World. Death was what made them what they were.
From knowledge of death they made up love,
Whose shape we see, acting against oblivion.

Encounter in Antioch

Your God became a man, our grandest men
Have trouble becoming Gods. You've got
Three Legions now and their influence grows
With the superstition of the Emperor.
And those terrible Alexandrian disputers
Always wanting to cut their balls off
And everybody else's too. No wonder
Three-headed goats are coming out of
The desert. I met a man had three shits
A day in honour of the Trinity.
But one day this theologian's world
Of pain and dirt may surprise you,
The wind off the sea may bring the Tyrian
Scent to your garden, and then you hear
A million brainless jaws jarring the lawn,
You're fanned by a million ledger leaves
Turned by quilted, careful hands.
Drink down a cup of water and look out
On the town – the someone whose hat
You laugh at may stop and the great tide start
To come in on his stranger's gifted face.

Shopping Scenes

1

Huge heads of amiable malice
Hang across the shop in processed air
Saying: 'At Uncle Holly's Christmas Hollow, see Alice
Disembowel the Mad Hatter and the March Hare.'

2

Behind his half-moon glasses, the
Sesquipedalian don is triumphant.
He's found an 1870 Book of Nursery Care –
The same stiff-backed volume on his bare
Backside wielded by his arthritic aunt
Terrified his childhood. Terror warmly
Returns. 3/6 will set him free again –
Happy Return of guilt and certainty and pain.

3

Snubbed by that bouffant giggly girl,
All tit and bum drinking Babycham
At the office party, he leaves early
And dashes into the record shop, buys
'La Favorita' with his Christmas bonus.
Spending money is the kindest orgasm.

4

(An advertising man in the Palermo Catacombs)

Panthering here on handsewn turquoise suede,
He captions this Capuchin light and shade.

This Memento Mori floods Harper's Bazaar.
That 'overwhelming minority' of readers stares

At the mummies' now exclusive dust,
The season's silhouette, the witty bust.

The mask white model has a little heat.
Mr Avedon makes death famous. 'The feet

In off-the-shoulder shoes are real breath-
takers.' It's way out here at the House of Death.

Inspector Christopher Smart Calls

Dear Friends, I have to convince you
The world you stand on is no surer
And no safer than instant pie crust.
'Instant' – yes, when the signal comes,
(Perhaps two lemon-coloured crocuses
Will flash the word across antennae,
A striped ant ferry it to our depot
Under a saw-edged tin of condensed soup),
Then it happens. What is it? Your personal
Parousia, the Biggest Show on Earth,
Meggido or bust! But until it happens
It's the breath of life to investors. And
Haven't I invested: Mrs Midnight,
Grub Street garnishings, a seriousness
Of creditors? I warn you, don't try to turn me
Away from the door like a Jehovah's Witness,
I can put more than coupons through the crack,
I can give you sixpence off eternal fire,
Green Stamps for the furnishings of Heaven.
I'm investigating love. Holy Thrift!
What can you show me? Did you ever
Have a plan to fit metric to the psalms?
How about counting the D's in Deuteronomy,
The whole book? Too bad. Something simpler?
Perhaps a water clock that only dripped
In Advent? An hermaphrodite Pope
From the Joke Shop with working parts
To embarrass Catholic friends? A plastic
Missal leafed with Tote tickets? Come on,
There must be something mystical about you.
Did you ever lie about Sicily to your son's Headmaster?
Use your vowels on a pink paraffin man?
No joy? I'm trying to help you. Just say that once
You felt unhappy, that's how catechism starts.
You know that great philosopher on telly,
The one who still looks randy at eighty-five –
A million selfishnesses have oiled his skin,
A spark of light on his mummied eye
And he'll basilisk your girl friend – now here's
The point, get with him, he's history, he's life!
What've you done that's got a gasp from noses
Pressed against lace window frames? A few sins,

A few imitation jewels? You've not been big enough.
For in my nature I quested for beauty,
But God, God has sent me to sea for pearls.
Dredge the great main of your dreams,
Everything is fragile. The Captain
Of Take-Overs, that cutlass of the City,
Has a septic throat, his Renoirs offer him
Extreme unction; a merger's afoot inside
The liver of Lord M : you need facts, poor Klaus
Has gout, his toes are cut off from the Chairman's
Blood supply. But energy is conserved –
For I am in twelve hardships, but He that
Is born of a Virgin shall deliver me
Out of all. Join the Titus Oates Society –
No more Liberal Popes. Reform among
One's enemies is the start of decadence.
Hate gives warmth. Sea-cow's milk is the drink
Of Paradise. But are you worthy? I have
My foot in the door so don't push. That's despair.
Nothing you give me will be spent on drink,
You get a receipt. God's Kingdom is eternal
But what you do here is on a meter.
No man is a sea, each is a fixed island;
I'm set to come ashore, you see me waving
From the boat. Rub your eyes, beware the sun
That makes this semaphore. The palms
Are fruiting, the cross-bred parrots cry,
A shot goes in, the heart abandons home.

A PORTER FOLIO

The Last of the Dinosaurs

Chalky, you've gone –
the only one to see the last
stegosaurus, the blue-edged plain
with bald egg-eaters blurring it,
eighty days' rain
before the mating season
and parsley blades neck high –

nice to have known such niceness,
these Cretaceous days!
Tyranno – sore arse – Rex
and other thick necks
thrive. Where's the gentle
ninety ton nonsense
we ate mustard grass beside?

So much time and blue.
That great arc telling
the centuries with its pivotless
movement, tick, tock, tick:
you can watch evolution
in those hairy faces
and poor Protoceratops being sick.

Another gentle day and
nothing to do. When you've lasted
150 million years
you can stand the sound of time.
Some day a mind is going to come
and question all this dance –
I've left footprints in the sand.

Valete and Salvete.
I hear the wintering waters rise
under the hemstitched sky.
Put me in the anthologies,
darling, like Horace almost
killed by a falling tree;
life is a dream or very nearly.

The Three Dreams

The Bird Dream :
My feet turn out
so I am a duck,
no, a coot and I have a white beak
and suggestive walk.
You're throwing bread on the water,
I take a piece from your hand
and have to waddle over gravel to do it.
I'm a floating furnace of love
but I'm not adapted to walking,
You walk away over the pathway
and the statue-mounted grass.

The Egg Dream :
My white is cool
and slippery
and nourishing.

My yoke is rich,
half-way to red
and nutty.

All of me is yours;
a little bit of me
is left at the corner
of your mouth.
They had to cook me
before you wanted me

The Poem Dream :

> If the ink lasts
> this poem will get me finished.
>
> Not only the ink
> the inspiration must stay the distance.
>
> So I wait my blue epiphany
> between phone calls and trips to the kitchen.
>
> You're wearing a mini-skirt
> that's well-judged for a girl of thirty,
>
> You're making me on the page
> and smile at the pun.
>
> 'I was born of an act of love
> and now I shall never change.'

The Thirteen Couplets

I have found an opening into high self-love
Like a belly full of God in stained glass.

This is one of those parthenogenetic cases,
A new sweet for souls with a self taste.

There are no visions, alas: just as I was getting to know
Dirigibles we start to rendezvous in space.

But I must keep to happiness: happiness is possible
Though there's usually something sexual about it.

Flowers may do and parts of the country
No Liverpool poet has heard of. Joseph Haydn helps.

I thought of a definition: a date with Miss Albion,
The poor chameleon angel led by Blake,

Your small island of torts and friends
Moored somewhere off Radio Caroline,

A sort of Heavenly Donaueschingen
With concrete poets out in dancing pumps

And bewildered bees pulling at plastic flowers
In borders beside pubs with ancient names.

I had heard of your huge sepulchres,
Monuments to Milton and the sweat of stones.

Ah martyrdom, said the colonial, his feet turning out,
This is where they buried Arthur Mee and the remarkable things.

There's no art to find the mind's construction in the face,
My enemy and I both love Shakespeare.

But Time reports that God is dead. Long live God.
I am struggling with the pronouns me and my. I am happy,

My Late T'ang Phase

Unexpected sun on white icing terraces,
Little girls ringing my doorbell and giggling,
More than a lifetime between six o'clock and seven,
Enough loneliness for a novel, enough poise.
Ambition fights talent more than sloth does.
I sit in the warmer, the caramel darkness
Watching two worldly eyes: where is the inseminate
Of boredom, the Rilke of the inflamed will?

Why be beleaguered by nerves only?
Why not have tanned historical enemies?
My friends find new forms which make kites
Of confessions: whatever your taste there's
Blood here to back it. I take eight-hundred page
Histories of Florence from Paddington Library.
I know nine tabby cats, all pregnant. News?
They dug up the dead who were smiling.

Fantasia on a Line of Stefan George

I shall die if I do not touch your body.
If I cannot claim a small priest-like
Privilege at your waist, my masks
Of face will slip, no tides will work
Your body's shores, no storms rouse
That inland sea. On a hectoring day
I stood in the Natural History Museum
And couldn't breathe. The blue whale
And the passenger pigeon worried for me,
Surely my fingers were losing their prints,
I had no history in my bones, I was
Transparent as a finished gesture.
Where you are is life: this sunlessness
Is only inside my head,
The inverse paradise, rain forest where
Evolution's mother blocked with eggs
Waddles with beak aloft to spin
The thread of fear that leads back to you.

The Battle of Cannae

As a great wonder in a world of names
    the child picks Hannibal to be his hero,
outgenerals Rome on the southern grass –
    all day the slaughter lasts, the thrill
radiates to yellow bedroom walls;
    a cell of power is forming in his head
(a model of the battle worth ten
    thousand marks was commissioned by
the German General Staff): at three o'clock
    in the afternoon it ends; the boy
leaves the Carthaginian panthering,
    takes a sore finger and dislike of sport
into frightening Saturday commonplace.
    To bruise his mind upon the bloody froth
of battles he will expel the air
    from dove-clapped house and sandy street.
No right but clemency can save a life;
    he travels back to find the stretch marks
on history, arrives at the same eclipse
    white-mouthed, informed, explanatory.

81

After the Temptation

I come to teach stones
They need not reach for bread;
A thistle carries arms, a sheep's eye
Stands in Heaven for an opal –
Father, the world is only painted on!
No one's here, I am unprayed by prayer.

I laughed on top of the Temple,
To fall, dog-paddle in God's air,
What are the molecules, the molecules for!
Let that woman die, this bird might lose a wing.
Jump and you can look – Jerusalem
Is always underfoot, when will I be there?

The Travel Agent sent me
Pictures of worlds beyond the piers.
The dogged here has no vacancies,
No boat is leaving. Water returns
The only answer. Father of walls and wharves,
We move. The world is only painted on!

I lead the revolt of iron filings
In the magnetic field.
I am blue and yellow mixed, I am red,
I am God's knees he kneeled in
To kill me, I am dead Abraham,
Dead Isaac, dead star, dead dog dead.

Dorothy Osborne in the Country

Watching the doves in the drowned park,
Every leaf dripping its colourless wax,
The shine of water over the world's face,
I envy the slightest fish in its cold pond.
I shall take the waters of Epsom for my spleen
Among high ladies and their little dogs:
Boredom is like the great clock in the hall,
It writes the hours with unchanging face.

My suitors' wheels turn upon the drive :
Sir Entail and Sir Gravitas approach –
The one owns all a lake and half a shire,
The other is tone deaf and keeps a choir.
The wet birds still sing and dare to love.
Easy to arm against melancholy,
Hard to be true hearted at midnight
Alone in England under uncertain stars.

Fortune is a horse that must be ridden,
Fear a curtain to be pushed aside.
Birds build in soundest branches,
Precepts of love hang all about my eyes.
In a field a boy fights the wind
Whipping his kite to a corner of the sky,
The string still holds and the proud frame
Turns its cheek upon the dangerous air.

A Hoplite's Helmet

Inside this helmet
A brain known to great brains

Moved to kill,
The object was in the orders.

The helmetless lover
And boozer fathered as many

New skulls as any,
But he put the helmet back on. You can

Frighten the cat
Poking your fingers through the eye pieces.

When death's eyes
Make a play for me let him approach

In this helmet;
It's sat on some howling scenes –

Witness the old lady
Of Corinth who couldn't be parted

From her sponges;
A yellow bean drying – that was a chunk

Of Epaminondas's brain,
You meet the greatest people in battle.

The helmet's worth
A thousand pounds. Verdigris takes

A month to form
And lasts two thousand years. As many

Million dead
Must come again before this metal dies.

St John on Patmos

For the right visions
You need a desert or an island.

On an island the beasts will listen,
The groundsel sneak into your cell,

Evil done on the mainland
Will let down a bloody feather at your door,

You get a lion to boss your bestiary
And the best menagerie of all in your head.

What a ramshackle day! The missed heart beat
Reforms a whole landscape :

That sail is bringing pilgrims, a hymn to God
In your convalescence – the passion-fruit flower

In its sun-suit, heliotrope under the keel
And fish choking in unbreathable blue,

Closer than the enskied artillery of the Lord
Regrettable Emperors with gold hands

And at the right moment of routine
A sure verb to bind the vision to the rock.

Doctors. Doctors. There are things to do.
Kyrie Eleison. But with the world's help.

Approaches to a Line of Auden & Kallman

Murderer and matron have reached the *petits fours*,
    Warm wasps are filching our home-made jam,
Moons ago honeysuckle wilted at this wall,
    A Telford bridge is inundated by a dam.

Nature relieves herself at the Spastics' Home,
    Sun and righteousness have challenged many,
The tapeworm hatches on a red and rindless world,
    Monsieur Necker died clutching his lucky penny.

Munch, munch, the white ants address the throne,
    Democrats have tempers and renal faults,
The carabinieri are only doing a job,
    Yes, provincials may learn the Metternich waltz.

Brou, brou, like a fire ship comes the bull
    Into a land where even death is kosher;
The fountain of youth throws up new affronts,
    The God Dionysus has entered Bœotia.

First Scene from Dostoevsky

Whatever quantum of wrong awaits
Its avenger or guilt at the way
That house opens its doors
To the bandaged talkers stirs
The aristocratic lady who
Was rude to a bandsman coming here,

Whatever premonition of nothing
Flashes like a lifted blade
The evening is full of civil music,
The trees are huge with leaf
But will not drop tonight;
Some figures we don't know well
Are promenading down the planted
Lanes. Two of them are quarrelling –
A strain on the others this, yet good
Sense prevails. Only ten minutes before
She was expected, the girl arrives
At her mother's house; half an hour
Early the man picks up his neglected
Book. Someone else is watching.
He has taken up his pen to write:
Not the shot bear or the trapped wolf,
Not the peasant crucified to
His Christ or the madman walking
In blood like snow shall
Assassinate Holy Russia
But men coming in from dances
By moonlight on an evening
With nightingales and women laughing.

Second Scene from Dostoevsky

No sir, this is the patient.
Were you to ask him what
That carriage lamp was,
He'd say a mushroom or
A sticky toffee left under
The seat by a child. He's calm,
Sir, he listens to himself.
There's a man with a flute
Inside his head, his childhood
Plays at Patience with him,
His mother was mauled by a bear –
A ridiculous cliché but
We cannot order our lives.
Beneath his eyelids he has
A map of Pomerania; he'll write
You an essay on Gustavus

Adolphus. We're going
At fifty miles an hour
Through a countryside
Of larches. That other man
In the corner, the one who
Smiles and says nothing,
He may be from Smolensk indeed,
He may also be happy
But he's the man
When we come to the end
Of this journey, in some small
Hotel, probably before dawn,
My friend will kill
And watch with for the first
Light-stepping chambermaid
And the clean light of day.

The Shining God and the
God of Correction

I am haunted, how can I doubt it?
My taxi driver had the face of Anubis,
The thin and fat ladies in their flowing shifts
Passed in and out of doors and were bowed to,
I alone had the glass closed in my face.
Is it my accent, my self deprecation, my race?

I stood by the old sawmill where you said
The reign of felicity would start: I tore
The short leaves of spring with my nails,
Red sun shone through sawdust but
Ten pigeons could mate while I stood there;
Sensibility capsized on the air.

The yabby diggers were out at four in the morning,
The Shining One stood by a weatherboard house
Dressed in towelling, with roots of grasses
Plaited in his toes. He cherished a dry bone
And watched for dawn to roast the high cloud;
At Eventide Home the wakeful birds were loud.

Death will not save you, said the Corrector,
My mind can penetrate the landlord's formica.
I can work your self-loathing to a fire,
Only your cowardice will help you now:
Grey hairs marshal on your fattening head,
The smell of rotting poems fills your bed.

List the Sullivan operas according to merit,
Write parodies of Gray's two famous Odes,
Arrange Mrs Beeton as a Cantata text,
Find in Montaigne excuses for getting drunk,
The Watcher with the Code approves these games,
Hell has no faces but many proper names.

Locked in an expanding eye within an eye
The shining world streams out to its end
That's nowhere; it's as short a journey
As to the dirt that glitters at your feet.
Each graded star is polished by the mind,
The all is paraphrased in one line.

An impersonal dream, the kind you don't connect
With your condition: walking among the dead,
Fourteen corpses alone in Station Road,
Colonial architecture, wide verandahs, frangipani,
Kelpies, straw hats, squeak of the plague cart,
The broadcasting van is wired to your heart –

No chance for the Shining One to show a snap
Of the one person you love, no late pass
Could get you back to Pleasure Pale, the train
Over the Divide has entered Cancel Cutting –
Ahead lie wheat plains in three-coloured clays,
Behind, the Fit City warm with mini-praise.

What the Guide Book Said

Sited by gull course where the river swerves
    to fit a tendon of the Giant's Heel,
they laid logs to make a parallelogram
    and, balked of stone, from mud and wattle
built their church. St Stephen-of-the-Surcingle
    was always holy: there the blessed Cunegonde

88

beheld the Virgin dreaming in a crystal,
    the scholar Timoleus waited for the call
to Rome. Fra Geronimo walked here
    with the last Margrave – they summoned
The Golden Age with twenty sheep deep grazing
    and a chaffinch picking at the crust of sky.
Soon the city boundaries hove in sight,
    the banished architect's bald cupola
flashed like a gold tooth in the morning sky;
    encroachment on these holy perches
was so quick, a brisk cockaded visitor
    was misdirected twice by citizens
on his pilgrimage. He came to hear
    the silver pornographer lecture
on the city's poet, the circle of Christ's world
    like St Catherine's wheel turning
to light each face. Wars and quarrels
    lapped the low walls, working a patina
part smoke, part blood: at last the great exile
    rode here on a farting charger, portly
to his house's restoration – sullen chimes
    and lemon fire sat upon the Square of Penitents
and again before his adoring people he set
    the pose of copulation like a God.

Seahorses

When we were children
We would cheer to find a seahorse
Among the wrack the breakers lifted
On to the beach. Sometimes two or three were together,
A team to pull a chariot of cuttle,
Or like a suicide wreathed in fine
Sea ivy and bleached sea roses
One stiff but apologetic in its trance.
Seahorses were vikings;
Somewhere they impassively
Launched on garrulous currents
Seeking a far grave: wherever
That was, they set their stallion
Noses to it, ready to be garnered
In the sea's time at the sea's pleasure.

If we wondered why we loved them
We might have thought
They were the only creatures which had to die
Before we could see them –
In this early rule of death we'd recognize
The armorial pride of head, the unbending
Seriousness of small creatures,
Credit them with the sea's rare love
Which threw them to us in their beauty,
Unlike the vast and pitiable whale
Which must be quickly buried for its smell.

Competition is Healthy

Es wartet Alles auf dich

Everything. Yes. Some men holy enough
To have seen the Buddha may try to keep
His commandments – to clothe the ragged in lightweight
Dacron, to feed the hungry with milk bread
Or curious corn, to press salve of the sacred
Laboratories of America into sores
Too big to form scabs. Yet the underprivileged
Rich pray for a Goldwater victory
Within an ant's tremor of God's instep.
Your heavenly Father knoweth that
Ye have need of all these things.
He gives bells that walk the fields
When the unsteady rice is shooting,
He gives Sebastian Bach to the citizens
Of Leipzig. Out of reach of the philharmonic
That old man is planting his garden.
He nestles each seedling in the soil,
Contrives a cotton grid to keep the sparrows off,
Sweats in conscience of his easy goal.
Unknown to him his son has scattered
Radish seed in the bed and the red clumsy
Tubers shall inherit the earth.
Take no thought saying 'What shall we eat?
What shall we drink? or Wherewithal shall we be clothed?'
We shall eat the people we love,
We shall drink their fluids unslaked,

We shall dress in the flannel of their blood,
But we shall not go hungry or thirsty
Or cold. The old man writes with a post office nib
To his son. 'The Government has cut the quotas,
Here the bougainvillea is out,
The imported rose is sinking in the heat.'

Steps on the Way

Brought down from the organ loft six books
Landscape-shaped, the Tables of the Law,
Sullenly finding all the greatness out,
Otherwise talking only to the school cooks,
Peeling onions without crying, a bore
To everyone: mother mad, father devout.

Seven years on, Cousin Thomas reports that
You've just been voted Student of the Year,
At Carnival seduce a Professor's wife,
Jeer at your friend 'old gargle-orgel, cat-
arse cantor', pay for everyone's beer
With your idiot mother's savings. The toast is life.

You disappear. High in the oberland
A somewhat old pharmacy apprentice
On a cold day lies in a field with cows.
'The boat on Galilee rests now on warm sand
And there steps ashore a God. From this
Moment the larks starve which follow the ploughs.'

The Colonel-General offers you a smoke –
On your chest a small cross speaks black courage –
You must lead the Circus now, the Baron's dead.
A letter says poor Orgel's had a stroke:
They've smuggled in La Malandrine, the stage
Can lend her for a night to grace your bed.

Ten thousand unemployed are rioting
The night your viola concerto's premièred.
The light of diamonds speaks to your pale wits.
'I saw the host that sat and heard the king
Speak to them on death. We will not be spared,
Our country's a cold whore, a Gräfenitz.'

The town's on fire. The bombers will return.
A priest brings round the late-night watered milk.
The asylum clock ticks plainly in the dark.
'This is the sermon. Until our bodies burn
God can't see us.' In your last silk
Shirt by bomb light you are fingering Bach.

The Next Hundred Years
will be Religious

Sticky from repairing his seventh vase,
Mr Spark calls for hose joints and the smell

Of lilies of the valley. You know what
The great hunchback philosopher said,

This is an age of religion. Interpret it with flowers.
There is the first pansy my green hands

Ever trained to set down rated roots.
From the verandah the sun casts inch-long

Shadows, we are so close to twelve.
The milk of poinsettias makes rubber

On my palms. Keeping to great quantities,
I see no reason to think ill of things.

For a start more people are happy than
Ever were before. More are born whole, and

If out of the corner of your eye you see
Poor Stamp, thirty-five and of no

Definite sex, think how we set him off.
Our normality fills his nostrils like

Pollen. Poor chap, they say the bees kill
Their freaks. He lifts his head and feels

Pity peppering his nose: he smiles, he thinks
Humanists are lovely from the south,

He must feel grateful for perspectives,
His body leaks into his mind. In the drift

Of blossom over the window sill
He identifies the tower of history

Long on the slack land, queened by canals
And college grass – the wind lifts his eye

To a duckling train of monks smoking out
Devils from an innocent piece of death,

Up then to the corpse clouds whose light
Applauds two tears – somewhere else

In this unjust landscape a donkey takes
Two steps forward raising water in an old bucket,

The wheel moves a broken spoke a perfect circle,
The set bee moves through its archipelago,

Beside the AA box in dusty nettles
A dog leaps a dog and finishes too soon.

The Return of
Inspector Christopher Smart

There was, there really was a time on Galilee
Our Lord distrusted the lake weed, the little
liver-leaved plant with the speck of gold,
and Him the one that put the clothes on God –
consider the lilies and the talcum of the field,
these are the munitions of his majesty;
a top product like that needs marketing
so his strategy was bold: get the kids to want it –
those manic little bonbons on a stalk
ate the fat ears in the bugles of wheat,
they're blowing under the hill till resurrection,
they seed for Heaven; see the innocent eye
wait on them with names, stinking roger,
pee-the-bed, old man's balls – they praise
The Biggest Seedsman of them all, His beds of glass
shine past all the railway lines in Surrey!

This is just the start. It's wonderful to be back
with twenty thousand of you here tonight
Earls Court up in my spiel. I know you're waiting
to hear Avro Manhattan on the trombone
and the John Knox Chorale rendering
that mighty number 'Brays the Lord and Parse
the Admonition'.
                         Lie quiet James Joyce,
we're all Protestant spies here – wait till they've got
pessaries in the medicine cabinets in all the bathrooms
in Salamanca and the pill in a twist of blue
paper in every packet of Pacelli's Crisps
(that's how I like my Jews, he said, done to a crisp).
They've taken it all in their stride – Hildebrand,
sodomy, Luther, Pio Nono, Pacem in Terris,
they'll handle a bit of campus rut
in the Catholic West. Listen to that Vatican PR
'even when our boys sniffed that A-rab tail
in Aleppo, we could still get every man Bohemond
of them on parade if Christendom was growling.
Just now we're on a Management Consultant kick
but it's the Reader's Digest to last month's Mind
things have never been so jammy in Stateside
Outremer'
                         So I remind you, don't underestimate
the Papists. Here's a few hints to fix your catholic
friends. Show them that book of Fulton Sheen
demonstrating the Mass: if they're intellectuals
that profile should do for them. And for the trogs,
send a list of seventy avant-garde poets
from the Tea House of the August Moon, all of whom
are secret catholics (put in a picture of
Thomas Merton playing backgammon with the editor
of Fortune). For my grounds in New Canaan
shall infinitely compensate for the flats and maynes
of Staindrop Moor. Coming under the hammer
at Sotheby's, Maureen Connolly's copy of the Little Flowers
with notes on the Adversary's backhand sweep.

But I digress, friends, and out of the mouth
of a pun comes the stalling truth. How, in fact,
do you die? Die well, die old, die howling,
die drunk, Dai Jenkins? I've talked to you
About life and other such old hat and a pretty

sad sight it looks, just like last week's
Colour Supplement. But what is life but the new
Unit Trust for Death? That's what we're getting ready for.
Watch for it in Monday's Newcomers. What is it
leads you beyond micro-skirts to the underside
of a cowrie?
                        Back to the Wound.
                                    Back to God.
Your mother's lips as she squeezes on a peach
in her sunmilked kitchen and the tradespeople
at the backdoor taking bets on the afternoon meeting;
little Marie under the steps among the passionfruit
showing her Junior Chamber of Commerce, the wet
wide lick of the alsatian, the one leaf on the goldfish pond
coming round for the last time, manna from
the everlasting backyard, quails for grails,
hot corrugated iron on your backside and
erections receiving Heaven – the fingers climb
the scala peccatorum to the enskied Marina
where it's always soda time and the God-girls
in their yachting caps are willing. Miss Death's
got a cold in her whiskers and now the pilgrims
swarm to that sad spot. I left my crutches by her grotto,
carried her holy picture through the streets :
For I have seen the White Raven & Thomas Hall
of Willingham & am myself a greater curiosity
than both. If you're drowning those two puppies,
miss, I'll have the one with the pink nose.

So, you're going to die. What about HIM then?
I mean that one, der geist der stets verneint
(German's the only language I like to quote in)
The Adversary, the Accuser who is judge of this world.
There's a dead God if ever I saw one, a sort
of Nietzsche with the ichor drying on his arms
beside the duckboards the first day of Passchendaele.
He's your Uncle Mick that rested his big hams
on you by the ivy wall and talked of a fat man's love :
the Devil's the sun and this puppy world
has its tongue out, lap, lap! Parry the Adversary
and believe in death.
                        You've got the scene,
we're bursting out of our budget in one of those city states,
the organizer from Romagna has got the boys

95

on the floats, they're enacting the Battle of Salamis
and the banks are lined with Master Botticelli's
'won't-melt-in-your-mouth' girls, their hands
down the apprentices' fronts. Festina Lente!
Pico and Ficino are chatting up an old rabbi
with goose fat stains on his gaberdine,
time is burning in the ladies' cheeks,
the siege machines are rumbling through the celery
and where is il popolo grasso? Taking a holiday
from cancer at the end of a Spanish pike.
Death is like this, a custom-built carnival
with the bill just about to be presented.
I see you as God sees you: one at a time, His
little Willy, daytime owl blinking at the light:
we've been Europeans now for a millennium
and where's it got us? Doing piece work
by strip lighting in Waco, Texas. It's the Anglo-Saxon's
privilege. He has his catacombs inside his head,
Rotarian dead to clap the dust he raises.
For the ENGLISH TONGUE shall be the language
of the WEST. *Dark Eyes Are Tracking Him!*
His epitaphs are polished on the moon.

At the Theatre on St Valentine's Eve

Now the machines of art are more cunning
And the bar conversations more puerile.
Skill, great skill goes into the hair,
The tits, the teeth, the smiles, the heels.
We sit ranged in an hemisphere of dark
And the sun comes out on the stage. It's late
In our world, we cannot stand pain.
Though the author is ahead of us, we have
A sophistication better than his words.
Having taken the graph of pain to the top
Of the paper, we rule new grids with love;
Why should the line ever stop? These sweet
Washed girls are virtuosi of light,
Mutants of harm are lovely and come to the call —
The West is washing its dirty linen in blood.

Moaning in Midstream

You can see the Master's latch-key
at the University of Anaconda,
plus a note from a girl who wanted
to write poetry ('I feel vowels like peaches'),
the picture he bought at the Salon –
'Sardanapalus Prepares for Death' –
and several letters to a Normandy vet
about boarding out his dog.
I looked in one hot day in June
before rehearsing my Organa
for Thirteen Orchestras. Lucky Master,
I thought, living at the doomed end
of a serious century, and went off
to hear Knipper's Concerto for Farts.
But there in the library gloom go
the dark geniuses, dapper and intense
in their fin de siècle silences,
caught by the camera ridiculously
at Seine boating parties, or heavy-glanded
watching balloons go up: arrogant,
incurable, hell in the home –
No point in regretting them or lauding
their relics – still, how nice just
not to be here at the fifth concert
of the series, trying hard to be fair, trying
harder still to like something, feeling
only breath won too easily on closed faces.

The Eclipse of Lady Silvertail

Baffled by clarity, her last victims
Stare at us from library books,
Donizetti's fevers and syrup of digitalis,
Wolf's mask of rest at the end
Of a screaming century. Watch by
Your brother's bed for copy, the end
Of a man may have the most artistry.
It's all public now: never more
The spent genius wrapped in rugs
With mercury-blacked teeth, wheeled

97

To a yellow hedge, his amanuensis by.
The Lady's best incarnation was
A thin lighterman's daughter
Living ten summers down at
Teddington. She slipped a blessing
On a younger son for Calcutta's
Heat to hatch out. She was generous,
She sang. Little Lady Silvertail,
You whiten us by wish-light – fear
Of you is nesting in us still,
Up some worn steps we hope we never drag,
Some doctors' booming jokes
We'll never raise a laugh at –
We have a homage to pay to
Old daguerreotypes, to the eyes
Of Europe fallen in eclipse,
Noses pecked off out of empty air.

Futurity

If you could guess at seven
That the little girl with plaits
And the band on her teeth would be
Fata Morgana the great star and Alice
The most invited girl in the street
Would later turn her feast of eyes
On the recurring chianti bottles
Of the asylum wallpaper
Counting forever up to ten
With no crack in the world to follow,
If Sophonisba with the spots
Playing Czerny in the sun
Through afternoons of talc and zinnias
Could guess to what use a half-moon
Carving knife might be put,
If Ralph the even-tempered Saxon
Who carried his bat through ten
Summers could prognosticate
His two children and the pulp
He'd make of their brains with a new
Tack hammer – if all these could
Then perhaps you could have seen

Standing beside the mossy overflow
Of the rain tank that your nerves'
Carnival would sink to a smile
From Bridget, to three children
And a clock of dead chimes, that and
A three inch par in the local paper
When you saved an oiled seagull
From the Council boatshed, crying
And smiling for one death the less,
This strange fate of a tropical Nietzsche
Condemned to the Bizet of his dreams,
A silted sinus and two doctors
Casting short shadows on the lawn.

Homily in the English Reading Rooms

The plains people never liked this place,
Trapped here by an ethnic kink,
Unable to get away after their Augustus
Corrected the boundaries. The river is deep
But the marshes are too wide and just
In the wrong place. That great bridge
Would look magnificent if it weren't
Coated half the year with primer – a day
After alighting at the cement-winged
Central Station you find yourself drinking
The sophisticated one of the three beers
At the very café a film made famous.
Coke is dear, so the locals drink it –
You sit at the Drei Sklaven and tell
Lies over the new wine. Around those smiles
There seems too much prosperity – haven't
These people suffered, where is the shadow
On the plate of their souls? Across the Square
In the ugly building where the Negro
Basketball team plays tonight, wasn't that
The scene of the great Saalschlacht?
It's been a cinema since and a repository.
Something makes you quarrelsome – one
Argues over a tram number, the other fails
To find a lavatory on the Kai, the first
Remarks that boxers outnumber dachshunds,

The second that water feels the same fine-blown
From council fountains the world over. When
Did brushed pigskin reach this part of the world?
That book *The World of the Stingray* upsets you;
Although all you can say in their language is
Your room number to the fat lady behind her paper
You resent the internationalism: at last,
Lying awake in one third of a hard bed,
The dark lapping your chin, the hot
Body beside you feeling for your nerves,
The lattice shows one or two stars, alien
Like you but professionally filled with light.
When the person you love is as strange to you
As the nervous system of the frog, you may,
If your fate holds, arrive one day
At the ultimate non-connection – a room
Over a baker's shop, the landlord's daughter
On the stairs with two hot rolls and a cup
Of coffee for your breakfast; then the shot
And your dead body on the seersucker quilt,
Nobody's business but the Vice-Consul's
And the police's; a beautiful change
Of the soul's weather while tours come south
Over the passes and the Grand Expatriate
Takes his morning drink with the Mayor's son
In the café Norman loved and talks
Of his Prep. School under a red umbrella.

Three Poems for Music

1

A scandal is starting now,
look where Helen, shoulder-borne,
teeters to the see-saw ships.

A well-paid Florentine saw this,
a man in a soft collar
follows a girl to the next gallery.

100

2

A flayed skin keeps the features of a man,
  A star followed flushes out a God,
A foot in the ragged robin brings to land
  The Emperor's ship on his exiled shore,
A forgotten name bruises a girl's blood,
  The world waits for love to cast a claw.

3

Though this is not in Hesiod,
Music was stolen from a God:

Not fire but notes the primal giver
Paid for with helpings of his liver

And virtuosi of the earth
Outsang the Gods who gave them birth.

When Orpheus plays we meet Apollo,
When there's theology to swallow

We set it to music, our greatest art,
One that's both intellect *and* heart,

There war and peace alike depict us
(Drums and trumpets in the Benedictus) –

It sang beneath the Grecian boat,
It kept Pythagoras afloat,

It suffered poets, critics, chat
And will no doubt survive Darmstadt;

This brandy of the damned of course
To some is just a bottled sauce,

Its treasons, spoils and stratagems
Aleatory as women's hems

Yet beauty who indulged the swan
At death completes her with a song

And Paradise till we are there
Is in these measured lengths of air.

St Cecilia's Day, 1710

In memory of W. F. Bach

Having nothing new to say but born
   in the middle of a warm skill,
watching the animals of art
   grazing undisturbed as if
on the savannas of the moon,
   free by virtue of failure
of the egregious disruptions
   of fashion, you are the star
to hail across centuries
   of competitive rubbish:
marked by the small beast's
   epiphany, worn by the stair lights
of princes, the clubbable season
   of shiny trousers awaits you,
a firework of freeloaders
   day-tripping by the burghers' sea.

And this in your broad hat:
   the landladies are polishing
the black stained tables
   making a great ordinariness
which is like art; a light
   somewhere high on a buzz
of crotchets weans a face
   to misery: the milk of this world
boils over and a loved
   firstborn son arrives
on the planet death. We are all
   children lying awake
after the light is put out.

St Cecilia's Day Epigrams

1

Beaten to work, Caliban roars
His resentment to the stone ears
Of the hills, from whose magic hollows
A separate music blandly flows.
Energy is conserved: each sound he vents
Sets twangling that thousand instruments.

2

Annotators agree Composer X
Though always in love never had sex,

While a thousand motets and masses lie
To the credit of sex-mad Composer Y,

And that lover of life, Composer Z
In his operas wishes he were dead.

Each in his paradoxical way
Does a lot for the famous Critic K.

One Died in Metaphor and One in Song

Meridian fixed to walk out on death's crutches.
His hobbling made many fears dance: a vicar
Saw God melt into midday; short Mosaic law
Was ironed to ruin a man in print.
It came out straight, lines that didn't meet.
They make a grill for loneliness. Once bent,
The fire passes, the metal holds its shape –
Calm governors wonder at a world of wretches,
Healed liberals have read it all before,
Our darkness shows the exodus of heat.

Parallel went mad, lived thirty years
Devising antiphons and metric for the Psalms,
Put Mrs Perkins with her rose red hands
Through Job's afflictions: his cat received
A dictat playing with a mouse; God did this

103

While growling at raw meat. Then one laved
Skin made equatorial by sex,
Saw sin enfranchised in his spiralling hairs:
All Brunel's steam and spit of Freikorps bands
Only amplifies the hush of Genesis.

Why We Get Drunk

Pestered by wives and bells,
    Hiccuping regrets, we
Try to get these sulphur songs
    By heart to sing them
To smilers on the terraces
    And pallid experts
Who know how much of the moon
    Is rich in nitrate.
A useless pilgrimage and one
    To die on early.
Nice to be looking upwards
    When the blow falls, have
No name, no friends, no luck.
    How does this differ
From a gregarious face
    Stopped in the mirror
Waiting tidily for pain?

Pig in the Middle

(The Daily Express – Friday 15 November 1963)

Wallowing in luxury lay
A Most Important Pig –
Cornelius, Top Pig of the Year –
Pink and White, bacon-rich Cornelius!
Where a couple of weeks ago lissom young ladies
Were competing for Miss World,
Cornelius basked under camera lights
Like an odalisque in a Turkish harem.
'What a clean pig', we all exclaimed.
'O very clean', they answered, 'we washed him

For his debut in detergent.'
Cornelius is the first MDH
(Minimal Disease Hybrid).
Fat and fancy Cornelius grew to bacon-
Slicing size in only one hundred and twenty-nine days.
He derives from high-bred Landrace
And Large White parents. He wasn't born,
He was removed from his mother by hysterectomy.
His upbringing (bottlefed with a minutely balanced diet)
Ensured against infections which pigs are prone to
From the moment of his birth.
His cereal and fish-meal feed
Was carefully tinctured
With chalk, copper, zinc, molybdenum and other minerals.
For every 2½ pounds of food he ate
He put on more than a pound in weight.
But what about flavour?
Age and exercise put flavour into meat,
But the hard facts of farm economics
And a reasonable price for the housewife
Means animals must be grown fast and killed young.
Poor Cornelius!
He is the only pig that ever wallowed
In Waldorf luxury.
His debut in the Aldwych Suite cost £50,
All to make a better British breakfast.

The Recipe

Smelling of love like a piece
of oiled wood, I shaded
those bleached shores.

Pull back the sun under your belt
I said. An old lady is mad
among staghorns and potted maidenhair,
her family were sugar boilers of Huguenot stock;
now they have refined themselves away.

A new land has ghosts waiting
at the mangrove quays.
The journeys are all inland.

Ambushed by those little migrant eyes.

Baptised in their bellies, the sun men
strapped the country to their backs.
'Pendragon, Belinda and Jack, March '65.'

These are the wrong ingredients.

Take instead a veined and freckled man
with his ten-year-old son
treading among the uguary shells
talking about the world's drawn blinds,
the boarding house of hell where meals are prompt.
Europe has tipped these workings
on a spastic shore.
A dredge is called the Dauntless
and a road that runs nowhere
is named after the native pubis.

It was breadfruit in the books
and bread deliveries in the street.

The milkshakes are pouring
for the matutinal mass :
in the cool of the bush house
bulldog ants are rebuilding the republic.
On her ninetieth birthday Aunt Blin
thanks the cousins for their present of death.

When we're strong enough we'll make them call
this north and Europe south.

A picture of Ayers Rock was given to
everybody at the Press Reception.

I bless my ancestors in the name
of the cornucopia and the gibber plains.

Fair Go for Anglo-Saxons

(A near-contemporary gallimaufry)

1 *Provincial Messiah*

To be under thirty
and already have written ten pronunciamenti,
to think all older writers
only want to lay you
and boast of the girls you've laid,
to think no one is any good
except a poet from Alberta,
Catullus and some friends
who run a mimeographed magazine,
to misquote Ovid, misrepresent Pound,
misunderstand Olson and never
have heard of Edwin Arlington Robinson,
to have to print your girl friend's
things alongside your own,

to be all this is better
than to have talent and have to write well.

2 *At the Trat'*

The translator of aphorisms
is wining and dining the actress/playwright/
wife of the famous TV Producer.
Everyone in the restaurant, including
the determined client-suitors,
is eavesdropping now. Red wine
and vintage sex life spill among
Sicilian smiles. She's an old hand –
she can stick to Lichtenberg
and the hundred German devils
while he gets a feel in.
The waiters are sending money home.
Now says Old Ruby Nose topping up his glass
the goat-faced youth are knocking up the girls
in the randy grass of Agrigentum.
In her next play she retells the story
of Persephone: we winter with her
as she greets the God in jeans.

3 *Sibylline Stutterings*

After the New Emancipation
The New Rudeness,
After the New Heterosexuality
The New Cruelty,
After the New Live Art
The New Messiahs,
After the New Violence
The New Dandyism,
After the New Controversy
The New In-Touchness,
After the New Complexity
The New Indeterminacy,
After the New Toughness
The New Lyricism,
After the New Expressionism
The New Communication,
After the New Concern
The New Loneliness.

4 *Lines*

She's loyal to the marmalade she bought in Danzig
They found paddi-pads in the Chairman's trunks
Boethius or Bride to the Thing in the Box: two good reads
Wise old eyes have perused the small print
He told her he didn't love her in the Restful Tray
Proof of genius: fatty degeneration of the heart
She was buried holding her Tolkien books
Sunday and the fish are parsing the reviews
O for Pauline in the french nylon knickers
So neighbourly, a candid Canuck and a smiling Finn
God died underfoot – in the steps of the master
Köchel, even the fifth edition notwithstanding, the score
includes bassoons
The comic novelists' convention is ending

5 *Twenty-four lines*

A common cold wins
provinces for a man,
an arbiter of elegance
rides into town on a Bactrian camel

The ravines of this city
are full of gold and milkshakes:
a light box where the pain shows up,
I mean the world, our clean small world

Face to face with wise Inquisitors
I tore my skin in night despair,
I am the Quinbus Flestrin
of this louche Lilliput

A lot of religious black men
strip the air of its European clothes,
the occupying army leaves behind
a complete set of the Waverley Novels

Can you solve the problem
of the Pervigilium Veneris
or graft the Peace Rose
on the Lady Buchanan?

The forks are shut up in the drawer,
the word has come among us –
I that in health was and . . .
wounds healed forever leave a scar.

6 *Half-Mast Poems*

The quick brown fox jumped over
        the lazy dog. The MFH
had been up typing all night.

Open the window and let it in
        said the parson. I want a terror
applicable to my Sunday sermon.

Oxford Marmalade is American owned.
    Ten public-spirited Coopers
resign from the Telephone Directory.

The pollen count in London was 107.
    That was the day he caught the Speaker's eye
In the Westminster Public Convenience.

Now for the great work, begun among the ruins
    of Western Civilization, the start of the long return,
this morning in the ABC in Westbourne Grove ...

Two Nations!
The Rich and the Poor, the South and the North?
No, the Attractive and the Unattractive.

The Porter Song Book

1 *Wir haben beide lange Zeit geschwiegen*

We sit untalkative in a room
The light is leaving: after such words
The flesh cannot get close enough
To hold half-smiles. Love's angel
Will not come; the warm world
Of lime trees, madness and
Pianoforte albums has given way
To goadings in the yellow gloom
Of Gospel Oak. The silence after love
Is broken, not by the closing wings
Of the Nineteenth Century, but by
An article on topless dresses
Tossed into stale air. This severity
Is just to vex. From the fenced wood
A black spirit flaps up to our eaves.

2 *Story from a Travel Book*

They spent three months in the marshes.
Love and the water turned them into
Beautiful animals. They told their rescuers
The wide Delta sun steamed up
Like a river boat, each of them became
A soothsayer, sounds of struck brass
Were lost in the flattened reeds.
There was one death – baked in golden mud
He lay among a childish people
Caressed by keening. One great soul
Saw the light go out, reached for
The Akkadian dark: smelling a little of urine,
He was taking one step on to the stars
When a French engineer found him,
Blue-eyed, still recognizably European,
But suffering from malnutrition that
No river dog or girl of twelve
Could be companion to or compensate.

3 *The Sanatorium*

Flowers brought by the lying woman
Break from bud and sweep the room,
But die rightly with the scent gone.
By coughing light she comes, telling
Stories of childhood, of the long
Verandahs and the travelling aunts.
To the doctor she speaks of being
With him on his Magic Mountain,
For the man she wishes a mind
Not easily frightened by Managing
Directors' parables. Like lonely
Hangers in hotel wardrobes they rock
Occasionally at doors opening:
Turning his eyes to her, he sees
A wall without bricks lit
By endless sunshine brightening.

4 *Clairvoyant*

You've narrowed the horizon to a noose
And in anxiety bang about the house,
The enemy of vases. One or two people,
Your husband for a start, will die
When eventually they get past you
To the disneyland inside your head.
You're a spiky girl the children love,
You always settle with the milkman early;
But still you gaze through lines and dream
Of living: here is peace, the reach
Of an old river with lawns to its edge
And an opposite bank nobody has seen.

5 *Journal Entry*

Then when we stop the car deep in cow parsley
And strive against the epitaphs of love,
There comes a minute of peace – back to back
Hands pressed against our foreheads, we
Keep to the shallow end of shadows, not
Needing to think about the quick-built walls,
Guards with their backs turned or playground
Sand scattered to cover up our blood.

6 *Genius Loci*

Look, nothing has changed –
the great spoor have never faded,
the jugular tips blood from a new quarry,
    there is a parting by an iron fountain,
rays of water fan from the sun of this place
and there in his accustomed corner
    sits nature's godson,
nursing his face on the water's skin.
Do not come, love, if you are afraid
    to turn into a barbered shrub :
what we are now the fire will hold.

7 *In Hora Ultima*

At the final hour
Everything will be destroyed –
The trumpet's steel and silver throat,
The plated flute's garden note,
The plucking at the pelvis of the lute;
Waltzers of the Middle World
Shall turn no more,
The great bassoon joke
Die on the German tongue,
The émigré dancer leap
Beyond the compass of his mind.
This is when the one tune plays
Which only death sings descant to.

8 *The Visitation*

A night after Michaelmas, under
  The no-light of sodium, I
Foxed and sniffed at the stippled glass
  Of her door and scratched
With my claws for her. She had
  Kissed these tomb-robber's hands,
And now the pictured girl implored
  The god of the dead to find her.
Watching through the glass, I waited
  Her emboldened coming down
The carpeted hall, her body
  Like a document held out,
Night cream shining on her face.

9 *Lyric found in a bottle*

I'm locked in my own body.
Today I found a small worm
In the wood of my heart. Now
I'll push it through the bars
To freedom. Perhaps if you see
A crushed worm on the path
You will visit me. The words
I write are delicate:

113

Straighten these serifs of pain
And I will feel your body
Along their line. I'm your worm
Of love, I'm working towards
You in the sun: look down,
The land shines where I crawl.

10 *Late Lyric*

An area one inch by about
Three inches of his left arm
Is heated by the sun. Warming his nose,
He bends to kiss her in the sun.
An area one inch by about
Three inches of her left cheek
Is heated by the kiss.
She stretches out an arm from infinity
To take him apart,
Till he is one inch by about
Three inches of wetness on the skirt
And curtain of her perfect love.

11 *Poetry*

An old art spreading rumours about
Paradise, it begs outside the gates
Of the gods : the active gods come out.

12 *White Wedding*

At St Columba's or St James's, Spanish Place,
Before a congregation freezing in
Quant and quantities of ice and lace
Two butterflies are waiting for the pin.
The organ loft is stuffed with violins,
The pipes ascend to Heaven; they want to roar,
But do not give the cue for Mendelssohn,
See the bride's eyes are filled with tears and sore
With looking at the groom's dynastic nose.
Alas, alas, God's rosters are declared,
Tears dry quickly fanned by Prayer Book prose,
If love can't be, then hatred may be shared.

13

The mynah bird dips its beak
In the friendly man's pale beer,
Three salesmen talk of their careers,
Two feet play hide and seek.

The bird says suddenly 'dirty old man'.
I look at my finger nails – dirt!
I'm thirty-five, half the Psalmist's span;
If I took off my clean shirt

I'd stand before you pilled in fat.
Each day I clean the floor of my cage,
The body smells more at my age,
The words of love come pat.

14 *From an Old Master*

On the green cloth of summer lie
Bullrushes, water, ducks and sky.
There Christ, a sinless silver boy,
In his mother's lap sits like a toy;
A sapling lapped in pale green moss
Casts down the shadow of the Cross.

15 *Quick Frozen Poem*

God, she's wolfed two sides
    of gold-grained plaice.
    From that small fish and loaves
    we fed a multitude.

    My need is straightforward now,
    another pun to go on with:
    Of her bones are quarrels made.

God, let me die of it
    only with a temperature
    and violent telegrams.

Farewell to Theophrastus

In a boardroom panelled with founders,
chairmen and new brooms sit ten men
considering the colour of a toothpaste.

The Inventor of News has finished talking
    and the glassy silence is mottled
with his unchaste stories: it was
    Sir Gilbert took his secretary, Lord Moron
was cut down throttled by his braces,
    nine-tenths of unconscious choosers
fancy pink. *Chip on Shoulder*
    says the meeting's being held too late,
Production Department's hopelessly behind,
    these are the same cigars we had last time;

Overdoing It's lost a carnation but has
    two rosebuds in his right lapel;
he offers the table the name of an hotel
    in Amalfi and spends a minute on his knees
retrieving the Chairman's pen top.
    Petty Ambition knows that new photographer,
not, most definitely not, an East End Boy
    on the way up, absolutely middle-class
and a genius; he's surprised to hear
    the name McLuhan but is certainly orthodox
on Dichter, you've got to stop somewhere.
    The special memorandum of a hundred pages
before *Late Learning* is in an awful mess
    yet he promises copies for their next.
He reminds them of the dangers of gerontocracy
    but he goes too far when he talks of the Crisis
Facing Elected Government and the Failure
    of Social Democracy in Our Time.

Abominable Man is there, he's married
    to the Chairman's daughter. He's just told
the one about the Jew who wasn't circumcised
    and got a hundred little smiles from
the Agency Man for abusing the new campaign.
    He's obviously enjoying the smell
of one of his own farts, soon he'll be asleep.
    Love of Evil knows the world is shrinking,

he hates those latitudinarians, his friends,
    he's for napalm and white mercenaries
and has invented a pack of playing cards
    of murdered girls from Mrs Crippen to Sharon Tate.

Unseasonable knows a man who died three
    minutes after being diagnosed: it was only
encephalitis but if he were my son etc.,
    he thinks the last speaker quite correct
on the effects of the dock strike, he took
    the trouble to note these figures from
'The Economist': taking up another point
    his nephew spent a year in Zurich and made
the following observations on the banking
    system. Someone has complained
about the ashtrays being full, so they send

Demoralized Man to empty them while
    a secretary knits outside. He refills
his neighbour's pen nib to nib
    from his own, he speaks only one sentence
but contrives to give the impression
    he's suggested an improper approach
to a rival's client.
    The Chairman himself
is proud to stand for *Ironical Man*;
    he's rereading Pliny in the car
and is sure we need more hard-headed
    realists in business if only he doesn't
have to have dinner with them. He draws
    amusing caricatures and shows them
to his victims; he's interested
    in his wife's adultery, she has enough
money to run away but he knows she won't:
    coldness is catching, he smiles on death,
his one unswerveable friend.

Through the door comes their surly heir,
Unclassifiable, monkey-wrench in hand,
he says it's something in them pipes
and gets to work. No one knows
the future belongs to him, devoid
of qualities, not even clichéd, warm
in the colour of nothing, man

117

of the manageable world, staring out
on the gardens of this planet wanting
little, not even death, just to be let
stay in his skin while his health lasts,
propped on the face of wonder, paper
in hand, reading about screwing.

THE LAST OF ENGLAND

The Last of England

It's quiet here among the haunted tenses:
Dread Swiss germs pass the rabbit's throat,
Chemical rain in its brave green hat
Drinks at a South Coast Bar, the hedgehog
Preens on nylon, we dance in Tyrolean
Drag whose mothers were McGregors,
Exiled seas fill every cubit of the bay.

Sailing away from ourselves, we feel
The gentle tug of water at the quay –
Language of the liberal dead speaks
From the soil of Highgate, tears
Show a great water table is intact.
You cannot leave England, it turns
A planet majestically in the mind.

Civil War

Calm lie the plains of golden races,
Dark the forest where Europe died:
The Counter Reformation takes a bride,
The Container Revolution is a war –
No man's hand may be held against his neighbour,
Same against same is what the same is for,
The hire of death is worthy of the labour.

Elegy

Matriculated at last from strangeness,
inhabiting footfall and timetable,
not skirting broken glass or the well-kept
hedge that harbours a face in its midst,
     he launches himself on the city
     through a surf of man-made fibres,
     home again, the out-of-phase prodigal,
     ready to consume aggression and silence.

But things have changed in his absence –
the Commune is packed with priests and breakfasts,
talks on God are issued as supplements
and four times out of five the man-in-the-street
     recognizes Savonarola's picture:
     alas, the doctors are still over-
     prescribing, a furious novelist
     says she fucks for her health's sake.

What is he to make of Pan's Festival
where the corona and bays are awarded
unanimously to the Laureates of Low Spirits
and a group of formation dancers
     called Maud is interpreting scansion,
     where the vatic confessional
     is booked for the evening and Positive
     Evil is seriously on the syllabus?

How he hails them, the Comforters and Old-Time
Resisters he remembers from many a march:
they turn away and hand him a journal
with obscenities reversed out on pink paper;
     a page of the telephone directory
     serves as a libretto; someone says
     an American Machine is coming
     with Hot Gothic printed on its brow.

And even the home discomforts are not
quite what he remembers. The pigeons
still eat his herb garden and Consommé
the cat has bald patches – but, alas, the sweep

of headlights on his bedroom wall
is a flash of pain now, the porter's
habit of reading his letters and hiding
the envelopes no longer seems out of Gogol.

There is nowhere to go: the cars are nose to tail
along the ring road and every third remembered
café or pub is an estate agent's. La Bella
Bona Roba he had called her until he heard
 her order scampi and chips.
 Is it indeed time to attempt
 the serious novels he was keeping
 for his real old age?

Outside his window the trees perform their ritual
leaf-shedding in the month of the setting-up
of a Ministry of Technology. A world of lasars
has millions who must be blanket-bathed,
 and a species of rat-like marsupial
 is officially declared extinct –
 the Ars Nova sound is a special
 test of high-fidelity equipment.

A balm for these distracted times, he says –
a legend in my own garden, I shall stay
on the bench in what passes for evening sun
till I am stylite with air and crisis.
 Tell the neighbours the news –
 I come from a factory of the mad
 but I am at home to my mother
 the city. She will come to me.

A Meredithian Treatment

We knew at the time that he was dangerous,
I for one had an instinctive loathing –
The dirt, the bells, the glasses tied with string –
Yet we thought of this as something wrong with us.
The past is dead, the future dead, the now
Is here, an apotheosis of girls begins.
He who takes nothing stronger than aspirins
Leads us in worship of the Dulcet Cow,

A sociologist issues us with parts!
I am King Pentheus, I shall sort out Thebes;
It's not the queers and chewers of poppy seeds
I hate, it's that gammony gang of tarts
That's bringing normal sex into disrepute;
They've read the legend wrong, my mother's torn
Me apart already, now I am reborn
In huge respectability, with a gun in my suit.

Christenings

The Good Fairies have trooped off one by one,
Their strawberry smiles fading and their
Consumer Durables piled up on the floor.
Here come the Baddies with their stingy gifts,
Small genitals they bring, bow legs, catarrh,
A talent for crosswords and losing girls,
For overhearing insults, getting gossip wrong,
Their Diners Cards make fatherly waiters rude,
What mother says they weep away in bed,
They throw your hat from the ferry when you're drunk:
To us, their godchildren, they give this saw,
A starlight epitaph – *Here they belong*
Who died so young although they lived so long.

Short Story

Maureen makes a rope and ribbon model
of Nicholas, plaiting him a big member,
        then puts it on to cook.

Her stove is patented 'The White Goddess'.

Nick is, as the novelists say,
        an ordinary, young, good-looking,
empty, ambitious, self-fascinated shit.

        I think we'll give Maureen
a weekly Group Analysis session.

Dr Brandeis is away at a conference,
    what is she going to do?

Puts sixty-seven barbiturates in a tumbler
    just to look at them.

Nick's saying to Mr Ballantine,
    'terrific, I'm screwing this bird
and her bloody dog comes up and licks my balls.'

    Maureen enters a dream,
a pride of lions walks from the upturned glass –
    over their prophetic thighs
    puffs the angel of death.

'If she had to go for pills why couldn't
    she make it *the* Pill.'

The lions are in front of plexiglass
sunning in the architect's patio,
noiselessly they cross the nursing home
    and sip her quiet milk.

The Samaritans send her Norman O. Brown.

She could become an assistant
    with Abacus:
no, I'll set her up cataloguing
maiolica in a private collection.

    I'm going to give Nick
a mild dose, but I can't stop him
    becoming Brand Manager.

    I'm wearing God's shirt.

We'll leave Maureen under the departure board
at Waterloo looking up a train to Godalming.

The trouble is you can't write about dreams.

What was caught in Surrey in the headlights?

This all came about because I had
a strong letter asking me
why not write a poem where the woman
is the despised and loving creature
     for a change.

Diana and Actaeon

You only think you see them
     the dolorous dogs of conscience

You hear only yourself
     to have looked at the naked moon

The moon rises again
     under the quicks of your nails

That is the moon's music
     from the far side of a syringe

They are her officers
     the moon team under Doctor Lucubrare

Soon she will come to see you
     she has her times of the month

And memories. Memories of the sun
     things not looked at directly

You looked and fancied and she knew
     now there is no safety anywhere

She gives flowers to a nurse
     for certain she has seen your grave

From the bottom of the lift-well
     the howls of the baskervilles

The Workers

The people of the meniscus
see over the edge of the world

Valerie runs her hand along Hugues' bright creases
and takes her finger within an inch
of his sleeping penis in Independence Square,
she loves him over coffee and pigeons
and over the complications of her doubt

It takes a whole Black Country
and at least one new oxidizing process
to maintain the canals in her fallen eyelids

Justice of the sun, she says, on the water –
this was once the capital of the wool trade
when the bankers were the nouveaux riches –
calm of the duck-billed dawn
and the cerise and cerulean pills!

Their planes are honed on the sky
and they are together beside the *Geertgen tot Sint Jans*,
a torturer's and a peasant's descendants

On the broad back of money
are the fine moles of sensibility –
she reads that in a novel
and thinks how like a girl in a novel
she is –
        she knows how to
find a switch and turn the room
to a D Major landscape
        she has a vision
that all the rest are in the mines
where the D Major is dug,
the perruked miners,
workers at the star-hot centre
filling the hoppers with life
and she and her lover at the end
of the beautiful cables, fed and balanced
and warmed, thinning down, rarefied
and soon to have wings –

the libraries and the switches and the slurry
are programmed for this,
her delicacy and radiant quickness,
her crystalline migraine which they like ants
are the distant and decent makers of

The Widow's Story

Eight years old the week of Mayerling,
Given the theme 'make life a work of art',
A statue unveiled to Daddy in the Park –
How best use these gifts knowing nothing
That's first rate moves far from the heart?
The waters of death recede from the Ark.

The Styrian genius winks across a room,
Flowers, a *Liedchen*, Hinkel Dinkel the pup –
Great symphonies bleach like cherry seeds in May:
Madness in the sky, the Empress's womb
Honeyed with defeat – you're making up
Games of Europe the young will have to play.

Count Prosit brings the Emperor's regret,
'That Oberon was boiling with *Affekt*,
But why not try America, the Court
Must take cognizance of the Rupprecht Set.'
Forty staved paper for number six, cherries pecked
By blackbirds, love a trade and not a sport.

Memory sets in bits. Your great dead man
Will keep you warm in comfortable exile
But at his bier you only think of bed
With the painter with the stainless steel hand.
Vienna glows at your widow's Catherine wheel,
Sparks from your suttee turn the Danube red.

Peace to the architect with Europe on
His hat, peace to the angel daughter dead;
Study instead the little covert Czech,
Forty years a sallow tenor song
Like doctor's oil in your ears – it's said
He bit you where he reached, your pearl-strung neck!

Stars over Europe when the bourgeoisie
Get no work and the rumpish corporal plans
His twilight table talk are just the lights
Appropriate to Venice and your fee
For love, but those black stars your lover scans
Burn millions in their distant appetites.

New World and the Old in Beverley Hills,
Club of those that got out – even the Führer's
Favourites are reborn in delayed upbeats;
America is ignored save for two skills,
Publicity and death – instinct for the surest
Way quotes both Eichendorff and Keats.

Austria returns, the beach set fades
Out-exiled by fiacres in the rain –
Die Wiener Herrn are at the Studio,
Death sends his card, the little Mill Maid
Dances for the hunter, music again
Plots with the lovers before they weep and go.

Europe

An Ode

Breathe honey looking south, the mined land over;
   Tamed temples take the flash of rain
      Buckets up to their gone gods, their many
      Children born stinging like the horsefly–

No lark, no scrap of cirrus, canna flower
   But runs in the veined skull for sap,
      Saints blanket-thrashed to city samplers,
      Angels starved gold in high blisters!

Hefty the face of the Carthaginian, puce
   The blood-flower in his morning steps;
      Just a rock, towelled by tourists, yet sat
      Down there the bum of God and a gold cat.

Crossroads, too, injustice knows them
   Like its uncle's nose: hard men hived
      His sweet spittle, bright the honey
      Of rational Emperors, patrimony

Of ten pathic brothers; dust lies on
   Whig terraces, night road of oratory, mud
      Mentioned us among its peers –
      Lady Holland, operatic cards, tears!

Sun-high, valley-served, in his dressing gown
   Tussling with tyranny in dead March
      Remarkable for leaves, the great Glans foresees
      A million Fiats in the palms, water-skis

Ploughing by Procida, directors' gutturals
   On tape: 'Selfishness of the poor'
      Blows the market, money complains
      Under Swiss peaks, the S.S. Keynes

Founders in a mere fathom. Worm meat
   They all were but gave out with Gothic,
      Clawed from Cluny, struck the sun
      With big verbs – die for a pun

Was one rule, outlive any pain
   Another. Pretty Polis, lisped the Boy King,
      Back to back, whitebait, layer-cake;
      Promises make Jack's jaw ache.

But this was invective, had two ideas
   America and love, that the starved angel
      Blow right the great gold mouthpiece,
      A yes for everyone and the police.

Nations navigated too; who then humped
   Henry in his tower where the great west
      Started, over the black rim, the dark
      Gods and grief? In a letter, Mungo Park

Wrote the brown coast Augustan – alas
   Other evangelists erupted, the white man
      Found his fetish, truth and order
      For bare breasts and turned-on tape recorder.

Leave us love, they said, love is politics,
   Love is poets and prisons, love's
      A revolution, winter on a mattress
      Coughing up Europe's pound of flesh.

They were on a moving staircase and knew it,
  Knew the latter God as Progress and why not?
    A drained fen tins peas and we eat –
    Bulldozers fan out in the heat.

So they found a place to put the Mob!
  It built aristocratic porches
    But sat around psalming – each
    Fallen Fruit fancied itself a peach.

They god-hauled the railroad and they swam
  The capitalist rapids but ended up
    In Printer's Ink with a half a gimmick –
    Back to Europe, men, we're stuck!

There for the fallen Gothic Museums glow,
  Enthusiastic doubt like sun motes
    Turns to dandruff on old shoulders:
    At the start of the world, the beholders

Find the permanent kingdom and this
  Peninsula, its rational Europe
    Where the blood has dried to Classic
    Or Gothic, cinema names in aspic.

But the giant iron is ours, too:
  It flies, its sings, it is carried to God –
    We come from it, the Father, maker and healer,
    And from Oviraptor, the egg-stealer,

Launched in the wake of our stormy mother
  To end up on a tideless shore
    Which this is the dream of, a place
    Of skulls, looking history in the face.

There Are Too Many of Us

I see him there, the dedicated man,
His wife in her dressing gown boiling eggs,
Flinty smuts of indignation
Constellated round his eyes – he handles
A letter like a search warrant
And some must burn and some must pay for this;

His choler is how the gods of chance
Fixed the fringes of the world,
A paradigm of the judging sun,
To be a lemon eye in winter
Through liberal mist but finally
To plate the prophet's face with gold.

And victims sitting in the tireless hall
Before the second paper of the afternoon
Are answering shadows. Who'd start
The heron of the Eighteenth Dynasty
From painted reeds; who'd say Paul
To a persecutor from a quarterly?
The blind man is called in as
Adviser and the tone-deaf President
Buys Wagner's bed – our only protection
Sacred objects with a patina
Of fear. And that there are too many
Of us will never refer to one.

As the great theologian said
There are no special peoples or
Special solutions, only a tradition
Of mind going uphill and always
Getting steeper. The lucky genius
Refines his burden to one thing
At a time – his passenger friends
Are quacking in the beautiful
Incomprehensible languages: doves
Are at the feet of demon anthropologists,
Amazing earthquakes are on
Video tape, nothing is allowed to die.

I respect my red-haired adversary
Cutting his measured and
Unsatisfactory words. Even syntax
Falls from the bone, who would have guessed
That final seriousness is temporal?
The mystery of our sacrifices, our
Faustian bargains, the golden pledges
Of loves we've spent are only
Pitch-pine on a fire: we world-eaters
Are eaten in our turn and if we shout
At the gods they send us the god of death
Who is immortal and who cannot read.

A Consumer's Report

The name of the product I tested is *Life*,
I have completed the form you sent me
and understand that my answers are confidential.

I had it as a gift,
I didn't feel much while using it,
in fact I think I'd have liked to be more excited.
It seemed gentle on the hands
but left an embarrassing deposit behind.
It was not economical
and I have used much more than I thought
(I suppose I have about half left
but it's difficult to tell) –
although the instructions are fairly large
there are so many of them
I don't know which to follow, especially
as they seem to contradict each other.
I'm not sure such a thing
should be put in the way of children –
It's difficult to think of a purpose
for it. One of my friends says
it's just to keep its maker in a job.
Also the price is much too high.
Things are piling up so fast,
after all, the world got by
for a thousand million years
without this, do we need it now?
(Incidentally, please ask your man
to stop calling me 'the respondent',
I don't like the sound of it.)
There seems to be a lot of different labels,
sizes and colours should be uniform,
the shape is awkward, it's waterproof
but not heat resistant, it doesn't keep
yet it's very difficult to get rid of:
whenever they make it cheaper they seem
to put less in – if you say you don't
want it, then it's delivered anyway.
I'd agree it's a popular product,
it's got into the language; people
even say they're on the side of it.
Personally I think it's overdone,

131

a small thing people are ready
to behave badly about. I think
we should take it for granted. If its
experts are called philosophers or market
researchers or historians, we shouldn't
care. We are the consumers and the last
law makers. So finally, I'd buy it.
But the question of a 'best buy'
I'd like to leave until I get
the competitive product you said you'd send.

Stroking the Chin*

Some possibilities

At the same time
emit a thin bat sound,
sitting in the William Morris chair
looking at the Scandinavian blind,
the easiest way into the mountains
and the land of monkey tails.

*

Things don't happen this way,
I write them down this way
and I pull from my chin
two hairs I've allowed to grow –
so much for historicism, I say.

*

Remembering her sentimentally,
feel to see if I've shaved,
for she wasn't always good-tempered,
being a good fuck but a spiky human being.

*

* Spelt *Ch'in*, this is a Chinese lute. There are a number of acknowledged ways
of playing it, each descriptive of a mood or state of mind. They are called Ways of
Stroking the *Ch'in*.

If I centre my thumb
in the almost non-existent
dimple of my chin and touch
my four reachable moles
with my four free fingers
    that brunette
will leave her publisher
and cross the tiled floor
of the restaurant to invite
me back to Montagu Square
for the afternoon.

*

In the Lord High Admiral's style,
the other arm leaning on an astrolabe,
elbow on Mandeville and Marco Polo,
watch them bring aboard three trussed Indians,
some dull gold in a nest
of parrot feathers and a vein
of pox for the sake of history –
the belief in progress is worth it.

*

Caught between the smell of celery
and the sun's incandescence
on the polished back of a brush
pinch dry flesh at mean temp-
erature, my agreeable dewlap,
and curl up like a Degas print.

*

After the oven exploded
I passed for black
and wrote three articles
for liberal journals
and occasioned
a season of old
Eddie Cantor films –
my statue, chin in hand,
is to be erected
in a small South London park
to illustrate the First
Mode of Opportunity.

Two severed heads
with trailing beards
look out of a
Nineties photograph –
Chinoiserie!

Sunday

Where George Herbert would
Have seen this day the holiday
That made natural the good
In its six forerunners, I only play
A recording of a Lutheran
Cantata and lie in the thick
Enriched simplicity – man
In heaven and God in aspic.
The debate shifts to the garden. Where
Is Eden, the Marketing Man
Is inviting the press to the square
To launch *Summer Days?* In the Underearth
Of the Betrayed Biped I close
My umbrella eyes and it rains
Protestant tears on a big nose. Pains-
Taking love leaves me alone
With the *Keyboard Practice* and the *Great
Service.* We come to a place of stone,
Basalt sun on a granite street,
And the Prelude on the Chafing Blood
Is playing; the Holy Nuisance of
St James's Park stands in St Crud-
the-Great in the twenty-four colours of love
Chanting the *Song of David* to birds
And beasts and flowers and I wake up
To Sunday in London, to comfortable words
And the Grail filled with orange cup.

On Stonebarrow Hill

The whole population of England could fit
Under this gentle sloping hill, if some piper
Led them home to their ancestral shale.
The surf is all above me where the clouds
Race and lock about the pivoting sun:
I lie across the path of dogs and blackberriers
And silver-headed ladies carrying thermoses;
I am on a very infirm crust and doubt
The orthodoxy of this galleried field
Owing so much to God and to the National Trust –
Perhaps I shall be exalted like the noticeboard
Marked Danger or walk the midway air
As the invisible pink dog-rose does,
My mind still ministering to itself, resolved
To keep its grip on metaphors of death
And guessing shrewdly that those trees would say
They have a knack to last the better perhaps
For the growling of the sea beneath
And the panzer bulldozers circling on the hill.

Let Met Bore You with My Slides

It's this new colour process –
the world licks the back of our hands,
four of us on the winter sands
squinting at the soft-backed sea.

Brown for Hester in her aviatrix suit,
little girl in love with an iced lolly,
damson for Juliet and melancholy
sniffed and snapped at by the puppy waves.

And we two stand together on the wall
joined by the membrane of one life,
love's face peers between husband and wife,
a cautious colour like afternoon.

135

The Sadness of the Creatures

We live in a third-floor flat
among gentle predators
and our food comes often
frozen but in its own shape
(for we hate euphemisms
as you would expect) and our cat's
food comes in tins, other than
scraps of the real thing and she
like a clever cat makes milk
of it for her kittens: we shout
of course but it's electric
like those phantom storms
in the tropics and we think of
the neighbours – I'm not writing
this to say how guilty
we are like some well-paid
theologian at an American
College on a lake
or even to congratulate
the greedy kittens who have
found their mittens and are up
to their eyes in pie – I know
lots of ways of upsetting
God's syllogisms, real
seminar-shakers some of them,
but I'm an historical cat
and I run on rails and so
I don't frame those little poems
which take three lines to
get under your feet –
you know the kind of thing –
The water I boiled the lobster in
is cool enough to top
up the chrysanthemums.
No, I'm acquisitive and have
one hundred and seven Bach
Cantatas at the last count,
but these are things of the spirit
and my wife and our children
and I are animals (biologically
speaking) which is how the world
talks to us, moving on the billiard

table of green London, the sun's
red eye and the cat's green eye
focusing for an end. I know
and you know and we all know
that the certain end of each of us
could be the end of all of us,
but if you asked me what
frightened me most, I wouldn't
say the total bang or even
the circling clot in the red drains
but the picture of a lit room
where two people not disposed
to quarrel have met so
oblique a slant of the dark
they can find no words for
their appalled hurt but only
ride the rearing greyness:
there is convalescence from this,
jokes and love and reassurance,
but never enough and never
convincing and when the cats
come brushing for food their soft
aggression is hateful;
the trees rob the earth and the earth
sucks the rain and the children
burgeon in a time of invalids –
it seems a trio sonata
is playing from a bullock's
skull and the God of Man
is born in a tub of entrails;
all man's regret is no more
than Attila with a cold
and no Saviour here or
in Science Fiction will come
without a Massacre of the Innocents
and a Rape of El Dorado.

At Whitechurch Canonicorum

This is a land of permutating green
and can afford its pagan ghostly state.
Only from the recurring dead between
the well-dark hedge and talking gate
can mystery come, the church's graveyard,
where now the sun tops the stones and makes
shadows long as a man work as hard
to live as he did, rotting there till he wakes.

That he will wake to trumpets they believed
or tried to who bought him ground to hold.
His dead eye takes in the high coiffure of leaves,
the pebble-dash tower, the numbers in gold
upon the clock face. For once he has reason –
this undistinguished church, whose frown
lies in the lap of Dorset rebuking each season
its appropriate worldliness, has a saint, pale and home-grown.

St Candida, white in her Latin and cement tomb,
has lived here since rumour was born.
A woman's pelvis needs only the little room
of a casket to heal the flesh it was torn
from: an enlightened bishop lifted up her lid
and pronounced her genuine, a lady's
bones who if she healed as they say she did
I ask to help me escape the further elbowing of Hades.

I tried to put once, while no one was about,
in the holes for the petitioners' limbs,
the crotch of my trousers, for love locked out
not impotence, and spoke to that air which held hymns
like amber from the stained-glass sides
a prayer to the saint to be given love
by the person I loved. That prayer still resides
there unanswered. I gave the iron-studded door a shove

and stood again among the unsaintly dead.
St Candida is also St Wite,
the Latin derived from the Saxon misread,
the death clothes she sings in as bitter
to her as when her saintly heart stopped.
England has only two saints' relics confirmed

and hers are one. Three times now I've dropped
by at Whitechurch and asked her her easiest terms

for assistance. The old iron trees tend to roar
in the wind and the cloud seems unusually low
on the fields, even in summer. The weight of before
stands here for faith; so many are born and go
back, marvellous like painting or stones:
I offer my un-numinous body to the saint's care
and pray on my feet to her merciful bones
for ease of the ulcer of feeling, the starch of despair.

On This Day I Complete
My Fortieth Year

Although art is autonomous
somebody has to live in the poet's body
and get the stuff out through his head,
        someone has to suffer

especially the boring sociology of it
and the boring history, the class war
and worst of all the matter of good luck,
        that is to say bad luck –

for in the end it is his fault, i.e. your fault
not to be born Lord Byron and saying
there has already been a Lord Byron is no excuse –
        he found it no excuse –

to have a weatherboard house and a white
paling fence and poinsettias and palm nuts
instead of Newstead Abbey and owls and graves
        and not even a club foot;

above all to miss the European gloom
in the endless eleven o'clock heat among
the lightweight suits and warped verandahs,
        an apprenticeship, not a pilgrimage –

the girl down the road vomiting dimity
incisored peanuts, the bristly boss speaking
with a captain's certainty to the clerk,
      'we run a neat ship here':

well, at forty, the grievances lie around
like terminal moraine and they mean
nothing unless you pay a man in Frognal
      to categorize them for you

but there are two sorts of detritus, one a pile
of moon-ore, the workings of the astonished
mole who breathes through your journalism
      'the air of another planet',

his silver castings are cherished in books and papers
and you're grateful for what he can grub up
though you know it's little enough beside
      the sea of tranquillity –

the second sort is a catalogue of bitterness,
just samples of death and fat worlds of pain
that sail like airships through bed-sit posters
      and never burst or deflate;

far more real than a screaming letter,
more embarrassing than an unopened statement
from the bank, more memorable than a small
      dishonesty to a parent –

but to make a resolution will not help,
Greece needs liberating but not by me,
I am likely to find my Sapphics not verses
      but ladies in Queensway,

so I am piling on fuel for the dark,
jamming the pilgrims on tubular chairs
while the NHS doctor checks my canals,
      my ports and my purlieus,

praying that the machine may work a while
longer, since I haven't programmed it
yet, suiting it to a divisive music
      that is the mind's swell

and which in my unchosen way
I marked out so many years ago
in the hot promises as a gift I must follow,
          'howling to my art'

as the master put it while he was still young –
these are the epiphanies of a poor light,
the ghosts of mid-channel, the banging doors
          of the state sirocco.

The Sanitized Sonnets

1

Somebody must have been telling lies about Porter
for they took away his sense of pitch
and they wouldn't let him scratch his itch
and they put a strain on his aorta

and they said he suffered from Porter's Complaint,
i.e. an inability to feel anything when feeling
is the whole point of the operation – try kneeling,
they said, your old father's a secular saint.

And they told him to report to the tower.
It was all green and phoney along the Yeats-like land,
death was leaving on the hour –

the hand down the front, the trusted kiss was a lie –
he wrote this on his girl's letter in a shaky hand
'I haven't enjoyed life. I don't want to die.'

It's there, somewhere in the Platonic cold store,
the work of art all computers love,
very Greek, very rational, yet so much more –
a Mahlerian *Abmarsch* perfected from above.

And the perfection floats in professors' hair,
ends up as a well-displayed and priceless junk:
the luckier art is remade in the air,
holy bubbles mark where Schönberg sunk.

A page is turned – eureka, a snatch of tune
is playing itself, the piss-proud syllables
are unveiling a difficult prosody,

two unclean bodies are seeking pleasure – the moon
goes into Alcaics; at six bells
Agamemnon comes into the bathroom to die.

3

Heterodoxy's your doxy and orthodoxy's
my doxy. I scriven at my inlaid desk
in a too-new world. Now memory, cut and mix. The Esk
in autumn was cold gold with leaves. Biloxi's

been blown down by hurricane, Camille,
two hundred dead. Frightened of tumours
which were itchy spots, blessed by rumours
that Ad. Reinhardt is a poem pack. Veal

I won't eat, but otherwise I'm selfish.
I dream beautiful music with dirty words,
your legendary spoor. 'Beered and belchish

come I to the bosky core; none is near,
yet here entangled by the whiting birds,
on mark and fen find singletons of fear.'

4

Much have I travelled in the realms of gold
for which I thank the Paddington and Westminster
Public Libraries: and I have never said sir
to anyone since I was seventeen years old.

I've wasted forty years thinking about
what to write on my gravestone. Here lies
five foot eleven, thirteen stone, brown eyes,
who got his tenses wrong and his zip caught.

He had a high temperature called mother
and knew the Köchel catalogue by heart,
he is the programmers' A. N. Other

but I in my first person present will
do my duty as a consumer of art –
Milton! Dryden! Shakespeare! Overkill!

Ululate from high wires and the house eaves, doves!
You are my John Cage, my feet in the sky,
my everyday bit of Zen. *Man you must die
like us Turteltauben and our tufted loves*.

This sonnet picks up words like a comb
does paper; *bei Spiel und Scherz bleibt
froh das Herz* and beer froth has wiped
away tears of *Gesellen* far from home.

Ut, re, sol, la – In hydraulis – virtuosity
of the west nowhere near Vilayat Khan
on the sitar – the height to me

of western melisma is the oboe ritornello
of the soprano aria from Cantata 187 by Johann
Sebastian Bach. I would not cook on *my* cello.

6

Now it's in all the novels, what's pornography to do?
Stay home where it's always been – in the mind.
It's always been easier to wank than to grind,
yet love is possible, palpable and happens to you.

It's nice to have someone say thank you afterwards
goes the old joke. But are the manual writers
right, are masturbators nail biters?
(Even the Freudians are anti, albeit in long words.)

Don't burn *Office Frolics* and *I've a Whip in my Valise;*
in other disciplines the paradis artificiel
is considered high art and not mental disease

and if your mind arranges tableaux with girls –
e.g. strip poker with big-breasted Annabel –
it's a sign the world's imperfect and needs miracles.

7

Man is social and should live alone/
I disappoint you/what is hate?/hate is
this disappointment/we are here to quiz
the infinite/underneath is common bone

There are the smiling daughters/a linnet
surprises the starlings/the hot ball rides
over laughter/the sun has made two brides/
I haven't cried for years/I could this minute

Nasty the scrapes we get into/as Darby & Joan
told the TV Interviewer, we've been together
too long/death has an earphone

He sees a mistress turn into a judge/
marriages are made in the grave/bad weather
in the soul for ever/the door will not budge

8

Via the car radio Christ cries I thirst,
a stupid sheep has slipped in the ditch
and bleats to the indifferent marsh. Which,
asks the spirit of midday quarrels, came first,

God or Pain? Home is where the hawk rises
but I lie down with the panting dog.
I stay near the sun, dependent; in my log
I work on punishments and pardons, the assizes

of everyday. In a dream I told
my inquisitors I was a phrase in A Minor
and My Master's Voice. They said *Untold*

Variety and *Matchless Cider*, Hungarian Musicians,
were asking for me. Vanished world! I combine a
death with a life and am the sum of precisions.

9

Backwards went the barefoot sage: he chanted
to the hedge birds and fell over the cliff,
the chronicles showed what could be done with an 'if',
winds still storm the trees he planted.

Faster went the Athenian boat but faster still
went death. There will never be equality
until we are all equally loveable: I
won't allow it and history won't allow it. The last evil

is still in the box. The tourist holds his breath
as the white island with sails starts
from the sea. More death, more peace, more death.

The island is a sheet fold on fold
in the sun, the home of pruning and the arts:
sacred ground, so keep your god under control.

10

Anima of birds, I enter at your face/
you walk greenly belittled, the Venus
of ships and men/to invent the world with your penis
is god-like/will it be your place or my place?

I made love to my own body to make love
to yours/we are two people lost in the sweet
of ourselves/under the table our knees meet/
the nearness burns/like a god, keep off!

The blowfly drowns in the measured pot
of jam/the barley sugar never gets out of
the bottle/the iron will not stay hot.

A lover took nothing to bed here/
the pain is in the words/'I fell into love
like a cockroach into a basin'/love is fear.

11

Put me in the abbatoirs where the electric poleaxe
runs/I'll be steak and glue for your sake,
hide and blood for your blue hands/take
me to the tax haven of twenty heart attacks.

My tongue strokes you/I am the machine
that works the holy pen/I need time to please/
analeatorypulseofpossibilities/
there are four seasons here and yet the scene

is always winter/waughs and lecturing!/
homeoftranscendentalmiddlemen/
be loving then/then loving be/be then loving.

While the heart lasts the search is sex/
U/2/my heart is yours to hold again,
'luxuriously bound in rich red skivertex'.

Real People

1

Swallowed a bottle
of turps substitute
and did irreparable harm
to a masterpiece
    in his stomach
leaving an inexplicable
fashionable rectangle
    on canvas

2

His tenure
raised the Merrieweather
Praiseworthy Bank
to top position in the county
    alas, it did nothing
for the game of a country boy
who had been handicap ten
    at seventeen

3

This Swordfish pilot
survived Taranto
and three reshuffles
of the B Directors
    when the nerves
of his colon failed
they put in five inches
    of inert plastic

4

What is symbolic
of his thrusting nature,
his pointed nose
and supporting bone structure
    is rat-like
timorous but assertive
and conducive to asthma
    in his marriageable daughter

5

With Rimbaud and Schönberg
as heroes, he was considered
for ten years after university
the authority on Neglected Genius
Vindicated by Time
        his later personality
is just as authoritative
being a demonstration by career
of the alarming corollary
Sponsored Mediocrity is
        Always Up to Date

6

Why a stone garden
in an iron town,
cheap clock, rare rain,
        elastoplast on a knee
and an empty swing
        slowing down?

7

This is a little girl
and she lived in a house
with a cat and a terrapin
and a big sunflower
        called Mummy
and the sun was shining
and there was a queen
who caught crabs with oxygen
but Daddy didn't come
because he lived too deep
        even for oxygen

8

The choice was there
Socrates or Jesus
        or Insurance
or to be discovered

Heaven's lightning conductor
with only his feet
sticking out
    of a bed of asters

9
Stella had a journal
written for her
the star of the world
    our Stella
had a journalist
write about her
when she got off the boat
in mid-crossing,
the water
    a field of stars

10
The irascible poet
with weak eyes
accuses these reasonable
faces in the street
of being merely
imitations of the perfect
collection of monsters
in his heart

11
Even the 'way out'
doesn't get a cheer
in this reviewer's
piece, but he's worth it
to the magazine,
the way he tells
how he lays
his girl among
the review copies

12

In the chartreuse
glow of the tropical
fish tank, the doctor
tells me his good news:
the better the new cures
the longer the teeth
of the thing that
gets you in the end

13

Where his grandfather
was speared by natives
the young farmer takes
parties of tourists
water ski-ing

14

Uncle Stefan likes to choose
his trout from the live tank,
Uncle Max is kept alive
by a lung in a tank

15

How can one represent
one's profession,
being neither the smelly
monster from the Sleeper's Den
with his prize pile of bones
nor the beautiful young man
landing miraculously
on one lung?

Japanese Jokes

for Anthony Thwaite

In his winged collar
he flew. The nation wanted
peace. Our Perseus!

William Blake, William
Blake, William Blake, William Blake,
  say it and feel new!

Love without sex is
still the most efficient form
  of hell known to man.

A professional
is one who believes he has
  invented breathing.

The Creation had
to find room for the exper-
  imental novel.

When daffodils be-
gin to peer: watch out, para-
  noia's round the bend.

I get out of bed
and say goodbye to people
  I won't meet again.

I sit and worry
about money who very
  soon will have to die.

I consider it
my duty to be old hat
  so you can hate me.

I am getting fat
and unattractive but so
  much nicer to know.

Somewhere at the heart
of the universe sounds the
  true mystic note: Me.

Applause for Death

Hello everybody here today,
Death has come to say his say;
I'm sure you'll all join with me
In welcoming him to our comity,
So a big hand please, Rotarians –
He's the blondest of Aryans,
The zingiest, stripiest Wasp in town,
He beats Guinness hands down
For Black Power, his Civil Rights
Are sexy as a pair of stretch tights;
We're lucky to get him, I know he's scary
But there's no one so contemporary –
He's a documentary on the pox
Complete with interviews on the box,
Or a brave face smiling at the screen
On the other end of a kidney machine,
He's ten sparrowhawks laid in a row
Where the ICI insecticides go,
He's the British Farm, that *tabula rasa*,
As flat and hedgeless as a plaza,
He's a foggy evening on the M4,
That Biafran you found a bit of a bore;
Have you ever received his mailing shot
Both for and against the use of pot,
Or read his 'plague on both your houses'
Or 'who in your marriage wears the trousers?'
He thinks Mr and Mrs Oedipus Rex
Classic examples of Unisex,
His hand-held camera rather blurs
The charnel distinction of HIS and HERS
But let him loose in a catacomb
Where the infant dead are still in bloom
And the lawyers hang in debating rows
As grave as a line of Latin prose,
He'll draw you the finest possible lines
Through putrefaction's visible signs.
He keeps his iconography
As orthodox as the BBC
But he'll let religion and priests transfigure
His nature (it makes his triumph bigger)
So there's mileage yet and a clear road
For German composers on their *Tod-*

In English he only rhymes with 'breath'
To poets' annoyance, that is unleth
You lisp your way through the double esses
(His favourite poet's the one who confesses).
He has his happenings: the ICA
Honours him almost every day
For it pleases the healthy and well-fed
To take their symbols from the dead
And tycoons relaxing on the ranch
Have each his imported Totentanz,
Grocery Kings love painted tumours
As bankers devaluation rumours
And many an art-collecting Tory
Keeps as his pet *memento mori*
Autopsy sketches by a Master
Or amputations worked in plaster.
Death's personalized and custom-built
And sanitized and purged of guilt;
He's mid-atlantic as Sargasso,
As everlasting as Picasso;
Death is a cheap-flight, short-hop Jumbo,
The home-brewed whisky of Colombo,
The Reverend Paisley's wild Oates
And Paul VI's more dreadful quotes;
Death dictated *Humanae Vitae*
To the frightened heirs of the first Peter,
Injected a couple of million mice
With toxic blight for Vietnam rice;
He's given a thousand Oxford lectures
And named a score of noble Hectors
Who left the earth like Hemingway
Lighter in animals for their stay;
His policy of defoliation
Gave Concrete Poetry to the nation;
His critical triumphs are recorded
In the ten books Leavis lauded
And he'll be there at the wheelwright's shop
When modernity shuffles to a stop.
Things he resembles are: Dr Husak,
Nixon, factory farms and Muzak,
The edible novel (in marzipan),
The Common Market, the non-stick pan,
Zukofsky's Catullus, anyone's Lorca,
The next long-distance protest walker,

Reformers who finish every speech
With *delenda est* or else 'from each
according to' et cetera,
Sci-Fi Porn, All Bran, The Car
Of the Future, reviewing dons
The *Spectator* takes for silver swans.
Death is as boring as Music Theatre,
Impedance, baffle, Herz and tweeter,
As natty and nasty as Enoch Powell,
Ambivalent as Roberta Cowell;
Death shares the news with Françoise Hardy's
Sex life, Lady Antonia's parties,
Mr Wilson's thousand days,
Plots of the World's Most Famous Plays,
Book Club Medals of J.B. Priestley,
'Your Bed Manners, are they bold or beastly?'
The Customs let him through Heathrow
With a thousand tons of hash in tow;
We need him for our heart transplants,
Our Bollingen, Ford and Fulbright grants;
His corgis and his Christmas speeches
Are reassuring as Doctor Leach's
Praise of our libertarian land
Or the Black Dyke Mills or Foden's Band.
I know he's going to tell us how
It feels to be Mister Here & Now –
Don't twist your fingers in your lap
But give him a really thunderous clap
And remember just one thing before
I let him have the speaker's floor:
When next you meet him after this
You'd better give your wife a kiss,
Pack a few things for eternity
(Polaroid glasses and Pekoe tea)
And say as I'm saying to you now:
I'm ready to go, please show me how,
Is this the place, I think I'm right?
I've finished. Yes. Thank you. Good Night.

PREACHING TO THE CONVERTED

The Old Enemy

God is a Super-Director
who's terribly good at crowd scenes,
but He has only one tense, the present.
Think of pictures –
Florentine or Flemish, with Christ
or a saint – the softnesses of Luke,
skulls of Golgotha, craftsmen's
instruments of torture – everything is go!
Angels are lent for the moment,
villains and devils are buying Hell
on HP, pain is making faces.
In the calmer sort of painting,
serenely kneeling, since they paid for it,
the donor and his family keep the clocking now.
They say, Lord, we know
Lazarus is king in Heaven
but here in Prato it would be death to trade:
the death of God requires a merchant's dignity
and so they tip their fingers in an arch
that runs from Christ's erection
to a *Landsknecht* leaning on his arquebus.
Those centuries were twice the men
that MGM are – God loves music
and architecture, pain and palm trees,
anything to get away from time.

The King of the Cats is Dead

The light on his thigh was like
a waterfall in Iceland, and his hair
was the tidal rip between two rocks,
his claws retracted sat in softness
deeper than the ancient moss of Blarney,

his claws extended were the coulter
of the gods and a raw March wind
was in his merely agricultural yawn.
Between his back legs was a catapult
of fecundity and he was riggish
as a red-haired man. The girls
of our nation felt him brush their legs
when they were bored with telling rosaries –
at night he clawed their brains in their
coffined beds and his walnut mind
wrinkled on their scalps. His holidays
were upside down in water and then
his face was like the sun: his smell
was in the peat smoke and even his midden
was a harmony of honey. When he stalked
his momentary mice the land shook
as though Atlantic waves were bowling
at the western walls. But his eyes
were the greatest thing about him.
They burned low and red so that drunks
saw them like two stars above a hedge,
they held the look of last eyes
in a drowning man, they were the sight
the rebel angels saw the first morning
of expulsion. And he is dead – a voice
from the centre of the earth told of his death
by treachery, that he lies in a hole
of infamy, his kidneys and his liver
torn from his body.
                    Therefore tell
the men and horses of the market-place,
the swallows laying twigs, the salmon
on the ladder that nothing is
as it has been
                    time is explored
and all is known, the portents
are of brief and brutal things, since
all must hear the words of desolation,
The King of the Cats is Dead
                    and it
is only Monday in the world.

Preaching to the Converted

Calling down the funnel of your mind
News the charnel chords make *larmoyant,*
The Pretenders come, of black and silver face –
The Old is painted on an eye, he's Sleep,
The shadow of a never-noticed death,
The New is pictured on a box, he dreams
Of Ever-Afternoon, Ego-Eternity:
Great Abstracts, which our thin vocabulary
Strains to make real: and this is poetry.

Strung down the classic nave of San Lorenzo,
Gouty and gorgeous as the flesh puts on,
Howls of the damned, the stretched-out cries of love,
Heard all before and when the wind blows heard
Over water to the Marble Island: never
Like Mother or the Moon to rise in state
Casting their grave clothes, no territorial
Imperative remaining – only to huddle close
Under the sermon shower: God will be verbose.

Preaching to the Converted is preaching Time,
The only subject that memorials hear;
They wink their Latin letters, listen at angles
To rhetoric till their sculpted knees are knocking –
This is the height God's words have risen to,
Beyond it you are free – you poet, you philosopher,
You driver on the autobahn – the base is fixed:
A *Grundrisse* for the dead – have marble fun,
Put on your shoes and walk into the sun.

Timor Mortis

As Schopenhauer's coach rolls
the worms in the panelling
start a schottische –

Sister and brother in the mitral dark,
when we go we are single,
our handclasp's broken –

But clocks are still clocking,
strangers are dreaming
identical dreams –

Hailed out of nothing and with
nowhere to go but a spread
sail of theory. Ever and ever –

We would escape if
the raft could hold all of us:
I'm in the painting –

Touch is the touch paper,
the fuse in the tail,
the sermon in silver –

The plague town behind him,
relaxed with a nosegay,
Schopenhauer mutters –

Man is ridiculous; if
it weren't for his death,
he'd have no value whatever –

Fossil Gathering

Armed with hammers, we move along the cliff
Whose blue wall keeps a million million deaths;
The surf is low, the heat haze screens the stiff-
Backed searchers for imprisoned crystals. Blind
Eyes of belemnites watch from narrow clefts,
Jurassic sun shines on them while they're mined.

The children look them up in paperbacks
And break an Ancient with impatient ease.
Sorted and cleaned, the fossils are in stacks,
Prepared and dressed for classrooms and jam jars –
At night in cupboards the reassembled seas
Break over England, straining for the stars.

A Little Guide in Colour tells us how
These creatures sank in their unconscious time,
That life in going leaves a husk the plough
Or amateur collector can displace,
That every feeling thing ascends from slime
To selfhood and in dying finds a face.

May, 1945

As the Allied tanks trod Germany to shard
and no man had seen a fresh-pressed uniform
for six months, as the fire storm
bit out the core of Dresden yard by yard,

as farmers hid turnips for the after-war,
as cadets going to die passed Waffen SS
tearing identifications from their battledress,
the Russians only three days from the Brandenburger Tor –

in the very hell of sticks and blood and brick dust
as Germany the phoenix burned, the wraith
of History pursed its lips and spoke, thus:

To go with teeth and toes and human soap,
the radio will broadcast Bruckner's Eighth
so that good and evil may die in equal hope.

Evolution

for D. J. Enright

From Minneapolis and Rio, from Sydney and Hendon South,
    they will tunnel through the soil
    (old mole in *Hamlet* and the kids' cartoons)
    and eventually they'll end up here.
This is the Jewish Cemetery at the foot of
    the Mount of Olives. From my point of view
    (and I have been calling myself a residual Christian),
    a cemetery without crosses and headstones
looks like a stonemason's junkyard. But
    just beyond the cemetery is the Garden

159

of Gethsemane, the Vale of Kidron, the Dome
    of the Rock, and the Eastern Wall
with its Gate for the Messiah to come through
    (decently bricked-up). Staring in sunlight,
I am conscious only of the Jewish Resurrection –
    Christians can resurrect anywhere,
but every Jew has to go by underground:
    out of Cracow or Lodz, with his diary's
death, from the musical comedy stage of
    New York, from the pages of fiery
Medieval books – he dives into oblivion
    and comes up here to join the queues
as the millions swapping stories enter Heaven.
    How hot and dirty and pale are olive leaves,
how one's heart beats above the golden city,
    which really belongs to architects,
archaeologists, and such Sunday Schools as we have left.
    None of it's as real as a carved camel
or a smudgy glass ring, except this Resurrection:
    I can see this easily, and if the boys
flogging panoramic views would just keep quiet
    I could hear the first tapping on a plate.
Now we are changed: I haven't an atom
    in my body which I brought to Europe
in 1951. How beautiful is evolution,
    that I am moving deeper into my own brain.
The air is filled with something
    and I will not call it light –
stay with me, my friends; truth and love,
like miracles, need nowhere at all to happen in.

Sex and the Over Forties

It's too good for them,
they look so unattractive undressed –
let them read paperbacks!

A few things to keep in readiness –
a flensing knife, a ceiling mirror,
a cassette of *The Broken Heart*.

160

More luncheons than lust,
more meetings on Northern Line stations,
more discussions of children's careers.

A postcard from years back –
I'm twenty-one, in Italy and in love!
Wagner wrote *Tristan* at forty-four.

Trying it with noises and in strange positions,
trying it with the young themselves,
trying to keep it up with the Joneses!

All words and no play,
all animals fleeing a forest fire,
all Apollo's grafters running.

Back to the dream in the garden,
back to the pictures in the drawer,
back to back, tonight and every night.

Notes to a Biographer

I've only sailed through the Mediterranean –
eight hours in Naples, three stops
at Port Said; I didn't even get off the ship
last time at Gib –
I've never been on Ulysses' island
or on Isherwood's
or skin-dived with Swedes
and galley-slaves off Lindos –
if then a Prince would pay for it
my *Italienische Reise* is ready to go –
let the mad Cambridge cyclist
and the randy archaeologists
precede me: it can be Hamilcar
or Horace's farm or the Last Stand
at Syracuse, I don't mind.
There are important nerves telling my
unimportant imagination
that the dirty sand is more
than a hatchery of cockroaches,
that a rotting pier is rich in injustice –

161

saddle the nightmares and let the driver
move off into the night;
I want to watch the Emperor's fish
in their pool at Baiae,
the exhausted hills, the horticultural bones,
the olives of death.
I've never been so depressed
as when I saw the Florentine
National Library on television,
and there are so many more books to come!
I shall write only a few of them,
but at the movement of timid breath
on the page this provincial passion,
this unreformed ignorance
will glow again
and the famous carriers of sadness
appear beside my writing hand.

Story Which Should Have Happened

There should have been the Old Manse under creeper
with half a sermon lying on a desk,
the vague light reaching in to touch the roses –
   there should have been herb gardens and poppies.

Upstairs in the attic we should have found,
pressed in prizes, petals of bold wildflowers
and Uncle William's primus stove, initialled –
   there should have been picnics and smoke-smelling clothes.

The Monopoly Set should have dated from
Nineteen Thirty-five and the silver kitchen spoons
heavy enough to weight down a bag of kittens –
   there should have been afternoons sweet as verbena

We should have known the pain of finding
goldfish floating bloated under lily leaves
and father with a burnt hand smoking wasps –
   there should have been hedgehogs in the tennis net.

The novels by P.C Wren, though read, should soon
have yielded to the Brontës and Thackeray
and *The Ancient Mariner* with coloured illustrations –
   there should have been intimations of love and hate.

After closing the door the doctor should have whispered
what brought tears to father, while the tray
grew lighter carrying buttered toast and soft-boiled eggs –
   there should have been standards to measure death by.

We should have come back in manhood to
a new and vulgar family with a Rover outside
and the conservatory packed with magazines –
   there should have been paradise to be expelled from.

What should have happened happened to other children
in other places: I meet them, tall and fair,
at ease with psychoanalysts and women –
   there should have been fictions to be real in.

Seaside Resort

With her nose turning from her shroud,
smelling of onion and Osborne,
the small black rained-on Queen
stares with disciplined eyes at the sea –
    between her and it
start and zebra-stop the export-worthy
cars, call the corpse-coloured gulls,
toe-tip and rock-a-nore the great
public and its implacable children.
    She can see fishing boats
and tankers, the only Imperial things
in her lawful eyes and even they
dribble tar like old incontinents
dripping it down their flies.
    She is more than a square –
she has all the Squares of England
and all the cats and hydrangeas at her call!
To be in two minds about her is right:
gone and for good riddance the Raj –
you ice-cream your mouth under her

undersized pedestal while the Eastbourne
Brass Ensemble showers its *Showboat*
Medley on the American-owned air,
but you regret Mr Mendelssohn
and the plant collectors of Udaipur.
          The polemic here is death;
the old people are flaking away
beside the model village, the three-
hundred-foot embroidery and the eighteen
hole Miniature Golf Course.
The scorpions never move all day
in their glass case in the Zooquarium;
so many nuns come to the beach
to test their black against the wind
and in the rain the Marina drops
its yachting posture to look
like an abandoned 'Thirties Aerodrome.
          There will be stone on stone,
say the bells, whatever happens to trade,
and we have so much burying still to do –
you cannot withdraw from our
Christmas Club and it's not yet
time for the Resurrection.
          But try to be serious
like bombed-out Number Three of the terrace
and the bombazined Queen.
          In the hinterland,
important things like electrical farms
and literary shrines are showing up well;
further off still in London, the life of
statistics (while hiding from Germany
and Japan) is a big deal.
          But what can happen here?
A new Ice-Cream Flavour or a boom
in Rabbit's Ears, the visit of a hundred
skinheads or a Television Team,
a Conference of Escapologists,
Christ walking on the water to claim
the record Channel Crossing?
          Nothing but the calm
of history dying, the beautiful
vulgarization of decay –
Empire gone, the pensioner
will ask for a single stick of gladiolus

in a laughing shop.
　　　I am almost in love
with the small black Queen in the wind
and I will not notice that the beach is full
of mussel shells and crab claws
and the smell is unimaginable
yet like your mother's corpse,
that the torn feather is a terrible
catastrophe, and I am cold
and lonely on an unimportant strand.

Dream Restaurant

In this restaurant the flowers double-talk,
they have overheard our dates to die:
my side-plate is a schism of the moon.

Why is everybody leaving, elbowing aside
chafing dishes and napkin barbicans,
why has a nimbus ducked the world in blue?

These radical ends of thought: my liver
is excoriated from my back, I have hidden
my pain like valuables in a vase.

I must be firm on vulgar instances –
a bell ringing like spiteful rain at sea,
a photograph that bloodies my right hand.

Where we eat is the world, I didn't dream it:
my mouth is full of eucharist, forgive me
if I've swallowed the words for love.

They will come back, the pain comes back,
return of the native at dusk or dawn,
private, without flowers, sicking up his words.

Dark and dark, the inside of the dark.
I am the world's digestion, I am love,
I eat and am eaten perpetually.

165

An Open and Shut Case

He was hungry, he said, which was why
he'd come to this house, and the pink rose
tempted him up the path – a dusky carmine
like his mother's old dress – immediately
he'd noticed the knocker, Silenus's face,
strange for a modest country door,
and the eyes were polished bright in the dark
brass: he walked straight through the hall,
slightly aware of cats and pictures,
till he met her, entirely naked, at
the kitchen door, humming *Va
pensiero* and carrying a dish
of strawberries

         Amalgam of gold and ice
         his hard ring colophoning
         her back as he pressed
         down on her: to carry
         back to Meredith Grove
         that adulterous sign
         was marvellous – she felt
         the breeze from round
         an avenue of urns, gardeners
         clipping at the back, this
         moment with a stranger,
         uproarious as brass,
         tender as vanity, making
         tomorrow that much
         less certain

                  I am glad
                  said the voice
                  when you come
                  to me; I
                  show my face
                  which my friends
                  say is nice,
                  but you can't
                  go back now
                  that you've seen
                  me. It means
                  nothing at all;
                  life must stop,
                  I want to

warn you, I
want you to
be happy!
Someone to talk to, slip the strap
round the small of her back,
watch the carbon sun in windows
set at regulo seven, soon to
be done to domestic brown,
a science of the heart to frame
with the childhood certificates.
Strangers now to all the tenses

even the chattering present,
met for a moment in a comic
schloss, for which at least
Ulysses and his dog felt some
gratitude; 'if it moves
make love to it, you may be
asked to die at its side.'
Once again he found himself
in that hall of whiskers and darkness –
how can you resent the familiarity
of hatstands? A woman who takes you
into her may still love the wrong Verdi.
The maplewood door swung open
at the broken ray of his dream
and he joined the gardeners loading
turf on hexagons of lawn. Rooks
boiled in a villeinage of trees;
kicking a democratic stone, he tasted
self-love, licking off her salts:
the owners of the world had gone away.

Between Two Texts

In you my lif, in you might for to save
Me fro disese of alle peines smerte;
And far now wel, min owen swete herte!
                    Le vostre T.

The scene is made, encarded on a play,
Our sunny afternoon, an autumn's gift;

Eyes down in ransom, trembling fingers lay
On hers, knuckled with rings – we lift
The tone of hoping with a rush of words
(The consonances lie, the trembling thirds) –
After thirty, nothing really happens:
Programmes from the fire are lower lights
And if she lusts at all, it's self-defence,
The drawing-in of these and chronic nights.

Yet every gamey gesture tells a story –
The boozing is a boast, look at her glass,
She sips a little lying inventory,
The husband detail of a lambent farce
(Somewhere beyond the hell of restaurants
Our epic artist gilds his Hellesponts)
And double double lays you for the dark –
The girl you love is traffic for all myths
But you sit flabbergasted: *he'll* embark
At dawn and leave you with the million Smiths.

I'll take him up – he's heir to Gilgamesh,
The death worm from the nostrils softens him
And then he's made the Dragoman of Flesh –
The Inundator with the Morning Hymn
Storms to the tomb of the desert's conqueror
(His international speech an actor's blur),
An Eden comic strip that ends in green
Among the Crematorium flowers and tapes
Of Solemn Melody – and I have been
Beside him showing suns to light his rapes.

This sound of anger is our childish urge,
The cluttered attic where the mind goes mad –
How well the spite of pain, the drunken splurge
Match confession: enlightenment is had
By saints and tyrants but by none so well
As lovers (we have entered them for Hell!)–
No afternoon is wasted if locked hands
Gesture alarm at premature burial
And Tolstoy waiting at the station stands
Lamenting the approach of Ariel.

Up at the Front, *nichts neues;* little's clear
Except the corpse shine and a broken sound
Located in the conscience of the ear –
Unhappiness is real as turning round,
It takes you to the grave (that Cressid-shed
Beneath the stones of Troy) – not to be dead
Consists in feeding life; feed hope like bees
With sweetness of survival, privilege
Of vanity and metamorphoses,
The crossing not the jumping from the bridge.

This said, I take the gift and smile on you
For suffrage of the afternoon. We're sexed
Like gods whose wishes never can come true
Unless the mortal part is burned – who's next
To feel the air's obsidian knife?
(Staying alive is now a way of life)
The Communicator's Charnel waits for us,
We have some pictures which will make them stare,
A marquetry of bones, a flame of dust –
Death is not peace but permanent despair.

Ek gret effect men write in place lite;
Th'entente is al, and nat the lettres space.
And fareth now wel, God have you in his grace!
                    La vostre C.

Affair of the Heart

I have been having an affair
with a beautiful strawberry blonde.

At first she was willing to do anything,
she would suck and pump and keep on going.

She never tired me out and she flung
fireworks down the stairs to me.

What a girl I said over the telephone
as I worked her up to a red riot.

You are everywhere, you are the goddess
of tassels shining at my finger ends.

You set the alarm clock to remind us
to do it before leaving for the office.

You are classic like Roman gluttony,
priapic like St Tropez' lights.

She put up with a lot: I forgot about her
and went on the booze – I didn't eat or ring.

I borrowed from her in indigence.
I was frightened and fell back on her.

An experienced friend told me in his flat
among the press cuttings: they've got to play the field!

Of course, I said, but I knew where that was –
down my left arm, my left side, my windy stomach.

She was sometimes late and when alone
hammered me on the bed springs like a bell.

She was greedy as a herring gull and screamed
when my dreams were of Arcadian fellating.

I woke in her sweat; I had to do something,
so called in Dr Rhinegold and his machine.

Meanwhile, the paradigm was obvious:
it's me that's in you said a polar couple –

me, the love of hopeless meetings, the odd biter;
no, me, the wife by the rotary drier

with the ready hand. Dr Rhinegold moved
mountains for me and said the electric hearse

might not run. But you're sick, man, sick,
like the world itself waiting in Out Patients.

I know how the affair will end –
but not yet, Lord, not yet. It isn't hope,

it's being with her where the scenery's good,
going to concerts with her, eating Stravinsky.

It's something more. I haven't finished explaining
why I won't write my autobiography.

These poems are my reason. She knows
she can't leave me when the act's improving.

She could imagine our old age: a black-
fronted house in a Victorian Terrace

or a cat-piss Square. Working on Modernism
while the stark grey thistles push to the door.

She can't let me go with my meannesses intact,
I'll write her such letters she'll think it's

Flann O'Brien trapped in a windmill. I'll
say her the tropes of tenebrae (or Tannochbrae).

I'll squeal in fear at her feet – Oh, stay with me
I'll plead – look, the twentieth century

is darkening like a window; love is toneless
on the telephone with someone else to see –

only memory is like your tunnelling tongue,
only your fingers tinkering tell me I'm alive.

On the Train between
Wellington and Shrewsbury

The process starts –
on the rails pigs' blood,
lambs' blood in the trees

With a red tail
through the slab-white sky
the blood bird flies

This man beside me
is offering friendly
sandwiches of speech:
he's slaughtered twenty pigs
this morning –

                                    he takes away
the sins of the word

I can smell his jacket,
it's tripe-coloured,
old tripe,
drained-out, veteran tripe
that has digested the world

I shut my eyes on
his lullaby of tripe
and the blood goes back to bed

(Someone's got to do it
and I'm grateful
and my neighbour's grateful
and we say so,
but thank God it's only
fourteen minutes to Shrewsbury)

Fourteen minutes to consider
the girl reading Scott Fitzgerald –
she has a red cashmere top
bright as a butcher's window

Shut out the sun and the cameras –
I want to talk to a doctor
about Circe's magic circle –
'you see, it was on the woman herself
the bristles sprang
and the truffle-hunting tongue'

What is it makes my penis
presentable?
hot blood –
enough of it, in the right place

With such red cheeks
my interlocutor from the abbatoirs
must have hypertension

On his knees he has
a lumpish parcel, well-knotted
with white string –

it makes all the difference
when you know it's really fresh

At one time our species
always had it fresh;
one time there were no cashmere tops
or butcher's shops

It consoles me that poems
bring nothing about,
it hurts me that poems
do so little

I was born after
man invented meat
and a shepherd invented poetry

At a time when there are only
fourteen killing minutes
between Wellington and Shrewsbury.

In the Giving Vein

The evidence, like the weather, is from
An inner storm; the poem, like every poem,
Will be merely a beginning, the daring work
For Venus's mirror, a heap of ashes,
Never to be finished though complete:
The mirror must be walked through
And the one of many million crosses
Borne – the pollen cloud dispersing, spruce
Sadists and armorial villains stand
Plausibly among scales and trumpets,
Violence and punctilio masked by falling
Almond blossom; then from the dream
A voice proclaims the flag and day of evil,
Indifferent to irony and liberal shame.

This is the gift I would refuse – I'd take
Well-water from a town of towers,
Make history of grey femurs and hot
Processions watched from reedy rivers:

The ingredients are myself, a nuisance
In a marmalade tomb grinning at
Centuries of cards, a savant with
A Cockney grammar interrupted as
The aristocratic plane drops, a storm
Of poets landing like Columbus' men
To bring back a pox to infect the twenty-six
Letters of the alphabet. There'll be no home
But that low-water amniotic
Whose sounds are caucus to the will to live.

No pressure on my chest and yet I'm not
In the giving vein. I have about me
Those moveables of eyes that dreams
Have sanctified. The weather is dull, no mist,
The lake is flowing in the wrong direction,
Early to work and the postman with
Words that fall down if they're leaned on.
Extraordinary that victory can be snatched
From such small things – a shift in
The weight of nouns, a new nickname
For God, a flower lasting an extra day –
We're in a fire, singing; I'm the one
Whose voice you can't hear; perhaps my round
O is agony, I shall insist it's praise.

A Hint from Ariosto

Hoisted on its great crane, the world laughs
As it goes upwards. One philosopher at least
Will picture in his hanging garden the yellow
Helmets and jackets of the hardworking gods;
It will take the rest of time to finish this
But thank Heavens the idea is working. Father
Helios is a bone merchant, yet we shall see
Life in the paper veil of a fontenelle. This
Is preambulum. It was the moon I wanted to tell
You about. American feet have walked on it
And Russian wheels trundled over it. Moon
Has no madness or even phosphate – it lowers
A lamp inside Mankind's memorial dark.

Erstwise it's all comic strip. Astolfo lands
The Hippogriff and signals back he's A-OK
To the warring lovers in the Marches. Negative,
Little Italy, with your Papal rages and your
Pretty learning. Touchdown is achieved
On a floating fairground. Beyond his unctuous
Steed (who's grazing on some aldermanic grass)
He sees a lake of quite unblemished purity –
All around, at every point, historical egos
Silver their reflected lips; the willing air
Is squandered on waves of lovers' words,
Truthful to touch and grammar: I die,
They say, and live to die again. No world says no.

Not just lost contracts and lost looks are found:
Bigger things, like souls, come swimming in –
What you fished for in sly intimations, woke
With on the salt of mirrors, here is real estate.
Solid as Sandgate are the Gothic passions,
Youth's exaggerations, suicidal tearducts;
Murder's gas a puff of birthday talc; most
Notably the silver words are real – those poets
We call holy or phoney find their clauses ring;
A bit of theatre cracks in a round bell;
The word *darling* pulses ceaselessly,
Comes in from the rain to put its arms
Spontaneously round the warm recorded heart.

Can Astolfo take it? He writes a letter home –
'No, eternity's not boring and the sounds
Of love are even smoother than a Florentine's;
Kindness for constellation and not cancer –
That's something to write home about. Love
Requited makes a garden without sundial
And all the madness which fills up earth
Is playing croquet here. Yet, my Paladins,
I am harnessing the Hippogriff once more
And shall sail for the sun. Look up from Hell
Upon my comet: earth and moon are merely shapes
Of the great plainness: you win a few, you lose
A few – only imagination is yourself'.

The Dust

How many divisions has the dust
as it drifts upon the lukewarm land?

We have matched it with our treaties,
our helicopter shadows;
when it shifts formation
there will be lights on after midnight
in several hexagonal rooms.

Plural, it plays with the calm of men.

The mortal magnolia has it like moth's wings,
it's shaken out as salt from a tablecloth.

The Two were formed from this,
according to instructions
in the Scout Book on that first of campings-out –
the cuscus looked and the slow worm sat
in a circle with itself: fasting, magnetism,
courage: they were our signs.

The Saviour of the State was accoutred
in his people's love, but a detachment of dust
rose from Spanish wheels.

Oh, but the dust, the gold-faced dust
from the Valley of Kings and Aunt Teresa's atomizer –
the aphids and the asteroids of change!

These are the priest's raised hands
and the lecturer's special slides
(for metropolitan audiences over thirty) –

As Doctor Danvers said – the cycle has one constant –
from the grub to the cyclone, the beta particle
to Donatello's chisel, the incorruptible body
to the pains of Hell –
only this milky dust.

Only dust the worm loved
singing at the river's mouth,
dust in the church of little spines,
dust where the library was burned.

Such clever men to start at starlight
when the dust lies low.

To know that when we land
the dust will be waiting.

Just as now a turn of wrist has sent a jot
of it over the rail to April.

Clear like a beast's old eyes
or Aphrodite's sweat-drops:

To please the dust by dying,
dying and returning –

To be worthy of the knowledge
that dust is only windows –

Not like the frightened Wit, brushing himself
ceaselessly behind sealed doors,

Nor the space in the crystal
where dust can never gather,

To live the while we live
just in this word, a dust.

At Scavanger House

We're here today by courtesy of Mr Eye –
     forever and forever, with the lint,
          the bathing box, and eighteen Centigrade.

Nobody may leave the building until
     the larder and the lavatories are searched,
          comments to be *sotto voce*.

While you're waiting, a tape of a run-over cat
          will be played,
a German Interviewer is approaching
          at 33,000 feet.

They'll tell you it's rehabilitation of the senses,
        all are to be sent to dig irrigation ditches,
we have rejigged the major scales and Bannockburn.

If it were possible to be with the Skalds
and have heroic syntax, that would be well –
        watching the mast as the helm goes over,
        fish in the panel of a wave –
no, it's not possible, and neither is New York.

We shall prove to you that blue is not a colour.

We defy you to say that this is just a dream.

By courtesy of Lichfield, migraine has hit Europe,
        trains at Rohrau are turning back,
        grease wanted for the guillotine.

Make it new! This afternoon you can choose
        between *Malleus Maleficarum*,
The Scratch Orchestra, and *Persuasion on Swings*.
Correction, there is also a Ballet Concrète
entitled *Pluralism, Compassion and Social Hope*.

I was under a yew tree in a churchyard
        when a poem crawled on to my collar:
it's in a bottle for the children;
we must find out what it eats,
        God will be pleased.

Calling Mr Ear, there is a call for Mr Ear,
will Mr Ear come to the Front Desk please?
News from the Moon, an opal outcrop of tears,
        Unrepeatable (suggestions?)(bargains?)

And Judges job, and Bishops bite the town,
And mighty Dukes pack cards for half a crown.

Now melancholy walks the mossy Grange,
quiet and birds contend in multiple leaves
beside the White Garden and the piled-up banks
of rhododendrons –
                        the stars are thinking
thoughts which may be mercantile

178

                              so grave a night
for loving and repairing love.

'The muscles of the under-dead are stirring,
rippling like roots that lift the concrete path,
straying from the house to track the goldfish
who rise to question Kipling's outheld hand,
then scatter to seek fantails of the dark . . . '

Something has been found below the elms,
        it's on the billiard table –
please call for Mr Nose, will Mr Nose report
        to the Matron immediately!
We need his expert knowledge,
we think this soft and jellied thing is death.

Oh, Mr Eye, Mr Ear, and Mr Nose,
we'd like to introduce you to Mr Mouth
who takes all things into him.

He's the owner of the house, his family
has all fishing rights, his books
are rarer than Monckton Milne's –
when you get to know him you'll agree
living and dying are his business.
A toast to Mr Mouth, the good and bad,
our benefactor, Mr Mouth. Last Georgian,
Last Aristocrat, he shuns the demotic
vagina but he'd lend his toothbrush
to a friend. A true soul, Mr Mouth.

And, as in Peacock, they went on talking through the night
        till the postman brought
    sun and thunder to the door –

The goldfish woke for another hundred years
        and a tip of ivy reached
the highest brick on the sunless North Façade.

The King of Limerick's Army

On the left flank a brigade of nettles
defying the corn-ingesting hens,
On the right, athwart the pig-yard,
squadrons of righteous cow parsley,
In the centre, unperturbed as Hannibal,
bracken already gold with epaulettes.

Serene, they flutter over the stone-cooped dead,
they bear American Researchers shoulder-high –
Aspirants to Namesakes are pageing Synge
among memorials to a weird hunger:
Yes, these are oaks that Edmund Spenser saw
destined to ambush floats of pretty kings,
And the stirrups hang, the stirrups hang at ease
from horns of clay, from long prolonged pursuits.

Here fell the noblest, the brave O'Byrne,
strung to a side of bacon in his grief,
Rowing on swan water, the platitudinous priest
asked of the virgin death a little flower,
Upside down hung Hahessy for a bet,
three quarts of the stuff draining from his throat –
Nonpareils that had the magic in them
gone under the sincere soil with nothing done.

Grey paths the clouds make over everything,
a shadow corrupts and the thinking wind relents –
I was in service in the war of damp,
that was the famine year, the failure of the sap:
We export Crosses to the Bronx, our politicians
are plural as the grasshoppers in June,
The Universe is ending, a million thoughts at once
sealed in a collapsar till eternity.

We can face such concepts here, our army
has its rations, the weeds, the jokes, the softening air;
Down a black hole to tumble; well, the church
was there before us and Father Fogarty understands –
If it's a matter of years, the Lord has many,
and a field or two of Limerick besides.
Spacewards fan the radio waves, scientists
tingle like small boys with tadpole jars,

180

Ninety per cent of the Universe is dead
but our king's army is in acorn time
And blustering by the stream his powerless horde
undoes tomorrow what is fixed today.

The Great Cow Journeys On

Standing here where prophecy peers out
from breasts of rock, I see the turnpike
furies eat the flesh of soldiers killed
in battle – the Gate of Scythes, the Tank Upland –
next under bossy palms the Holidaymakers'
Hell, fused by speedboats and the halcyon
furnace: there the old pus of Europe weeps
for what was tears, the carpet of easy love
shrinks limbs to ricket shapes. Along the Gulf
of Time huddle the former empires, cold states
now peeling frontages for the tanned police –
some lost souls there still show the hero's
strutting jaw, the last heritage of his eye
in fallen witness. Along the Bastion
of Monorails, I see the future in a skin
of lights, the breathless people sacred to
the God of Fracture. Prometheans at ease
among the stolen fire, they filter the sun
through their transparent hats and
walk about with conferenciers' smiles.
Then the domain of Merely Magic, static
between the feeling creatures' nerves, these
odes of men in paper palaces outbalance
the engineering deities and are wise with awe.
My mind can go no further. At the foot
of a fetid lake the latest Herakles
rubs oil in his hair – as the stinking waters
fade, the hero rises up to new insanity –
a race of Titans without glory, pulse
of the future in their salt-packed fields,
they have no purpose but to start again.

181

Delphi

There is a view of the sea through three tall trees;
We are not more than an hour from the best beaches
And the sun is so hot you might think a special
Lens hovered perpetually over our precincts.
Magistrates, families, and spinsters have learned
Extreme things here: pilgrims too have plodded
Past meaningless walls, the eye of a place-god
Watching from a piece of broken glass. NEVER
ASK . . . says a torn poster which doesn't intend
To be frightening – we have advertised the heart's
Wants since Aphrodite was a girl. You can have
A bathing hut and a packed lunch and if you speak
Quietly and take the occasional hand of cards
With the doyen of landladies she may utter through
Her muslin one of the aboriginal truths.
Our gardens are planted too late again
And the jittery clock at the Town Hall has forgotten
If Salamis or Mafeking was the time of its life.
The oldest resident, summing up sanctity and
The bracing air, says we have the seediest of
Perihelions, our tone of prophecy is due to
The prevalence of sunburn and the number of
Vegetarian restaurants. The many Conventions we have!
Addressed by bishops and conjurers –
The ladies with streaky hair who study gin
Through 2 p.m. light, the serene hum
Of vacuum cleaners always in another room,
The documentary film makers downing vodka
And lime, shouting how marvellous it is
In such a god-forsaken place! They are wrong,
We have never been abandoned: truth
And health are neighbours of death
And we know the home addresses of both;
Also we can make eternity seem like
Sunday afternoon. Our Kursaal and our
Public Gardens are haunted by butcher birds
And lovers' conversations – between us
And Olympus are plains of model dairies
And many unpolluted trout streams, yet a cloud
On the face of the gods will be clear to us
By breakfast, a shift in the balance of power
Exclaimed along the mole by frantic gulls.

182

What's worrying them in far-off Athens and Rome,
Where is the fleet becalmed, which hybridized
Plant will open up a hinterland? Ask by all means,
That and when your girl will learn to love you
And the weather and the trade figures. The statues
Of flayed Marsyas and the Generals of the Ashanti War,
Cross-pollination attributed to Hermes Trismegistus,
The Labours of Hercules in the *Arcana Arcanissima*,
Miss Austin's walking shoes – these and every notion
Will worry you in the Tower Museum. Our advice
Is to climb the hill to the giggling grotto
And hear the waves (just like cheese grating),
Take a good book (*The Childhood of Alexander
the Great*) – before dropping off, try alternately
Following squadrons of bees in the Corporation
Poppies and the shark fins of speedboats zizzing
Through the bay. Love? Money? Time?
Perish the thought! We assure you
There are no matters of importance left
And no questions worth asking. The clouds
Are parked in the fields. This is drowsy D . . . . i,
The happy haven, a good place to come to die.

Two Poems with French Titles

Le Théâtre de bruit

Down they come from Valhalla,
The Noisy Ones with outsize noses
and phosphorescent breasts. The gold
piles up around their golden hair
(not one but has a numbered
account in a Swiss Bank): this
is going to cost someone a lot
of gravy. Be quiet in the Wings –
the other wings are beating; this
is nothing less than Apotheosis
and from the Burgtheater to
the Opéra Comique good sense
gets a beating. It's just as well
or how else could laurel help
a flying girl or the wonderful
skin of a diver bargain for
peace at last on the floor of earth.

183

The gods look after us well
but they're not exactly economical –
indeed no, Peer, but their faces
have the new wet look and one day
it may even pass for tears.

Mort aux chats

There will be no more cats.
Cats spread infection,
cats pollute the air,
cats consume seven times
their own weight in food a week,
cats were worshipped in
decadent societies (Egypt
and Ancient Rome), the Greeks
had no use for cats. Cats
sit down to pee (our scientists
have proved it). The copulation
of cats is harrowing; they
are unbearably fond of the moon.
Perhaps they are all right in
their own country but their
traditions are alien to ours.
Cats smell, they can't help it,
you notice it going upstairs.
Cats watch too much television,
they can sleep through storms,
they stabbed us in the back
last time. There have never been
any great artists who were cats.
They don't deserve a capital C
except at the beginning of a sentence.
I blame my headache and my
plants dying on to cats.
Our district is full of them,
property values are falling.
When I dream of God I see
a Massacre of Cats. Why
should they insist on their own
language and religion, who
needs to purr to make his point?
Death to all cats! The Rule
of Dogs shall last a thousand years!

184

The Isle of Ink

'Es gibt ein Reich wo Alles rein ist . . . Totenreich'
Ariadne auf Naxos

The final purity is to have nothing to say.
  The portals of Carthage crack, burnt umber spills
Among the bees. Art is what should get you a lay.

They don't (the young don't) like these lazy frills –
  The approximations, *terza rima* (loose),
Garrulous on wine and priggish about pills.

Why sod about? Blood's running down the sluice,
  Napalm in the knickers, if I may quote Jeff.
We need a new art, with angles all obtuse.

Our Oxon. must be oxen, loveable, tone-deaf,
  And masters of *non sequitur*. Why not
Fold in bird music, too? Birds can't read a clef.

Joy the Holy Fool, the Bombed-up Buzzard – what
  Do we need with Dostoevskys? Play
With the big boys till it pours and you get wet.

Alas, there's a kingdom among republics, where
  You have to dry your eyes and face the sun,
Someone's left you, why else would you be there?

But it's too bad each tear weighs a ton,
  Too bad the god is late, the ferry passes by;
Purity is gas or tablets or a gun.

Across the island before Friday's footprint's dry
  A crabby old creature's got his easel out
(Not his prick, he'll do that by and by)

And cursing critics, friends, the time, the doubt,
  The headache, heartbeat, hangover, *et al*,
He's painting Carthage from a shit-redoubt

All pocked and wattled – yes, he's Romantic, pal,
  But he's taken the path away from the abyss
Towards the line I took from Hofmannsthal:

185

His proper terrain, while he lives, is this,
    The highest pile-up which our bones will make,
A ten-tiered city or life lost with a kiss.

He's not tuned in to Cage, he's on the Lake
    With Virgil's sulphuretted dead; it's like
A pond, man, where a thing armed with a rake

Etcetera – a million toddlers ride the bike
    Of Hardly Art. The rest of us will stay
On the Isle of Ink, postmarked *Totenreich.*

Can You Call It a Vocation?

In an age of fashionable innocence
when careerism is the purest career,
to have ambitions of complexity
and yet lack patience entirely . . .

They have their hands on the levers
of definition, they are synchronizing
their watches by Bashō's moon

To be unable to take ecology seriously
having polluted your own body
since childhood, including an island
of jettisoned trash called love . . .

They are playing games with new rules,
talking like foreign films, attending
Symposiums on the Great Leap Forward

Bothered by books like 'The Complete Wet Girl',
to try to get beyond all this fiddle
only to find it's concerned with rituals
of the braves and the bad-tempered bears . . .

They are taking the varnish off Shakespeare,
their oracles have pronounced: 'Anything too silly
to be said or sung can always be staged'

To dream of an Horatian present and wake
under a shower of bad odes written
by provincial sympathizers, the Festival
of Aniseed Balls having doubled its grant ...

They huddle in a space of starlight
ignoring the clever L and his memo to
his countrymen on sausage and compendia

Baffled by our age's revival of the art
of otherwise, steaming for love, to hear
a hot tail say, 'I won't sit on your face, Frank,
I'm talking to this guy about Dante Alighieri' ...

They have put the future on tape
and debate it while guns are raised
in wet provinces under a fanatic moon

Thomas Hardy at Westbourne Park Villas

Not that I know where in this changed district
       He may have walked under unwarming sun
Through a hedged righteousness already bricked
Up to the pale sky and the many chimneys clouding it,
       Nor where black steeple, tar-gate, and gun-
bright anthracite held back the spring and the exact green to
                                                    bring it.

Though the smoke's gone now, the old frailty shows
       In people coming unexpectedly out of doors
Hardly renumbered since his time: each house knows
As many stories as in the iron sublime we call
       Victorian. Suicide, lost love, despair are laws
of a visiting Nature raging against proof and practice and
                                                    changing all.

Here, rather than in death-filled Dorset, I see him,
       The watchful conspirator against the gods
Come to the capital of light on his own grim
Journey into darkness; the dazzle would tell
       Him these were the worst of possible odds —
ordinary gestures of time working on faces the watermark of
                                                    hell.

187

Chorus at the End of the First Act

After the hours of singing and the long vowels
which ape the roundness of the heart
after the apprentice thunderclap
presaging the Ebony God
after the maidservants with plain needs
and coloratura of fingers in the dark
after the arias of determination, after the soap-clean light
and windows of first communion

Since the flute is stalled on the still plain
and towers can be seen a hundred miles
since the shattered jug is evidence
of complicity at the highest level
since the box is locked and the key in the river
and the mattress of fire is given to the guest
since the wolf's belly is filled with stones
and the pot of fat is hid in the rafters

Now the watchmen publish the hour of death
commending the citizens to love their wives
now the prophet is shown his face on a tray
and stone weeps and the blanket speaks
now the stout lovers are naked as naphtha
and watch is kept and is not kept
now the wound is fed, the betrayer enters
the city at the rising of the moon.

Tending towards the Condition

The news has reached the frogspawn,
our world is ransomed, spring rain
brings down a veil of weed, the Arno
the colour of Advocaat, another round
of tasks performed. To have nothing to say
fills large books with responsibilities –
as I said to the man in *Niccolino's,*
do away with form and you drown
in the infinite chances, especially
as darkness and other persons' phlegm
puts such a strain on you. As I sit,

slightly drunk with change from a thousand lire,
I hear the pens of cataloguers circling
the evening: in this episode the ghosts
of Hoboken and Pincherle remind me
how much time there is in sixty years.
I will put out sugar for the scholars
and steal their honey – a sort of happiness
is tombed in the *Volta dei Mercanti,*
a breeze springs up and fluffs the sparrows,
another half carafe sets the moon sailing
or a blaze of rain to cool the customers –
there is a shape to the world, more real
than time, more absolute than music.

The Tomb of Scarlatti

Average depth of graves, four feet –
the illusion of allegro in our light
is hard: that Iberian heartlessness
is still with us but not such sweetness.
What miracles for the twentieth century
among castrati, melons, and the dribbling kings!
Average length of sonata, four minutes, with repeats.

I hate the idea of Spain, yet for Domenico
I'd round each corner with its urine smell,
tickle the garden fish with a martyr's bone,
sit in the shadow of a cancered priest.
So many slaps of black! The old dust jumps
for American recordings, keyboard clatters
like cruel dominoes – E major fills the afternoon.

Santo Norberto gone: cat stalks complacent
pigeons. The old gods swim for home.
What are the conversions? Scholars' rules
and lace handkerchiefs become duennas' breasts
leaning from all top windows. A tourist bus
is draped with moonlight while the sounding notes
go past like carloads of the glittering dead.

La Déploration sur la Mort
d'Igor Stravinsky

1

From Colleoni's shadow
in a final purple,
out of the grinners' black,
an old man in a box
is carried to a gondola
and warped to the Isle
of the Dead: the cypress dark
must come to everyone
or the refining fire.
This is the death of Europe,
this is the eclipse –
an oar rises on the lagoon,
the flies rise from the camera-
man's breakfast. Pray
for all who have not known
such love and energy;
we are all guilty of dying,
we have gone under the trees
in the buzz of water,
expatriates of godsend
lamenting the machine
of genius and the Great Chute
of Twentieth-Century Death.

2

Plorans ploravit in nocte,
But he was not a tearful man.
You must praise God with
a little art if you have any,
et lachrymae ejus in maxillis ejus.
Converte nos, Domine,
ad te, et convertemur.
God promised us prophets
who would not cry in an orchard,
the clockwork was all sinew
and Fabergé disintegrated
on the moon. 'Sunless
as a mushroom farm',
Los Angeles and death!
Innova dies nostros,
sicut a principio.

190

I've sugared all this verse to please Persephone
whose face is lacquered with her occidental tears;
she loves and praises in her petty underground
all those who do not shun the major modes.
Art is not religion, if death is –
one chord will carry us home: I bless the imps
of time who set his brain to ring before
self-murder got into aesthetics and the God
of Lyre-Strikers was known as Environment.
Praise to the end, an apotheosis by augmentation –
even the Georgics of Factory Farming have a place,
the new simplicities inherit complexity
to train against; we shall not talk of God
though Devils live; Marsyas' skin speaks for Civil Rights
but Apollo won't leave Heaven, his divine injustice
leans like a tall light among the cold immortals.

Postcard Poems

Orcagna – Detail from the fresco, The Last Judgement, The Inferno –
Santa Croce, Florence

Repentance comes too late. The camp fiends
put on a fashion show. Oh wring your hands
in eau-de-nil regret. Toasted with friends,
the damned tiptoe on the burning sands.
Orcagna, Florentine, your sexy smell
is semen frying in the pans of Hell.

Sir Joshua Reynolds – Lady Mary Leslie – Iveagh Bequest, Kenwood

Mary had a little lamb,
four plump little lambs and a band
of blue about her waist –
insipid Mary was whey-faced,
Daddy spent all day at the kennels,
yet I praise this picture for the sake
of once-fashionable Reynolds
and to spite now-fashionable Blake.

Domenico Veneziano – Profile Head of a young Woman – Kaiser Friedrich Museum, Berlin

Daddy's got the top interior decorators
at the Palace. Mummy's the best-dressed
woman in Tuscany. I met a poet
with good manners, called Poliziano.
It's hot today and the sky's hardly ever
so blue as in this picture. I look
as though I've got the collywobbles or
I've swallowed a Latin Grammar:
you'd never guess the things I can do
with my lips. I'm seventeen and bored again.

Pisanello – La Principessa di Trebizonda – detail of fresco, Santa Anastasia, Verona

I have dreamed of green bishops
and almond-flavoured air,
I have seen devils hi-jack
the nimbus of a minor saint
from an Ossuary by an Inland Sea –
the Post is very bad, the wind
is making tourbillons around my hat,
it ruffles my cat Jesu, the four legs
of impassioned platitude;
from the depths of my calendar
I send you two words – MUCH LOVE!

J.M.W. Turner – The Parting of Hero and Leander – National Gallery, London

Love was always like this: a broken egg
in the sky, dawn with its regulation
heartbreak and evening with a train to catch.
The high buildings are not real, only the hopes.
Nous sommes aux mois d'amour.
Instead, the painter goes back in his eyes
and the poet dreams he sees this incredible sky.
Then the water breaks over his head. Praise
on your birthday from the swimmer and his gods.

Peter Phillips – Random Illusion No. 4 – Tate Gallery

Like the dove said, when you got
a military-industrial complex going
for you, you can blow rings round
any old abstract scruple and have
enough left over to endow the arts.
Big nations have wingspan and it ain't
Chrysler alone that mows down midgets.
Now all you liberal poets, get off
your blocks and come on hawkish!

*Albrecht Altdorfer – Landscape with a Footbridge – National
Gallery, London*

When the hermit heard about Nature
he'd forgotten he'd been living off
dung and berries for half a century.
What a wonderful invention, he said,
God has given Man a perfect frame,
but I wouldn't cross that bridge
into the picture for fear philosophers
would devour me like wolves.

Richard Hamilton – Interior II – Tate Gallery

The world is enormous, as the old
lens-grinder knew, inhaling fine
flour of death in his twilight room –
the home fleet of the past dresses
along my lifted arm and wherever
the archons shift their weight
a bruise of power shows. I am
becoming perfect in a room,
salvationist veal, nearer
the heart of truth, the wholly
responsive, appropriate number.

Piero di Cosimo – detail from The Fight between the Lapiths and Centaurs –
National Gallery, London

The Race Relations Board should issue this
as their Christmas Card. Just for a paradox–
since even here nature and gentleness connive.
Vanity and monsters will abort, classic certainty
is mere placenta. Mid-picture, a cormorant
or some such dive-bombs the sea. Let them
rend and bite and bash, Darwinian heroes
are hiding in the bush. All shall be well,
the monsters end up on a frieze
with genocide on rollers at the farm.

Masolino – Adam and Eve – detail from fresco in the Church of the
Carmines, Florence

Only the snake's erect –
the man's planning to ask his secretary out,
the woman wants a refrigerator –
a frightful row is brewing:
Prometheus on the Rocks
or The Wreck of the Deutschland –
thank God for a good chair and a view
of pollution on the box.

Giotto – Portrait of Dante – Bargello, Florence

This serious young face, so like a Kennedy's,
poet and plenipotentiary and always
a citizen of Florence. Forgive them their books
and treatises and universities – not many poets,
even horrible Goethe, have argued a whole
town over to the true wing of the Guelphs.
I've eaten in a restaurant named for you
and seen your posthumous life-mask. You tell us
we never get home but are buried in eternal exile.

194

I cannot work out this allegory
of men and women on a crumbling cliff:
bare breasts with a sail, one foot on a globe
and one on a boat – no one seems worried
and the detail is very beautiful.
I'm writing this with experimental music playing
and suddenly I see how all art is aggression –
behind the brotherhood of man
creatures with shears spit and wait.

James Joyce Sings 'Il mio tesoro'

Something to warm your back teeth
even if your shirt's making its presence felt,
some piece of calculated impertinence –

My theory about *Hamlet* can drop
until I get these divisions right,
I mean the way McCormack gets them :
che sol di stragi e morti
nunzio voglio tornar
The Peace of the Fathers be with you
and all the browning photographs of Europe

Among the clean mountains the mad
are trained like roses on a trellis
                              pruned for love

My books are easier to write than read
and by God that's the proper division of labour

Nobody but me has produced literature
as great as music
                              (I make an exception
of the author of *Hamlet*)

195

Do I hear some ijjit asking about
Proust and Synge and Pound
                    and a lot of names
I think I saw on raisin packets?

A fine tenor voice
the peace of great art

I never knew when to stop

If I'd been christened Stanislaus
I'd have claimed the throne of Poland

LIVING IN A CALM COUNTRY

At the Castle Hotel, Taunton

Today it's not scones but tea-cakes
    (And the sound of ambulances
    in the reconstructed streets) –

Rich voices are discussing the new Warden
    (The Show is the best for years,
    the architects' watercolours outstanding) –

Pearls and brogues survive, cashmere clings
    (Is this the Ark of Adultery
    or two old friends killing time?) –

Interlopers must wait for their tea
    (There's only one waitress on today,
    her footsteps are masked on the stairs) –

Hands want something to do, eyes won't idle
    (*Country Life* in a rexine folder:
    who buys, who sells all these houses?) –

O impossible England under the modern stars
    (Mr Edward du Cann thanks the voters
    of Taunton for their generous support) –

So much beauty, so unexpectedly preserved
    (And we two strangers have today
    honoured gentle Eliot at East Coker) –

Not only the pheasant eating by the road
    (And the cider factory, the industrial
    archaeology with the rural) –

But the pattern of beauty changing in the air
    (Fields painted by history, a steam
    of seasons softening what lives) –

Somerset for survivors and a good thing too
   (*Seventeenth-century farmhouse,*
   part-converted, owner abroad) –

Seen from Ilminster spire, everything is safe
   (It is being kept for posterity
   but where do the people of England live?)

His and Hers

Mornings weaving through the mud
Gave his high boots a cracked glory,
And she, crying where she stood,
Heard the hardly bothered-with story;
Each not knowing that pain clings
To the cleaned surface of things.

The greenhouse overspored with seeds
And the motor mower dried of oil,
Over the garage virginia creeper bleeds,
The lawn has patches of bare soil –
This is the Estate Agent's concern
Since he's in a box and she in an urn.

Behind a door missed by visitors
High boots and binoculars stand –
The arrogance his, the unhappiness hers;
Neither can get the upper hand,
The doing and the watching part
Outliving the torments of the heart.

Anger

In long lines
about the hill, crops are at war
with evening

The moon high,
glimpsed then gone,
a drift of upper leaves
in the dark wind of Cornwall

To give no part
of oneself to death
before the time

Only to sit
with one's back to music
and no forgiveness

Colouring
the air and scattering
flakes of fury

Living in a Calm Country

Each picture is a comic strip condensed.
You stare at Santa Fina on her bench
And the palisades are packed –
Looking is locking up, eyes are a fence.

A change of element to wallow in!
The swimmer wades through words – to him
Come doves and office pigeons,
Tu quoqueing his music, pinking his skin.

The difference is (again) the fact of time,
Such a lovely word that rhymes with rhyme:
Pictures stand still and still
Music composes the world, poems set lines.

Living in a calm country, which is me
Is not like architecture or the sea
Or diligence of diction or
Any Mixolydian matter, it's green, grey, green.

Then back to Santa Fina who gave up
Her life by giving up her seat, the luck
Of those the gods love, unlike
Myself at the window now, calm as a cup.

Playing with selfishness, I propose
Rules for the game, the most outrageous clothes
On truth, a cunning heart
Pumping in praise of time, as the world goes.

Ode to Afternoon

A command to the middle-aged,
you shall write disguised love poems
so that the young may respect you
when the truth is known

They will ensex your abstracts
wink knowingly at all
the stale erudition
which so enrages your critics

You must make capital out of despair:
real pain is never art,
turn instead to quotidian tasks,
Grub Street at the obsessional!

In your review of *The Romance of Linear B*,
notice that all the texts are Official Art,
the numbers of the king's combs and cattle –
their songs you must imagine for yourself

Of *The Eighteen Chorales*, there is much love of God –
you alone have cracked the cypher
and know what he meant when he told the soul
to bedeck itself for its bridegroom

In the middle of *The Children's Crusade*
you may put two adolescents under a tree
poking bits of bark down each other's front,
music by Puccini, the sun declining

Having set the scene, you are in the Land
of Afternoon. Sex, if it comes, will be late,
up some stairs following a nervous lunch,
her eyes like a Florentine postcard

In the afternoon they came unto a land
in which it seemed always afternoon:
The fathers were at the races
and the lawnmowers ran all over the hills

Afternoon men in the morning of the world,
we donate our three score and ten
to a beleaguered maturity –
province of afghan hounds and honeydew

Mother, the girls you warned me of
are waiting behind the rector's hedge,
I can hear their voices: they are content
with the usual menagerie

Home of averages where human kind
cannot bear very much reality
but the sun is always over the yard-arm
and we are for the dark

Der Untergang des Abendlandes
is still a best seller though it sounds
better with a stierhorn's blast
than a song at twilight

These quotations will keep nobody warm,
so put away the deck chairs
and the half-finished poem
and return to your research

Which was into the lineaments
of great fiction, and began
with the motherless boy
circuiting his grown-up garden:

Huge tears are in the pond,
every hurt has a face like a flower –
that will be music across the road
from the long-dead birthday party

O sprays of scent and my blue aunts,
I am coming with my excuses ready:
I was reading down in the boatshed,
how shall we get through the afternoon?

Good Vibes

for Shena Mackay

If you hadn't noticed the unprominent sign
We'd have missed Adlestrop, missed the gone
Railway and the bullock raking his back
In the hollow holly-bower. Missed, too, the sky
So intolerably lofty in its beakered blue
And the loping dog which frightened me
(Which is how I know he was friendly) –
Most noticeably missed the station bench
And ADLESTROP, the railway sign, with Edward
Thomas's poem on a plaque for pilgrims.
Not a great poem, but rich in names
And heartache and certainly a focus for
A sinisterly fine October afternoon.
Down one lane adjacent the Home for Children,
(With what impediment we never found),
All the day-labourers of Oxfordshire and Gloucestershire
Were about their honey-making masonry
Of Cotswold stone, and the bullocks were nifty
In the meadow by the creek. There were no
Devils in the landscape, exhalations from
Ponds and dogs' breath and graveyards after rain
Could only be imagined in such unexpected sunshine,
But we felt them, felt a new humidity,
Oppressive like the self. This was a short halt
On two pilgrimages, a look-back out of Hades,
Such as the gods provide for laughter in their
Chronicles. Yet that sound, that risible division,
Strikes mortal earth some otherwise – such as
Gravel flicking from a low-slung bumper,
A trailing jet above, a jostling on the eaves
Of sycamores. It was as if the well-intentioned
Dead were breathing out and blessing everyone,
Vibrations of the minute, without franchise,
A pointless benediction. Thinking again, I feel
Grateful that you saw through uncleaned windows
A name which meant the same to all half-educated
Persons. To have trod on ground in happiness
Is to be shaken by the true immortals.

Seaside Picnic

Here where sprawl the armed persuaders,
    Denizens of three-inch oceans
    Who rage as Genghis over sand and rock
    Ignoring only the anemone's motions,
    Its meatless, beautiful tick-tock;
Here, scaled down from the world of waders,

Whose holiday gingerliness is as remote
    As God, the relentless law
    Renews itself: the soft-backed crab
    Ventures too far from its lodge, and claw
    And life both break at one stab
Of an old need and like seaweed are left to float.

This terror is enacted in seventy pools
    Of a single rock till the tide
    Renews like Deucalion's advance
    Another flood of darkness, and to hide
    Is the victim's and predator's equal chance.
This is a world without self-doubters or fools,

Egregiously unlike the pretty playground
    Of its kindhearted great
    Who might say to a clambering child
    'Don't leave that sea-snail to its fate
    But right it on its shelf so the mild
Worm can cling, the life platform be sound.'

For they are swayed by such overreaching waters
    As they do not recognize
    Along the bristling beach on afternoons
    Of sun, and having learned to prize
    Hope, pass each other plates and spoons,
Unpacking love for their murderous sons and daughters.

To Make it Real

After having written verses in tight corsets,
verses inspired by German Idealism
and random, thin, self-justifying verses,
I feel the need to trap a piece of real.
I started the trochaic motor up
some lines before but now I slip the clutch –
trochees and iambs are so Janus-faced,
I leave our virtuosi of the Classics
to startle us with Choriambs and Sapphics.

Despair might get some music into this,
poetry must do up its own laces.
Somewhere beyond my window (shall we say
in Pessary, Ohio) a widowed lady
rocks like acacia fragrance in the night
and lets a naked light bulb close her eyes,
the neighbour's dog her psychopomp, the
ruttish evening full of floating dust
as she is candled inwards, yet not fussed.

I made this lady up: my cat ascends
the curtain wildly clawing till she falls;
non sequiturs of heartburn and despair
are felt like persons in the early dark.
My mortal lady with the finished eyes
will not be named and will not need a grave,
but for her benediction London kneels –
our well-lit world goes in the Word Machine,
chaff in the jaws of God, blood in a dream.

The Story of my Conversion

I have begun to live in a new land,
not the old land of fear
but the new one of disappointment.

At forty-five I am at the right age
to appreciate that my new country
enjoys good relations with death.

But I am also returning to the surprises
of childhood, the sun-slatted boredom,
castles of the kingdom of bananas.

Not me, Lord. The summons is not for me,
I am considering my student's albums,
girls' addresses, hours of drinking, anger.

A marvellous mustiness surrounds me;
The Book of Useless Knowledge in my hand,
I salute the thousand green horrors, the self.

In the Eighteen Eighties, Freud
applied for a job in a Bendigo hospital –
it's enough to make Tasman miss the boat.

Nothing is alike in my familiar world.
The boy of the unwritten journal
would get my prig's sneer. Good God, his prose!

If he had a cypher for things not done
he'd write *halek* for the Greek girl
who went to the same Communion classes.

I might have been born in Galicia,
in the poet-killing provinces:
the olives look to me outside Cortona.

Instead, my vote went to verandahs.
What has this to do with the land
of disappointment? A style, or lack of style.

I am fond of the overdone. Of Luca Signorelli
and Castagno. I'll never learn simplicity,
I don't feel things strongly. I was never young.

I asked my friends how they swallowed the world.
They said, you will only learn by doing it.
That's why I would sooner be asleep.

I must use passive verbs. Describe death
as matter being re-cycled. I feel like someone
in a German play winding up the moon.

But this new land I was talking about –
it has a vocation for mad creatures,
they live by arguing with the sea.

I, too, am licensed to produce a masterpiece.
I start: 'In the Eighteen Eighties, Freud applied
for a doctor's job in Bendigo – or was it Ballarat?'

Night Crossing

The old charm dies hard, the vicious moon
A yellow mango and the ferryman saying
Some oblationary rune above the rising flood;
Night and silence have always been indoors,
A provincial pinchbeck still extraordinary
Among the duodecimo principalities
And me the hidalgo of all self-esteem.

I listen to the Time-travelling Schoolmistress:
Avoid simplicity, she says, that
Shakespearean gold made of short words.
You are a tyro of untrusted syllables
And your pretence of knowledge comes out
As dreams, like these, distorted, polychromed,
All about sex but more of neaps than nipples.

He comes closer daily, the white-winged visitor
With his pouch of riddles. If we stand close
To the bar and swear undying friendship, he may
Go away. It's just another reconnaissance
As is this life which Shelley said
Stains the white radiance et cetera –
I won't die young to make my language work.

But I am haunted, not by books or notes,
But by disparate refuse of a species' mind.
Where the diamonds of our race show clear
Light from the Father, I fudge murky red:
I go to sleep to greet the myths, pure comic-strip
With serious charges following, father and mother's blood
Upon the always shamed and always bachelor sheets.

Never to be what I say as never to know,
For instance, if the ferryman will be the same
Across the river, or whether a voice reading
COSMO MEDICI MAGNO ETRURIA DUCI
Is my old headmaster or the floating oracle
They promised me when I renounced my love
To become a good resentful husband.

The questions the Customs ask are quite unclassical,
The names unknown to Pope or Plutarch –
Some words this hand will try to set in place
Changing the mixed-up facts to meet the case.
In the bright morning of night I pay my way
Into the Great Exhibition: from here on
The gods are dead, I meet their proud originals.

Family Album

Tenable in dreams, here they are twice
as plausible, holding court to the lens,
with nothing to say but the truth.
            Myself, my mother,
culled from the caucus of summer
by a relative's whim: how did the fat woman
keep so many bees off her howling son?
            That man, chained to
his gross watch, wearing his waistcoat
like Prometheus his rock, did he edge
to the aerodrome to show he was too
frightened to enter the twentieth century?
            It makes a good fiction
to leer at their confidence. Something else
would fit in. The light, acid but milky,
along the near shore and the ironclad ferry
touching the stage; Cousin Timperley
walking an ice-cream up to the pines,
Beethoven for supper, everyone upright.
            Later, dispersal may offer
your motorcade stopping en route to Tiberias,
'This is Cana, so don't check the water
in your radiator'. Over us looms Mount
Gilboa where Saul fell on his sword,

a mortar lob from the red hibiscus
kibbutz, its blond children playing
through the collective afternoon.
                    Pictures from a lost
exhibition. Not the pianola and
the telescope, but a high-backed
Russian chair and the brilliantined
bridegroom asleep after venery.
Or this tribute: 'How we brought
the Good News', key of F Minor,
the house in the corn.
                    That hand, that brown face,
now papery, channelled with heart
disease, the transit of Venus.
Mother and father met here in me
ascribing a terror of photographs
to the lingering snake in the garden.
                    Made objective now
on the lake where the red-eyed fish
walk on wallpaper. O sails of death
that we watched on the river, weeks of rain
when we came to our father's house,
the pictures are ready, shall we walk in?

An Australian Garden

for Sally Lehmann

Here we enact the opening of the world
And everything that lives shall have a name
To show its heart; there shall be Migrants,
Old Believers, Sure Retainers; the cold rose
Exclaim perfection to the gangling weeds,
The path lead nowhere – this is like entering
One's self, to find the map of death
Laid out untidily, a satyr's grin
Signalling 'You are here': tomorrow
They are replanting the old court,
Puss may be banished from the sun-warmed stone.

See how our once-lived lives stay on to haunt us,
The flayed beautiful limbs of childhood

In the bole and branches of a great angophora –
Here we can climb and sit on memory
And hear the words which death was making ready
From the start. Such talking as the trees attempt
Is a lesson in perfectability. It stuns
The currawongs along the breaks of blue –
Their lookout cries have guarded Paradise
Since the expulsion of the heart, when man,
Bereft of joy, turned his red hand to gardens.

Spoiled Refugees nestle near Great Natives;
A chorus of winds stirs the pagoda'd stamens:
In this hierarchy of miniatures
Someone is always leaving for the mountains,
Civil servant ants are sure the universe
Stops at the hard hibiscus; the sun is drying
A beleaguered snail and the hydra-headed
Sunflowers wave like lights. If God were to plant
Out all His hopes, He'd have to make two more
Unknown Lovers, ready to find themselves
In innocence, under the weight of His green ban.

In the afternoon we change – an afterthought,
Those deeper greens which join the stalking shadows –
The lighter wattles look like men of taste
With a few well-tied leaves to brummel-up
Their poise. Berries dance in a southerly wind
And the garden tide has turned. Dark on dark.
Janus leaves are opening to the moon
Which makes its own grave roses. Old Man
Camellias root down to keep the sun intact,
The act is canopied with stars. A green sea
Rages through the landscape all the night.

We will not die at once. Nondescript pinks
Survive the death of light and over-refined
Japanese petals bear the weight of dawn's first
Insect. An eye makes damask on the dew.
Time for strangers to accustom themselves
To habitat. What should it be but love?
The transformations have been all to help
Unmagical creatures find their proper skins,
The virgin and the leonine. The past's a warning
That the force of joy is quite unswervable –
'Out of this wood do not desire to go'.

In the sun, which is the garden's moon, the barefoot
Girl espies her monster, all his lovely specialty
Like hairs about his heart. The dream is always
Midday and the two inheritors are made
Proprietors. They have multiplied the sky.
Where is the water, where the terraces, the Tritons
And the cataracts of moss? This is Australia
And the villas are laid out inside their eyes:
It would be easy to unimagine everything,
Only the pressure made by love and death
Holds up the bodies which this Eden grows.

On First Looking into Chapman's Hesiod

For 5p at a village fête I bought
Old Homer-Lucan who popped Keats's eyes,
Print smaller than the Book of Common Prayer
But Swinburne at the front, whose judgement is
Always immaculate. I'll never read a tenth
Of it in what life I have left to me
But I did look at *The Georgics*, as he calls
The Works and Days, and there I saw, not quite
The view from Darien but something strange
And balking – Australia, my own country
And its edgy managers – in the picture of
Euboeaen husbandry, terse family feuds
And the minds of gods tangential to the earth.

Like a Taree smallholder splitting logs
And philosophizing on his dangling billies,
The poet mixes hard agrarian instances
With sour sucks to his brother. Chapman, too,
That perpetual motion poetry machine,
Grinds up the classics like bone meal from
The abbatoirs. And the same blunt patriotism,
A long-winded, emphatic, kelpie yapping
About our land, our time, our fate, our strange
And singular way of moons and showers, lakes
Filling oddly – yes, Australians are Boeotians,
Hard as headlands, and, to be fair, with days
As robust as the Scythian wind on stone.

To teach your grandmother to suck eggs
Is a textbook possibility in New South Wales
Or outside Ascra. And such a genealogy too!
The Age of Iron is here, but oh the memories
Of Gold – pioneers preaching to the stringybarks,
Boring the land to death with verses and with
Mental Homes. 'Care-flying ease' and 'Gift-
Devouring kings' become the Sonata of the Shotgun
And Europe's Entropy; for 'the axle-tree, the quern,
The hard, fate-fostered man' you choose among
The hand castrator, kerosene in honey tins
And mystic cattlemen: the Land of City States
Greets Australia in a farmer's gods.

Hesiod's father, caught in a miserable village,
Not helped by magic names like Helicon,
Sailed to improve his fortunes, and so did
All our fathers – in turn, their descendants
Lacked initiative, other than the doctors' daughters
Who tripped to England. Rough-nosed Hesiod
Was sure of his property to a slip-rail –
Had there been grants, he'd have farmed all
Summer and spent winter in Corinth
At the Creative Writing Class. Chapman, too,
Would vie with Steiner for the Pentecostal
Silver Tongue. Some of us feel at home nowhere,
Others in one generation fuse with the land.

I salute him then, the blunt old Greek whose way
Of life was as cunning as organic. His poet
Followers still make me feel déraciné
Within myself. One day they're on the campus,
The next in wide hats at a branding or
Sheep drenching, not actually performing
But looking the part and getting instances
For odes that bruise the blood. And history,
So interior a science it almost seems
Like true religion – who would have thought
Australia was the point of all that craft
Of politics in Europe? The apogee, it seems,
Is where your audience and its aspirations are.

'The colt, and mule, and horn-retorted steer' –
A good iambic line to paraphrase.
Long storms have blanched the million bones
Of the Aegean, and as many hurricanes
Will abrade the headstones of my native land:
Sparrows acclimatize but I still seek
The permanently upright city where
Speech is nature and plants conceive in pots,
Where one escapes from what one is and who
One was, where home is just a postmark
And country wisdom clings to calendars,
The opposite of a sunburned truth-teller's
World, haunted by precepts and the Pleiades.

Frogs at Lago di Bolsena

Having come down and run the car into sand
Not a foot from the reeds, the tense changes to
The Italian present and stories of Montefiascone
Are right for the first perambulation –
Only a few plastic bags floating and the smell
Of burning in the hills mild as eleven o'clock:
Then the frogs start – out there in the shallows, one
After another clamouring against official Nature.

For Nature is official here, its privilege extended
To recalcitrant weeds and momentous blossoms –
The Miracle of Bolsena struck from an open sky
And like a sunset the Host ran blood: what then
Can prevail upon the gentle waters, calm and bloodless,
When Christ's sanguinity fills the slaughterhouses
And the bone-dry churches? A corpse in damask
Holds the unsyntactical silence of despair.

Invisible and croaking in their plainness, the frogs
Speak of a similarly certain pain never
Lessening, and of the will to bring new pain
After, which this Italy has squared into art,
And which pilgrims with books in their hands try
To exorcize by long looks at lakes, judging
The far bank and marvellous islands until
The picture is captured and killed for their dreams.

212

An American Military Cemetery in Tuscany

Why, I wonder, are there so few cows
Amid the succulent green of the tracks
And the neat, staked vine-plants in their rows?
This is Chianti country,
The river mud a Helena Rubenstein pack
Ensuring through raging summer a beauty
Of self-possession, a coolness waving back.

What appears a castle is a convent
Endowed by Florentine ambition, then
Comes the Winegrowers' Co-operative, meant
To look democratic and new –
Its striped blinds and sun-dazzled men
Wave to the tourist bus through thin blue
Exhaust bringing them dollars, marks and yen.

Because the land's flat for some miles
The bus keeps the cemetery in sight
For two miles at least – set like dials
For the eye of the deity
The headstones seem to the overbright
Travellers disagreeable presences – the laity
Find, as inside Santa Croce, God is uptight.

Underneath, men of Oregon and Minnesota
Are learning to be as green as Tuscany,
That dark green which has always had its quota
Of the most courageous blood –
Afterwards, a man can be tall as a pine tree
Straightening for the wind, or like flood
Water disperse himself in the silent majority.

As the bus passes this geometric field
A shiver runs from it to the sun:
Each of these innocent worlds is sealed
Under pressure of love and hate,
Each named soul is a precise no one
Discovering the mystery too late,
It is not fulfilled, it is only done.

A Table of Coincidences

The map of self is a grid of crossroads –
The tanned garage attendant is also
The learned custodian of shards,
The unhelpful presider over a dozen
Phones stops your plane in time
To wing you back to love. They cross and cross,
The focus of care and the occasional nuisance,
The reed-stealer and the bald historian.
Lucky indeed to have a graveyard
In your head: walk by the wild hibiscus
Where an army vanished – through the haze
The low lake waves keep their tint of violence.

Even our rulers eat themselves to death.
A professor writes a book on the third period
Of his great composer; next door, the new genius
Creates relevant art with Woolworth balloons –
The solemn thinkers are the ones with hate.
The oracle's advice is to fake it well,
By which she means, learn to live with
Your imagination. You may desire universal
Love but your hand has obsession
In its curve. There is no Devil and perhaps
No God, but the walls are running blood
From the unsightly pictures of your dreams.

Still, every tomb requires two masks,
The slipping grin of terror and the running
Nose of irresponsibility. There, by the wand
Of magic, an Attic outline strokes its prick,
Hoping to come before the police arrive –
Better to face the dark with something to remember.
Stalled by the roses with your favourite uncle,
Thinking only of Dryden and the sinking
Of the *Emden*, you go to the universe
Of interchangeables – take this to heart!
The day Columbus discovered America
Was the day Piero della Francesca died.

Each wasted day lives on to waste tomorrow.
Three bitter seeds were put in Adam's grave
That the bright flags of history might unfurl.
The world is far away at this high window
Where jet trails chalk a pane of the cold sky.
'My bitter days do waste and I do languish' –
In the mirror I see the face of an old man
With a big nose; my daughter has dark
Celtic skin which shrivelled in the sun of death
When my mother wore it; the man on the path
Is our Hermes of the commercial smile;
Our plane is late, the courier calms our fears.

That Depression is an Abstract

That depression is an abstract
is my doctor's view, who watches me open
one ear on a hinge and looks with interest
at a countryside of flowers and barges
and squares of green each carrying a cow –
                    None of this is necessary
he says in his subtle lower case,
you have landlines to ten capitals.
                    Good thinking,
bring the calabashes of iced wine
and the little sausages, I reply.
                    Lie on this couch
and tell me what Europe said to you.
                    She showed me an olive hillside
with the minty dead trowelled in a wall
and scented black steadying itself
for picnics on Mt Erebus.
                    She took my brown eyes
for gristle, something she could never swallow,
they had held tears at one age –
                    She said, my son,
I would name a river for you
if only I had one left –
I loved your galloping through the evening fields,
your snout plating over and your gills
forming where the love-bites were.
                    I saw the old castle

215

where deformity took itself as subject
and wrote God into the moon. Aunty Dolour
was my university and our good dog
played the Wolf of Gubbio
at the back door.
            Eventually, doctor,
we must come down to cases
but my memory is bad.
            There are these polemics
you write against the new art –
'Why persecutest thou me?'
You have a cruel masterpiece
crying to get out, Saints Cosmas
and Damian healing a Rider
Haggard impi.
            Six pounds fifty
an hour should clear your head.
Indeed, as the sun stretched along my side,
I gazed at the advertisements –
            I do not feel depressed
although it is old in May and not
my time of year.
            I would like you
to use plain syntax and straight words
and to practise your left-hand scales!
            They fell from my eyes
in the first reels of eternity,
my bones were hollow before the lark's –
having paid and spoken and been listened to,
I have my certificate of going back,
guaranteeing it as it was then,
coming down a winding road of villas
to the Badia, the lodge gates plaqued
'Domenico Cimarosa lived here
in 1779', and then the black sky breaking,
seeing a face I loved and knowing
it had no respect for me, seeing my father
in the rain trying to clip the bougainvillea.
            Until death
the abstracts will have silver faces,
baroque lanterns like the moon,
terror pressed into depression,
            you and you and you,
father, son and lover of the world.

The Storm

There where it's endless, it has this form of age,
of the feet no longer willing to enter
the waiting slippers, the etiolated arm
tugging a little at a nurse's kindness
though reconciled even to this lost rebellion:
'we come out of the dark and go into the dark again'
as the Hofrat put it in his gently bullying way, nothing
of the heated moment lasts and yet nothing
decays. The heart of the storm is now,
God wrecking man on death,
the absurdity of pitching his tone so high –

And the storm-tossed angels
about the bright graveyards and the chimneys
of the Corporation fire-temples,
they have huge albums of memorials,
of Hannah, dearly beloved wife,
of Lieutenant Sanderson, drowned on a boom,
of Grey and Gander, who fell asleep in infancy,
of names unnamed that do not feel
the drip of autumn leaves –
                                   they know
a barometer from a loving God
but what can they do crouching in His corner?
                                   Millennia
stop short at three score years and ten
and the only thing on earth which will never
wither away is the state.
                                 They ask
forgiveness for joking outside your sepulchres;
sometimes the sun shines and it seems
the storm is just a passing thing,
captains of industry smile on white terraces,
the regatta sails like drops of blood
fleck the blue estuary –
                            Back in the Nursing Home
a change on a chart is recorded, the angels
are tossed in its turbulence.
                               Why write poems?
Why, for that matter, march on Moscow
or ask your daughter if she loves you?

The calm. While it lasts, there is man,
and suppose him a creature it's worth
making God for. In that calm, as at Babel,
mercurial masons are singing the truth,
serene diapasons of business and profit,
university judgements, priceless preferments,
courage and cowardice. Perhaps it did happen,
the Renaissance, when even the maggots
had Humanist leanings.

                      The storm will return
but before it claps down on the foreshore
and harbour, put out the lights, the nightlights
and phosphorous and turn the sea upwards
inverting the stars – the long winking banks
are like Mozart or Nature, carrion-joy
that the dumb in the fields pay the price of
and grieve for; a central unfairness
which looks good to the living, loving
on bones of the dead with basset-horns
maundering, and flushed by their faces,
happy as stopwatches, unlectured
by sick-beds or dreams, awaiting
the tempest, the null epicentre.

A Study of a Bird

With completely retractable sail
he has an ocean surrounding him;
his surface is at all edges
and everywhere the reefs wait
with their yellow surf: he lives
in a cube drawn by a mad artist,
his eyes are along diagonals;
perspective is what we invent
to be like him: he is not like us,
he would never expect an epitaph.

Brave on a tractor while they lunch
he is as vain as a place god,
an inspector of three hundred tall
stalks and the ants' deep shelter.
That sound now – is it the frogs

218

in their safe swamp, or the crickets
down on their knees? No, it's
the bariolage of useless terror
made by all things born to die –
he dips his head, they are wiping their mouths.

Traction by Leonardo, costume by Audubon,
habitat by John Clare – the Establishment
of creatures chairs him to the top.
There he passes with his flaps down
plumb on a winter tree. We may
take his eggs and measurements
but we cannot levitate. A ring on his leg
will match him to God's census –
only his watching superiors leave
paradise, trailed by a flailing sword.

Fields at evening hold the honey
of the sun. He 'fleeth as it were
a shadow', the bird of the Angelus
among the gleaners of Nature:
it is all dark and light to him,
a scene by C. D. Friedrich to us.
Heavier-than-air machine the poet
loves, he overhears these pointless
poignant words: *I am a child of the
Enlightenment, I expect to be happy.*

Three Bagatelles

Under the grassed and general earth a space
Of two contending shadows that are still –
This private darkness was a lightness once
Which sinned against its native fantasy,
A hinged desire which swung below the sun
And closed forever: here the words persist –
Your amorous dust is flesh to my chill dust,
Your page of tributes printed on my heart,
I am your resurrection, you my lust,
Lipless, we kiss and never move apart.

*

The unseeing eyes are not within the world,
Their orphic stare is cataracted here.
Of trinities, beauty, love and pleasure
Have faces which philosophers adorn;
The Venus Pudica has two small mouths
But the gale of innocence is not blown out –
A small cadenza on the skin of sex
And see a burning world defy the odds!
Voluptas dies and Caritas will vex,
The gods are loveless, yet they are the gods.

*

Make speed by sloth and give the tortoise wings
As in the perfect day a dead fish floats,
Blood flows from wounds and from the menstrual ditch
The future runs: the childlike lovers age,
War on its knees petitions peaceful love,
A rabble pelts the stricken King of Swans –
The open box of mystery commands
Only such truths as memory puts in.
The eggs of death are warm, futurity stands,
Like the infinity of angels, on a pin.

Studies from Lemprière

The Feast of the Gods

In the perfect weather of their soft plateau
The reasonable deities deployed
Their human hungers. What was there more to show
To creatures who never had enjoyed
Freedom from death, but paying with their lives
Bought golden faces, a marble of archives?

It was a pleasure to imagine pain,
The circumstance of love, the stars far out
Which touched them little, and to feel again
That classic innocence when any doubt
Brought wonder to their finished universe,
The tessitura of man's dying curse.

220

One laid a hand upon his consort's flank
And felt by proxy every warming glance;
Birds of paradise and peacocks shrank
Into the polished fernery; the midday dance
Of animals to please their masters took
A warlike gesture from an open book.

The painter found them at post-prandial games,
Helmets worn askew and breasts exposed,
But having second sight he fed the flames
Of war which lay behind their lovers' pose:
Those long marches were not to any bed
But to the Fields of Fear, the Isle of the Dead.

Not to be moved by misery, not to know
Relish in loving, discontent in age –
Their thoughts were crystalline in sun or snow,
Their history atoms on rampage;
In place of good and bad they had fortune,
An aspect of the clouds and sliding moon.

You see this scene only when very old,
A vision of the unremitting gods
Picknicking as in the Age of Gold,
Not adding to or taking from the odds
But having eternity to live through
Looking beyond the face of death at you.

The Zone of Venus

This was the Attic picture when she drew
Her ribboned waistline to its narrowest.
These things her liberators understood,
The covetable radiance of the New,
Impressive art which might renew the West,
A stranger's touch conferring Neighbourhood.

Her guerdon seemed far otherwise to those
Who entered by the dark sulphurous door;
Would there be light again and would their names
Be heard once more or left beside their clothes
Upon the banks of Hell? Their feet were sore
From running and there were still the Games.

Her daughters found her picture in their hands:
'That was the Sunday night when I was laid
By a man from the Agency.' The goddess turned
To view her imprint in the shining sand –
Where love had been, a grave was freshly made,
Letters were strewn, a votive candle burned.

My darker side, she said, to switch the part,
I have these other gifts, that when I tread
On gorse or waste land, fields of pleasure grow
And this I call the landscape of the heart –
You find that lips can do what you have read,
Words are true, the honeyed anthems flow.

But barbarous fate to wake up in a place
Where everything is narrowed into love,
Your tongue her agriculture, war
Between day and night upon her face
And simple sleep murdered from above,
Possession being nine points of the law.

The pictures are deceits, Zephyrus blows
On the nymph's neck to bring up flowers,
Wounded Adonis whistles off his dogs –
Her mischievous girdle on, the goddess goes
Out antlering the world, her playful powers
Serve civil lovers for death's catalogues.

The Descent into Avernus

Coming down from the serious hills upon
The Campanian flatlands, then we saw
The black lake where the stars reflected shone
Among the stagnant argosies of weed,
Small sulphur roses knocking at the shore
And swollen pumice jammed among the reeds.

This was the Leader's promise, a lake without
Birds or any living creature, fanned
By volcanic breath, the home of doubt;
Here we would camp and wait until a sign
Gave presence to the statutory land,
Blood from the earth or voices in a vine.

One of our purposes was to trace the smell,
That all-pervading smell of misery.
Some said it was the heroes dead in Hell
Smothered forever in their victims' flesh,
Others the pus of gods, rot in the Tree
Of Life no mortal creature could refresh.

That it was human where nothing human lived
Was everyone's hypothesis. The shades of armies
Stood behind the midday dazzle, sieved
From a glut of contours by the sun;
Beyond the line of salt some spindly trees
Waved like souls whose torments had begun.

The Leader made survival rules for all —
To be observers of the scene was our
Responsibility. In the long haul
To darkness, man would need supplies,
Rations which the dead could not devour,
Signals beyond his rational faculties.

And so upon the poisoned earth we sat,
The air itself a teeming oracle:
Man's soul might leave him like a cat,
His body come to carbon, yet somewhere
Behind this valley or that clambering hill
He'd find his true and disciplined despair.

Dreamtime

To the short-of-breath an apotheosis,
To come upstairs behind some Metternich
Of the party-giving world and still be
Recognized; your hostess, her rings shining,
Ready to rescue you out of corners.

This might be the door opening on a dream
Of a prosperous terrain where at last
Scenery germane to the heart is displayed:
Silos with clocks, the Norman church deaf
To the procession with the lilied corpse,

Half-Cockaigne among the seaweed grasses
And the animal moon awake all day,
Severe streets opening suddenly after fields
Of grain, the calm citizens ambling through
Huzzahs of troops for a near-sighted heir;

The parturition of the Princess golden
With balconies, and the revolutionaries' smithy
Watched by a bored spy; melancholy hours
In the cafés without even a betrayal
Or a sexual touch of foot or finger.

That is the scene, but it may change.
We may hurry to some Horatian outhouse
For the evening reading and discourse blood
On the pink-faced terrace, someone nearby
Playing the flute at a lizard listening.

Hate in the hills where the rebels practise
Games with black gourds, boredom in the library
At any time of day, but fear always,
Fear in everything. Responsibility for this
Is the question on each person's tongue.

They will try to get you to dream a new world
For them, one made clean by courage. You
May need to give a hostage as you do now
When you see approaching the perennial bore
Who is host to nature and a lord of change.

Meanwhile

Doch unverständig ist
Das Wünschen vor dem Schicksal.
Die Blindesten aber
Sind Göttersöhne.

– Hölderlin

The source of all things is in themselves
but there must be pictures to hang in Heaven –
    the whale flensed in a chalky sea
    to make a dawn;
    craters of the afternoon
under eaves of the Fichtelgebirge;
    a mouth patrolling
a million eggs knowing its time will come.
    Simplicity, complexity
    and the words between!
Such pretty critics of our carelessness –
    what if we say
'I have tried to give up abstracts
but I cannot tell a laurel leaf
from a collar stiffener.'
    The soul
might look out through the eyes if only
all incoming traffic ceased a while.
    Till then, judicious murder.
Ruins run the landscape. Lodges
of Unlikeliness where dickering birds
inspirit sundials, a chequerboard
of turf above Moravian sleepers,
love leaving and arriving through
a gangster's ganglia, and then that music
which asks an amnesty of death.
    Mixed feelings
no less than metaphors.
    The wickedest dream
    man ever dreamed
    showed him to himself
    as pure spirit:
we live still in the horror of it.
    The gods come tumbling
to repair the damage, flattering us
with little evils –

a sculpture of snot
and Daphne's earwax,
payola for the trumpeting
of blood, the carcass
of a tear.

This riddling tone
is for the fierce enthusiasts and drumming
critics: theirs is the lust of change,
the module of imagination, but instead
we enjoy and through eternity
a breakfast after dreaming.
In the German
Meanwhile we lie down with words,
shaped into silence or thronging
to accuse. Our only health
is to be moved by movers, hearing
in stark quiet the order to conduct
the once-living through our lives.
This lifts the gods
from grovelling
at mortal spoor
and faces them
with loneliness and blind amenity.

Down Cemetery Road

The wind brings the Sunday bells. Come to church
good people. But for me they're simulacra
of the great bell in my chest, clouting out the end.

This comes of keeping one's nose to the moral north
where gods go when they die. Oh how pleased
they are to leave their Babylonian captivity.

And how strange that religion comes from the East
where tourists see only commerce – fanaticism
seeking blue-eyed converts in the claggy fens.

But not the point of this poem. The chorale of Bach's
which moves me most is a tune of *1713*,
a real contemporary, *Liebster Gott, wann wird ich sterben?*

226

The tune is Daniel Vetter's, the treatment Bach's.
There's the soft flush of earth when corpse and men
move among the matutinal flowers.

Bells like teeth touching, the towers of Leipzig
carving a Lutheran world in friendly slices,
that warm sententiousness we know as death.

Almost chirpy music, but don't ask the corpse
his view. Perhaps he sees that transcendental
radish bed promised by the tame Tibetans.

After a lifetime of blood letting, we deserve
a vegetable future. The flutes and oboes pilfer grief,
we have earned this joyful gruesomeness.

I think I was six when first I thought of death.
I've been religious ever since. Good taste
lay in wait and showed me avenues of music.

Which opened on the road to Leipzig's cemetery,
the alder trees in leaf and the choristers
waiting for their dinner. *Herrscher über Tod und Leben!*

We Northerners are really Greek. Stoic, old
and held by oracles. Tears are running down like soot.
My daily prayer, *Mach einmal mein Ende gut*!

A Toccata of Muffat's

The Herr Burgomeister is mining his teeth. Keep pressure
Up in all the bourgeois organs, this is God's sanity,
        Blowing air at calibrated lengths,
        Voiding Heaven for South Germany.

You will die not young, nor very old, but dusty on top:
Pleasures in the Palmengarten, the brass taste of logic
        And the graveyards holding a pedal
        For the repeated Fs of Jesus.

Darkness and the smell of wax snuffed out! *Zum Grünen Anker*
Where they ride on seas of blond wine, tasting self like sugar –
   The masked hours moused by my fat cat
   With all of Sunday to come home to!

It is forever before the cataclysm, hermits
Are boiling the state, but one gentle mad poet discounts
   The *furor teutonicus* with swan-
   Polished sails on the Swabian dusk.

Tiptoe through the granaries and old lead workings –
This is the bridgework of a Protestant Book of Beauty,
   The flowers Luther leered at, types of
   Forgiveness for aunts and abbatoirs.

Being translated into pretty Music Programme vowels,
A morning canto for Anglo-Saxon reasonableness –
   The thundering of bells overhead,
   The rendering of praise overheard.

Storm cones, conical icons of the middle element,
Hang like mad sausages in the organ-builder's brain-box,
   A wind to swell out Dorotheas
   And cool our diary-keeping cousins.

Witches are baking, hares sleeping in the stubble, ravens,
Black, unglücklich, cawing for the chance of further mischief;
   Now time is turned to drops of music,
   Apollo on *Posaune* and *Gedackt*.

The pebble in the stream is run from by the sun. Listen!
One is one and all alone and evermore shall be so.
   The air is arguing with itself,
   The gods are in the room, eavesdropping.

Cat's Fugue

  What a clever moggie to tread only
    in the keys of G Minor and D Minor,
  but then the gifted walk with care and flair
    as if on hot bricks; their bloodless

sleepwalking looks like exodus
    and the daggers are such dashing
footnotes. I chatted up a puss about Scarlatti
    but he had his Mason's secrets
and all I got was whiskers. Worthy men
    were walking by the gothic tulips,
sparrows purloined ears, so obviously
    the world was wired for sound.
Before you make your poem seem too twee
    I'll warn you, said the cat,
it's knowing when to stretto, how to keep
    your counter-subjects simple,
What to do when grandeur blows your mind –
    also, you'll notice that my fur
lies one way, so please don't brush it backwards
    and call the act experiment.
That sour cat was dead against our century
    and I was so ambitious,
I bought a cosmological notebook,
    Zinoviev's new machine
and a glossary of the German terms in Joyce –
    I'm in retirement till I make
my violent masterpiece; it's about a cat
    bigger than Bulgakov's, east
of Jeoffry in the night sky of the Lord;
    it stalks like plague along the grass
fathering history on the post-diluvial age –
    named Jesus at the whole Jerusalem,
the Day of Modernism dawns; professors touched
    by wings fly purring to the moon.
These are its juvenilia and in Horatian
    retrospect I see the cat
restored to its domestic stalking one salt
    Iberian morning in the light
when genius saddened at the cold keyboard
    is jacked with white and black –
again our dainty-footed man's companion
    strikes a balance with the dust
and props the world against its weary gravity.

The Settembrini Waltz

Time was, the fund of knowledge
Led to the barricades
And not, as in this college,
To making higher grades.

That was the great Cenacle
When dew formed in the night
Would coruscate and sparkle
On police boots polished bright.

When pages out of Balzac
And things the Fathers wrote
Were more than some Old Pals Act
Or urban guerilla's quote.

But polish up your Fanon
And keep your Brechtwerk gay,
The latest sine qua non
Is Ethnic Shadowplay.

Hearing the Appassionata
Sapped Lenin's will to fight,
But Cage's cool self-starter
Sits squadrons down to write.

Let's end it one cold morning
With bullets in a bed,
All ironies self-scorning
And liberal Europe dead.

Print Out: Apocalypse

When the army of ecologists
has scraped the last shellfish
from the lagoon,

When all the cars on
the urban overpasses are towed
to adventure playgrounds,

230

When the phrase 'fossil fuel'
is considered too holy to be used
in crossword puzzles,

When 'Thirties hats and hairdos
have come back into fashion
for the tenth time,

When archivists have stored
reserve prints of every manifestation
of popular culture,

When software and hardware
have swapped places in our
advanced computers,

When these words are fed in
for me to consider, I will come again,
says the Lord . . . .

Baroque Quatrains dedicated to James Fenton

Morning Song of a Court Dwarf

Dollops of iodine ease the fuming king
As De Guzman tells her maid to lace her tighter,
Epic lapdogs treadle on a swing,
The fountains' susurring grown still politer.

Organ pipes are cradled in a skull
To stall the clouds above the ferrous plain;
Our new tientos are obscene and dull,
The roof of Paradise lets in the rain.

The War of Widows buzzes somewhere off.
Sophistication leaves court etiquette to
The portrait painters: the Infanta's killing cough
Halts bald kanakas at their war canoe.

Ambassadors of northern countries stand
Impassive while our hierophants intone
Long canticles of Christ the Contraband:
Our grandees' hearts are shrunk to kidney stones.

To every morning task its discipline –
Some to make our skyscraper sorbetti,
Others gazump the price of prunes, and in
The boat all Europe waving from the jetty.

Death of a Comic Opera Composer

Balmoral balconies are tossed in gloom;
The short-lived whimper at a world which needs
Soap and some psalming. 'I like a billiard room,
The National Geographical Magazine, nasturtium seeds.'

Nonsense has corners, has a sense of focus,
Especially when the entracte thumps too long,
I say the magic names, *Keeling or Cocos*,
Esarhaddon, Klopstock, Suzie Wong.

Don't let a stanza come between your God
And you, and don't rely on stale *Rossiniana*,
The Music Critic who is not a sod
Can't black a knuckle at 'the grand pianner'.

Enough of dicing, playing 'crack the finger'
With Mephisto inside *Le Père-Lachaise*,
All men must feed their balls into the wringer
However few or many are their days.

The light is fading, randy darkness waits;
I am inviolate, 'grâce à mon plongeon' –
Those beaks above the bed, are they the Fates?
Tell Death I'm not a man to mix his genres.

The Queer Assayers of the Frontier

Our scene shifts to a Hunting Lodge in which
A clutch of pretty primpers is on points;
Doubtless we'll breakfast in the tombs, the rich
Are so macabre – cold plovers' eggs, veal joints

232

And liquorice lollies, sitting by cadavers –
The band has brought its timbrels and the boys
Are melancholy thinking of lifesavers
On Palermo beach and other departed joys.

The provinces are either wet and wild
Or dusty and disgusting – boarding houses
Full of loud galoots, their bathrooms tiled
With funny fishes, hung with dripping blouses.

If I weren't sick, I'd leap upon my donkey
And leave this place for good; if I had cash
I'd buy a cliffside villa with a wonky
Punkah and Solarium – I'd have a bash

At beating Claudian at his panegyric,
The Classic and the Christian at a blow,
Take nights off at the *Roxy* and the *Lyric*
And watch the ferry chuntering to and fro.

Exit, Pursued by a Bear

Others abide our question. Thou art free.
Art not an artist but an industry,
And to a nation fallen on hard times
Worth more than North Sea Oil or Yorkshire Mines:
Indeed, our Bardic Tours and Shakespeare Tomes,
With the Royal Family, Scotch and Sherlock Holmes,
Convince the USA and EEC
That though we're not what once we used to be
If there's some sale which needs a bit of class
An English accent's all that you can ask –
Our actors, raised on Bolingbroke and York,
Can hold their own at late-night TV talk,
Directors trained by England's classic teachers
Bring something more to Ads. and Second Features,
And poet-dons, with ear and taste defective,
On sixteenth-century love-life turn detective,
Track amorous ladies with Italian looks
Through sonnets, diaries, letters and part-books –
Our GNP, from Inverness to Flatford,
Could take a hint from tourist-battered Stratford;

An asset nursed need never be depleted,
The English Language cannot be defeated.

We owe this to the man for whom we're here,
Our Superstar, our J.C., our Shakespeare,
And if one's heart sinks in the London Library
Or trying to work the BM without bribery
Confronted with the Shakespeare section looming
Above us like a ship's hull (that's assuming
This metaphor impresses jet-age readers)
The mind, that most debased of dirty feeders,
Is more than pleased to see four hundred years
Of parasitic comment raised in tiers,
Unsought, unread, uncared-for and undusted,
The whole life's work for which dead men once lusted,
Grabbed office, wheedled, schemed and struggled through,
Reduced to Nothing after Much Ado!
But exegesis lives and dies, it's not
(Whatever you may think, you clan of Kott)
The point: we've got the plays in fine editions,
We know interpolations and additions,
And may, setting scholarship among the sins then,
Say Shakespeare wrote *The Two Noble Kinsmen* –
At least the very best bits, and then stretch a
Point and reassign to worthy Fletcher
All that tedious play, *King Henry the Eighth*,
Like Wolsey's bladders, not much puffed of late.
While praising Shakespeare, let us not forget
Contemporaries who left us in their debt,
Those men whom Swinburne praised in Mermaid dress –
The more of Middleton's is not the less
Of Shakespeare's glory and *The Broken Heart*
If not quite *Antony* is stunning art.
May they receive as many new productions
As teenage Romeos their set seductions
(See Martin Amis's *The Rachel Papers*
For the latest slant on young love cutting capers):
Let all the kudos this great name has stored
Be used to recommend the plays of Ford.

But now, alas, I reach the nasty part
Of this encomium – dramatic art
Is only half alive upon the page;
What then of Shakespeare on the modern stage?

I've sat through *Troilus* in the Second Empire,
Lear in local government, 'one that gathers samphire,
Dreadful trade', but surely not of Dover's
Since Edgar's dressed to play for Bristol Rovers;
Macbeth in trench coats and his guilty Lady
Somnambulizing fully-frontal, Brady
And Hindley to the life, as if the Bard
Were playing understudy to de Sade –
Then *Hamlet* 'en risotto', lines all diced
And dished up like a bowl of savoury rice –
Still, none of this is quite as bad as what
TV has done – sans time, sans lines, sans plot,
Sans everything but window dressing, got
Through with much relief: since money's time
The classics on the box can be a crime.
Then there's Shakespeare politicized by Brecht,
Hung-up by Brook, portrayed by Bond and wrecked
In any one of twenty thousand ways –
The mortal genius of some thirty plays,
Whose 'lives' as Mr Schoenbaum rightly says
Are many as a cat's, since each enhancer
Sees him like himself, a necromancer,
A Catholic, a crypto-queer, a Cornish Warlock
(He only lacks his own 'Person from Porlock'),
But always there behind that Stratford bust
Or in those undug feet of common dust
The Grand Enigma of each generation,
Surviving even fashion and translation,
And like his favourite Ovid ever changing
Gods and Men in Nature, rearranging
The world we others fancy is opaque,
Or cannot understand or simply fake
Until it seems Creation's paradigm,
A timeless dream which yet unfolds in time.

I'll finish now this commonplace recital
By just explaining why I chose its title –
It's from, of course you know, *The Winter's Tale*:
The man the bear rended tooth and nail
Was loyal Antigonus, the child Perdita,
One of the nicest heroines by far,
Too good to serve up as an ursine entrée –
But think, the man who put her in the play
Had daughters of his own, and how did he

Treat them, his wife, his son, his family?
One fact alone I dare to say tonight,
Shakespeare's younger daughter couldn't write,
Her mark is on some document, a cross –
Imagination must be at a loss
To think his mind, though blackened by his spouse's,
Cared less for daughters than for Stratford houses!
It opens up the way for royal Lear,
An avenue of anger lit by fear –
The bear is death which chases him so long
And never can be quietened with a song,
Each creature of the plays a funeral mute
Lamenting Orpheus and his broken lute,
And on some dismal shore the bones are cracked,
The genius of the universe ransacked.

THE COST OF SERIOUSNESS

Old-Fashioned Wedding

It was for this they were made,
The great present of their childhood
Kept unopened, the hard rules obeyed
And the grudged honey of being good:
A pure reward,
Better for being stored,
And, reached at last, seeming like the sea
Stretching after a dream of ice toward
The edge of reluctance properly.

So that the stunned moment now
When talk falls in the bright marquee
Is an elevation of hope, the drinks a vow
Naming everything which is to be;
And after this
The subtly twinned kiss
To start a carnal journey, and the night
Offering shining emphasis
Like crystal gifts emboldening the light.

To which the cynical, caught up
In the flurry of guy ropes let down,
And crushed flowers in delicate cups,
Pay tribute as sexual clowns.
After this huge
Joke, a terrible deluge
The speeding innocents know nothing of,
Mad hours, silence, subterfuge
And all the dark expedients of love.

At Ramsholt

The harvest is in early. Across the paddock,
where we raise the bull's head with mimic
bellows, through the salt-dead trees and thatcher's
rushes, yachts navigate on seeming land.

This is the Deben, not the Mekong, but a sail
curves round a copse; masts for Woodbridge
crowd three degrees of the horizon, edging
a painterly Dutch sky. Clouds are curdling.

A golden rain of ladybirds falls in the lap
of Suffolk. Drought has driven the wasps mad,
they butt the kitchen glass. A cucumber,
like Masolino's Satan, rears under grass.

To townsmen everything is like something
from a book – most noticeably in this
made landscape. The swan on the canal,
with nine cygnets, is the Home Fleet, 1936.

Ezekiel in church: shall these bones live?
The pheasants live another month and then
go plumply down. A nightingale sings
politely through the dangerous summer.

The Picture of Nobody

We are always being framed somewhere. A camera, an eye
Of memory is recounting inches along from the pea-trellis,
The cement-block fence, the rotary clothes-line: a leg
Is not quite where it seemed and an arm forward on the thigh
Strikes a posture more aggressive than the smiling face.

Then, beside the church where a clapped-out pigeon fell
To be picked up by a not-very-poor-looking Italian – was
She standing higher on the steps, or perhaps just out of sight
To the left? The Hotel de Beurs was surely closer to the canal,
The photograph should smell of cleansing and dark cloths.

Years after, another presence makes itself felt, someone
Who wasn't there when we bought the angle-poise lamp
And were snapped in the street, a shape which vanished
From the wharf-side beer garden and the Japanese bridge
Over an English river – now he seems so very like me.

A sentimental assumption. We put up our own coordinates,
The bars of our prison. Her own picture the doppelgänger,
She was already haunting those September stones with
Her death, just as at seven the teeth stick out which
Later slope in, rodent-like. The waves freezes at its crest.

Bring the coordinates together to get us out of unhappiness.
We are in limbo. And his picture is quite clear now.
He will move to the new album, the later, more hopeful
Photos over the same ground. Three cats on top of each other
Behind a grille in Venice, or a window of star-shaped ice-creams.

No wonder there are ghosts. What we leave behind is deadly.
The melody is played, a poisonous, long-lasting scent
Circles the garden. Spring again. Our friend has borrowed
A loved face to bring the bad news to the still living:
There is nobody else in the picture, yet fear looks out.

Waiting for Rain in Devon

Rain here on a tableau of cows
might seem a return to everyday –
why, you can almost poach
the trout with your hands,
their element has so thickened!
Something has emerged from dreams
to show us where we are going,
a journey to a desolate star.
Come back, perennial rain,
stand your soft sculptures in our gardens
for the barefoot frogs to leap.

The Orchid on the Rock

Two hundred yards from the house
Where the sounds of trees commence
With water always in descent
From the hundred veins of the creek,
The orchid rears its dozen necks
On a cushion of self: not scent
But a colourless colour, so intense
It eats the light, brings us up close.

Perhaps fifty years' battening on
Its own dead limbs have sent
Those roots like rivets into the rock –
The air brings stories of other lives:
Lemons returned to wildness, leaves
A hundred feet overhead which mock
The ferns, a fallen cedar bent
To the creek to kiss the sun.

Our sounds are the noise of feet
Unplugging from the grassy bog
And words at the service of botany –
We hush now for the daring orchid.
Art meets the world at an awkward
Angle, offering no harmony
Of fact and feeling – the sniffing dog
Butts through lantana foxing fruit.

The orchid blooms in perfect nowhere;
We go home to our electrified fort
To create relationships.
From the verandah, viewing the river
On its civilizing course, a fever
Of loneliness encroaches, grips
The mind. A clarinet has caught
The empty evening unawares.

The Charnel House, St Leonard's, Hythe

One of us, the prettiest,
would like a skull for an ash tray.
We who have flesh round our skulls
and can imagine the pain of dying
are proper company
for these generations of the sexes.

One is soon to be dead herself,
another wishes that he were,
self-indulgent, waiting for a voice . . .
A calm night after a blistering day,
the evening quiet with disappointment
and the apertures of death.

A bad opera on the radio,
proving that words and notes
make little difference,
and everywhere inside the summer room
the brilliant and disgusting skulls
with never a thought of names.

A Portrait by Giulio Romano

Dear long-dead lady,
what was it like in the world
of Aretine's postures?
The highlights of your beauty
are a blond tombeau
but you are in a cage.

Your white skin and your red
velvet dress – the uniform of love!
They have shaken out boxes
before your eyes, they have formed
letters on your lips, and held
your legs apart for the state.

241

We are wrecked on red dreams.
Eloquence is quickness,
the flying to extremes –
your pose and prettiness
are to keep off endings,
the highmindedness of hell.

Poem Waiting to be Translated

I have tried to stop drinking
because it makes me sadder
and upsets my bladder,
but evenings come on
and doubtless something unnameable is done
in some unlighted place.

Why not remember the heroes
of hard situations,
those who answered inquisitors
in fresh parables,
whose lyrical rejoinders
are assembled here
in memorial Penguins?

But not all are dead.
I met someone today
who said her years up to thirty
had been undoubtedly happy,
and I have seen with my own eyes
a dissident poet eating whitebait
and joking from the corner of his mouth.

Oh the lungs of poets
and their hunch backs –
They are looking for the chalk
of apotheosis, tutorial rooms
of some exchange agreement
where the homesick specialist
says hello to a lime tree.

There the moon walks over
the Marches and murders

small lives by stagnant lakes,
fireflies swing round the ears
of fishermen setting out,
the landscape is stoic
and policed by malaria.

At this point in our history,
everything is Un-English!
I say to the Japanese professor
who wants to know about Mateship:
we have reached a pluralism
of culture in our language,
and I should like my wise instances
subsidized and printed
with generous margins.

After the funeral of the drunken poet,
the busybody dogs disperse
on some business of their tails
and the dead walk the land
casting no shadow.

The Lying Art

It is all rhetoric rich as wedding cake
and promising the same bleak tears
when what was asked for but not recognized
shows its true face after a thousand breakfasts.

This, not Miss Moore's disclaimer, tells me
why I too dislike it. It is paid to distract us,
to tell the man disappointed by his mother
that he too can be a huge cry-baby.

Think of its habit of talking to gods
but saying only pastoral things. Real pain
it aims for, but can only make gestures,
the waste of selling-short, the 'glittering'.

I want you to be happy, you say,
but poetry brings in childhood on its horse,
the waves of parrots and the Delphic eyes,
and is never there when the scab is picked.

Music gets the better of it, since music is all lies.
Lies which fill the octave. Chromatic space
in verse turns out to be the ego's refractions,
truth always stained by observation.

So this argument goes in cut-up prose,
four lines to each part. I will not say
metric or stanzas or anything autonomous,
but keep to discontent, a nearly truthful art.

And what has this to do with poetry? Inroads
into rhetoric. The ugly and the disappointed
painting their faces with words; water showing
God's love to the beautiful – no way of changing.

Then we might as well make the best of
dishonesty, accept that all epithalamiums
are sugar and selfishness. Our world
of afterwards will have no need of lies.

The Easiest Room in Hell

At the top of the stairs is a room
one may speak of only in parables.

It is the childhood attic,
the place to go when love has worn away,
the origin of the smell of self.

We came here on a clandestine visit
and in the full fire of indifference.

We sorted out books and let the children
sleep here away from creatures.

From its windows, ruled by willows,
the flatlands of childhood stretched
to the watermeadows.

It was the site of a massacre,
of the running down of the body
to less even than the soul,
the tribe's revenge on everything.

It was the heart of England
where the ballerinas were on points
and locums laughed through every evening.

Once it held all the games,
Inconsequences, Misalliance, Frustration,
even *Mendacity, Adultery* and *Manic Depression.*

But that was just its alibi,
all along it was home,
a home away from home.

Having such a sanctuary
we who parted here
will be reunited here.

You asked in an uncharacteristic note,
'Dwell I but in the suburbs
of your good pleasure?'

I replied, 'To us has been allowed
the easiest room in hell.'

Once it belonged to you,
now it is only mine.

An Angel in Blythburgh Church

Shot down from its enskied formation,
This stern-faced plummet rests against the wall;
Cromwell's soldiers peppered it and now the death-
     watch beetle has it in thrall.

If you make fortunes from wool, along
The weeping winter foreshores of the tide,
You build big churches with clerestories
     And place angels high inside.

Their painted faces guard and guide. Now or
Tomorrow or whenever is the promise –
The resurrection comes: fix your eyes halfway
     Between Heaven and Diss.

245

The face is crudely carved, simplified by wind;
It looks straight at God and waits for orders,
Buffeted by the organ militant, and blasted
          By choristers and recorders.

Faith would have our eyes as wooden and as certain.
It might be worth it, to start the New Year's hymn
Allowing for death as a mere calculation,
          A depreciation, entered in.

Or so I fancy looking at the roof beams
Where the dangerous beetle sails. What is it
Turns an atheist's mind to prayer in almost
          Any church on a country visit?

Greed for love or certainty or forgiveness?
High security rising with the sea birds?
A theology of self looking for precedents?
          A chance to speak old words?

Rather, I think of a woman lying on her bed
Staring for hours up to the ceiling where
Nothing is projected – death the only angel
          To shield her from despair.

An Exequy

In wet May, in the months of change,
In a country you wouldn't visit, strange
Dreams pursue me in my sleep,
Black creatures of the upper deep –
Though you are five months dead, I see
You in guilt's iconography,
Dear Wife, lost beast, beleaguered child,
The stranded monster with the mild
Appearance, whom small waves tease,
(Andromeda upon her knees
In orthodox deliverance)
And you alone of pure substance,
The unformed form of life, the earth
Which Piero's brushes brought to birth
For all to greet as myth, a thing
Out of the box of imagining.

This introduction serves to sing
Your mortal death as Bishop King
Once hymned in tetrametric rhyme
His young wife, lost before her time;
Though he lived on for many years
His poem each day fed new tears
To that unreaching spot, her grave,
His lines a baroque architrave
The Sunday poor with bottled flowers
Would by-pass in their mourning hours,
Esteeming ragged natural life
('Most dearly loved, most gentle wife'),
Yet, looking back when at the gate
And seeing grief in formal state
Upon a sculpted angel group,
Were glad that men of god could stoop
To give the dead a public stance
And freeze them in their mortal dance.

The words and faces proper to
My misery are private – you
Would never share your heart with those
Whose only talent's to suppose,
Nor from your final childish bed
Raise a remote confessing head –
The channels of our lives are blocked,
The hand is stopped upon the clock,
No one can say why hearts will break
And marriages are all opaque:
A map of loss, some posted cards,
The living house reduced to shards,
The abstract hell of memory,
The pointlessness of poetry –
These are the instances which tell
Of something which I know full well,
I owe a death to you – one day
The time will come for me to pay
When your slim shape from photographs
Stands at my door and gently asks
If I have any work to do
Or will I come to bed with you.
O scala enigmatica,
I'll climb up to that attic where

The curtain of your life was drawn
Some time between despair and dawn –
I'll never know with what halt steps
You mounted to this plain eclipse
But each stair now will station me
A black responsibility
And point me to that shut-down room,
'This be your due appointed tomb.'

I think of us in Italy:
Gin-and-chianti-fuelled, we
Move in a trance through Paradise,
Feeding at last our starving eyes,
Two people of the English blindness
Doing each masterpiece the kindness
Of discovering it – from Baldovinetti
To Venice's most obscure jetty.
A true unfortunate traveller, I
Depend upon your nurse's eye
To pick the altars where no Grinner
Puts us off our tourists' dinner
And in hotels to bandy words
With Genevan girls and talking birds,
To wear your feet out following me
To night's end and true amity,
And call my rational fear of flying
A paradigm of Holy Dying –
And, oh my love, I wish you were
Once more with me, at night somewhere
In narrow streets applauding wines,
The moon above the Apennines
As large as logic and the stars,
Most middle-aged of avatars,
As bright as when they shone for truth
Upon untried and avid youth.

The rooms and days we wandered through
Shrink in my mind to one – there you
Lie quite absorbed by peace – the calm
Which life could not provide is balm
In death. Unseen by me, you look
Past bed and stairs and half-read book
Eternally upon your home,
The end of pain, the left alone.

I have no friend, or intercessor,
No psychopomp or true confessor
But only you who know my heart
In every cramped and devious part –
Then take my hand and lead me out,
The sky is overcast by doubt,
The time has come, I listen for
Your words of comfort at the door,
O guide me through the shoals of fear –
'Fürchte dich nicht, ich bin bei dir.'

The Delegate

In the garden (it was always a garden)
there is the punishment of remembrance.
I pray you love, remember. And quote me
the many things which might come to you
on your own death bed.
                                    I was there
even in our worst hour – the wreaths
and the mis-named name competing with
the other mourners' flowers upon
the crematorium slabs. I am divided
into an infinity of myself, pieces
for everywhere – especially that damp day,
that insistence on seriousness.
We shall never be so serious again.
But this frees you for levity today,
and perhaps a little licenced selfishness.
Take this gift of despair – what can
a ghost give but remembrance and
forgetfulness in the right proportions?

Never to puff up those sloping headlands
watching the children ahead negotiating
the lanes of the wide bay: never
the afternoon sun straining
the bedroom light to a tint distinctly
like gin: never more the in-flight panic,
refusing to see omens in our food
or the number of letters in the month.

These *nevers*
are just parts of my docility
as I go back. I am always receding,
my ambition is to accomplish
non-existence, to go out and close the door
on ever having been.
                            I am doing it in death
as I did in life – but it's so hard.
I cannot forget unless you remember,
pin down each day and weighted eye
with exact remorse. After fifteen years'
convergence, now we may draw apart
and face our different exits.

So I am your delegate
at the screaming hours: I walk alone
among the plains of hell. We dream here
in the skin of our deeds: such changes
as the schoolgirl saw in her body
are metamorphoses of the gods.
                            First I went back,
a quick change in the early morning
with my blood running into frost.
Now the reduction is set at smaller things –
I may even become the healthy strider
or flamenco dancer, but I must reduce, reduce,
become so small that I escape the eye
of god. There is no peace here, or on earth.
                            You will know
how the mind works at poems, feels ideas
as tissue – but, alas, the ceremony here
is different. I am not what you remember,
the snapshots in time and sunshine,
nor even the angry and accusing face
at breakfast, the suddenly delivered tone
of hope along a Venetian calle on a Sunday –
                            I am made fiction
by my needs: the brain changing in the garden
to a bush of thorns, a dream looking for
its dreamer, murder always at the end
of every vista. A letter now, headed
'Malcontenta, Orto Chiuso', a puff-adder's face
as I prop myself against the dying mirror
viewing disgust with satisfaction.

250

Breaking an egg-cup,
learning to give up, crying at the sight
of a withered seahorse pinned to the wall:
all those afternoons of hope and all those gardens,
no wonder I cannot escape now.
                    After a year in office,
your delegate has found this court
a place of ashes and the matches
played by moonlight cruel games.
But I have an immense truth to give you –
In the end, we are condemned
only for our lack of talent.
                    There is no morality,
no metered selfishness, or cowardly fear.
What we do on earth is its own parade
and cannot be redeemed in death. The pity
of it, that we are misled. By mother,
saying her sadness is the law, by love,
hiding itself in evenings of ethics,
by despair, turning the use of limbs
to lockjaw.
                    The artist knows this.
He is being used despite himself. The truth
is a story forcing me to tell it. It is not
my story or my truth. My misery
is on a colour chart – even my death
is a chord among the garden sounds.
                    And in this garden, love,
there will be forgiveness, when
we can forgive ourselves. 'Remember me,
but ah forget my fate.' Tell me like music
to the listeners. 'I would not know her in that dress.'
The days I lived through change to words
which anyone may use. When you arrive
I shall have done your work for you.
                    Forgetting will not be hard,
but you must remember still. Evenings
and mad birds cross your face,
                    everything must be re-made.

A Lecture by my Books

You cannot write tonight. We own all
the words you will ever need to make a shape
of permanence. But they were used by
men who felt along the lines
to life. We are dead
who kept the watch for you while your landscapes burned,
we stand like stelae
on the road to hell. Fear us.

And market us in dreams. We
are the finished phrase, the play of gesture stopped
before one death. See this gasping soul
declare a total library of meaning
less than a nerve end,
Anacreon's grave a house
of roots and the reaching out goodbye
your only poem.

From *Julius Caesar* and the laws
of aspic hardening, the heart will
snatch a vocabulary –
'I just want to be dead' – and all the novels
fry tonight. What did
poor Carrington find in her shotgun barrels?
Words for ending words,
the picture of nobody there.

In this garden of categories
a night rose withers –
it was the spume of Rilke,
words lying on the carpet where a planet
winters and the dapper genius
welcomes god to his
own twentieth century: a rich tapis
for tongue-tied democracy.

To be the actuaries of hope,
not so many graveyards of trees but gestures
in a terrible silence –
To be recognized,
a man, a woman
and a relationship. But the cat

has seen through their plan. He knows they have only
printed their hearts. He reads knees.

Here are the lines of a last conspiracy.
Listen to our words,   :
there are no others. Can you write now?
The brain's a neologism of rare aspect
but it isn't quite music.
We've sat on your walls and heard
the moon cry for the dead, poor centaurs,
poor Humpty Dumpties.

Scream and Variations

When I came into the world I saw

My face in my mother's blood
and my father crying where he stood.

A garden where a girl teased a man,
a man listened to a girl complain,
a boy wondered what a man could mean.

A house where children's voices rang,
where tiredness lived for each evening,
where a wife needed to be among
friends, and kids and a husband stayed wrong.

A party smiling for a photograph
one choking on the length of his life,
another ready to raise tears for a laugh,
one death harvested with a knife,
doors closing on a broken belief.

An ecologist painting Doomsday
for ten million watchers; tragedy
in the newspapers and poetry
in the schools; all style in a lie
and truth a shapeless story;
the lark ascending a poisoned sky.

My coffin in an unknown place
among enemies and the police;
my daughters trying to please
me in dreams with their replies;
a tear belonging to my wife ablaze
in the darkness of widowhood; peace
in her voice but only death's applause.

Myself in the world is all there was.

'In the New World Happiness is Allowed'

No, in the New World, happiness is enforced.
It leans your neck over the void and the only
recourse is off to Europe and the crowded hearts,
a helplessness of pasta and early closing days,
lemons glowing through the blood of Acre.

It is the glaze of galvinism – why are there
so many madmen in the street? O, my countrymen,
success is an uncle leaving you his fruit farm.
The end of the world with deep-freezes, what if
your memories are only made of silence?

In one year he emptied the sea of a ton of fish.
He wasn't one to look at the gardens of Greenslopes
and wish they were the verdure of the Casentino.
Living with the world's reserves of ores,
no wonder our ruined Virgils become democrats.

Masturbation has been known in Europe too
and among the gentiles. Why did nobody say
that each successful man needs the evidence
of a hundred failures? There is weekend leave
from Paradise, among the caravanning angels.

Here's a vision may be painted on a wall:
a man and a boy are eating with an aborigine
in a boat; the sun turns up the tails of fish
lying beside the oars; the boy wipes surreptitiously
the bottle passed him by the black man.

Rain strums the library roof. The talk tonight
is 'Voluntary Euthanasia'. Trying to be classical
can break your heart. Depression long persisted in
becomes despair. Forgive me, friends and relatives,
for this unhappiness, I was away from home.

The Cost of Seriousness

Once more I come to the white page of art
                to discover what I know
                and what I presume I feel
about those forgettable objects words.
                We begin with penalties:
the cost of seriousness will be death.

Not just naming death again to stoke fires,
                but thinking of suicide
                because life or art won't work
and words trying to help, Mallarmé-like,
                undefine themselves and say
things out of the New Physics: self-destruct!

Which is why the artist must play, but if
                he does he mustn't rule-change
                and say, 'Unless you agree
to Pound's huge seriousness I shan't go
                on living, and meanwhile we
are an élite of experimenters,

to whom someones in the city must pay
                homage, dons give neat memos
                and our correspondents pile
up hagiography in magazines – '
                A public worthy of its
artists would consist of whores and monsters.

So, to turn impatience into anger
                and want to punish slow minds
                or walk through our museums
with a clock ends up as despair or a
                professorship in exile,
the world as solipsistic as ever.

At which you may ask (ungentle reader)
                why does he avoid the point?
            After great vindication
coming through B Flat this way will never
            be the same, and so the earth
changes while we stand by a grave and mourn.

Yes, but the earth stays the same too, greeting
            leaves and their sons each season
            just seasonally; the boat
for Venice idles at the green-furred wharf
            carrying the body of
the composer Grimace (Ettore),

as timetable-conscious as if it had
            on board a scientist who
            could make a food crop of grass,
and I have come no closer to my goal
            of doing without words, that
pain may be notated some real way.

Seriousness – ah, *quanta pena mi*
            costi! I note from a card
            that hills are dyed purple by
a weed named Paterson's Curse. That is in
            New South Wales. The dead may pass
their serious burdens to the living.

Three Transportations

1 *Gertrude Stein at Snails Bay*

I am Miss Stein
and this bay is mine

I am Miss Stein (pronounced Steen)
and this sea is green

Americans do not like
European pronunciation

I live in Europe because Americans
do not like Europeans

I do not live in America
because Europeans do not like Americans

I am in Australia because
I hear you have an opera
and I am searching for snails

I am not here to buy your paintings

I am in Snails Bay to find snails

Although there are no snails in Snails Bay
there are buses behind me
and children in front of me
and sea in front of the children

They tell me this is Arbor Day

No, I do not drop my aitches

Nothing can be done in the face
of ordinary unhappiness

Above all, there is nothing to do in words

I have written a dozen books
to prove nothing can be done in words

A great artist may fall off an inner alp
but I will not roll down this gentle bank

I would not give a cook book for his alp

I have a message for the snails
of New South Wales

You will never know
which of you is Shakespeare

Yes, I am a disagreeable old woman
who talks selfishly and strangely
and writes down words in a peculiar order

It is to prevent unhappiness escaping
and poisoning the world

How do you define
the truth, Miss Stein?

A snail has not the right to say
it will or won't: it must obey

With the buses and the children and the sea
I have nothing to do

I am an observer,
I observe the blue and you

I see an immense rain
washing pebbles up the beach
and evacuating misery

The plane for America is a sort of star

2 *Piero di Cosimo on the Shoalhaven*

Through a banksia's cone the fire passes,
Aphorisms of the deities of time.
Here on a broad river's side, my glasses
Squandering the sun, I put rhyme
Into paint, Vulcan's and Venus's trespasses.

On a rock orchid, the roundness and gloze
Of a lapith's bum! Men hauled cedars
From these forests before their blood froze,
Making a camp for gods – our leaders,
We sighed, as we looked inside the rose.

My eggs boil on the electric stove –
Reincarnation of madness: one
Takes a mainline trip to Comfort Cove,
Another paints the rain forest in the sun,
A murder and a mating in a grove.

Drongo the dog is barking at a thing
Washed up on a sandbank by the tide –
A nymph, a suicide, something decomposing
Which his nose loves, and at its side
The mercenaries of life converging.

Up river the water skiers puff and plane;
I could not imagine more blended beasts.
The gods are husbanding our pain
Like all good settlers – the men of feasts
Will come, a Medicean super-strain.

Neither Adam nor Jesus ever laughed
But the serious earth is quite hilarious.
This is Eden as the cattle go past
The electric fence; the faces are so various
Of flower and shadow, which will last?

Only work can save us from night coming.
Newly-planted trees attest the faith.
On its dorsal, a monster is drumming
Messages for the new world – each wraith
Is a spirit of old Europe slumming.

Here I put a duck-billed wallaby,
A swimming jackass, abo-centaur:
So old a place has so much still to see,
There must be ghost traps. Shut the door
On dying, become a lamenting tree.

3 *The Boccherini Music Camp*

The widower as wooer –
no more awkward gesture
since Creation!

'Your refuge is your work',
but Signior Boccherini
is too fluent – he's forgotten
how many quintets he's written,
and he put a son through college
on a minuet.

As I said to your Arts Reporter
asking about myself
and Scarlatti and other
erstwhile exiles in Iberia:
'Out of Italy we come,
great talent, little room;
the hatred is for family.'

That portrait down in Melbourne,
scratching at the belly of invention –
you see me in servitude to sex and Prussia.
Each confrontation seems
another Right Wing Coup,
my cello as large as Spain.

Now for the Muse of Mittagong –
I like your lady viola-players.
I would not call this a sexy country
but they have pollen in their hair
and down upon their lips.

When I start an allegro
it's planned like those washing programmes
right through to the spin-dry.
In my view I should be called
Haydn's husband.

You can make sounds of sadness
but when the music stops
the heartless world will whistle –
every defeat stays on
as an examination question.

Do my children love me?
I doubt that any of my quavers
would bail me out –
I have been far away
all my life.

The call of strings through upland wattles,
my music recognizes me –
there is no time left
to outplay misery.

Evensong

Coming upon them suddenly,
the memorials of oh so long
ago, as tourists will do,
after a coffee and brioche,
the horseman galloping
in rain, the big dog
and the top dog locked
behind fine ironwork,
just as Ruskin saw them,
and hardly knowing they
were tombs, instances
of what was never far
from our own heads –
death outlasting love.

The scale, the Scala, the puns
of churches – that grinner
tip-toeing in brocade
and those martyrs' doilies
for their little-boned hands:
morbidity – see the river
run through its castled bridge
and a leaf jump to it
from a tree near us,
a career in air and water,
and from the top row
of the amphitheatre
the Alps chatter like
our gin-rinsed teeth.

Then to miss the way,
confidently stalking
past a prison – a real one
made of stone not days –
and take hours to find
the doors of truth, the old
benign image of hope
which couldn't fool us,
sky outside like the walls
of candle-smoked churches,
no other harmony for the night
but the separation of
sleep going on forever.

To Venetia's Shores Have Come

They say this state is sinking
and that its waters are a health hazard,
but boys dive into the canal
from the Fondamenta Bragadin,
the same boys every morning.

The cats are clean and hold convocations
on the silvery fish of charity.

What the Signore would give
to be back in Mann's and Corvo's days
when he might have taken a gondola
or imagined Ruskin on the Zattere.

An unlikely text rises as he walks
in sunshine to San Bastian,
'the state killed our mothers, they were depressed' –
To bring the world to your parish church
and lie there at the end,
that's a noble monstrance!

For the gods of the jewel-box
have come down from the clouds:
a favourite insight watching
the knife-flecked waves beyond San Vio,
the Pope to the Bishop of Gibraltar,
'Then I am in *your* diocese.'

The Signore joins those
who have had a vision in Venice –
The Last Days walking on the waters
in applauded levitation
and into his ears these words,
'Yours is the first and only death.'

'A city built by strong men
in the image of their mother.'
Not even this is the whole truth,
the corny stuff is better,
'I am afraid to visit the Lido
for fear I should die there.'

The light is moving away from Europe
and the Signore hasn't as much time as Goethe
who, after all, found the grave of Consul Smith.
Lost on a dark sea, he keeps in mind
a few relics – a toe, a claw of Venus
who ate her own placenta, an Eastern city
painted on the falling sun.

Looking at a Melozzo da Forlì

And in this instance we think of you, God,
You beard above all things,
Canceller of every fact except death,
Looking down on your grand intercession,
Orthodox, like the artist's vision,
Helpless helper of time and promise.

But we do not get closer to love.
The angel's admonitory finger
And the lily of greeting tell Mary only
That the clock in her womb is ticking,
That she will come sooner to sorrow.

And I can see too in the structures
Of church and family another death.
We are entered by the spirit
And thereafter comes such rich despair –
Sermons of the penis, oddities by the seashore
Where towns have sunk, letters lost
In the mumblings of a drunken alphabet.

What is Mary kneeling on? A yoke,
A box for Miss Plath's mad bees,
A stiff pew for a Protestant Sunday?
In one revolution her body shows
Disquiet, reflection, inquiry, submission, merit.

These shapes Melozzo put on a wall
Fade like the dove-voiced poet
Into a high wood of darkness.
From his flat-bottomed cloud, God observes
Earthly love and sadness, saying
After all, this is only a language of gestures.

263

Yes Mary, you are an actor in a play
Whose dénouement is now to be spoken.
I rehearse the lines myself to your angel –
The action is beginning, blessèd is the Virgin
Who shall be the mother of death.

The Painters' Banquet

They came with their gifts of the senses
And of the groves planted for them by God
In the retina; they knelt by sandy waters
And saw a violin shore, a fronded region
Of high responding light, rosella afternoon;
They gossiped in laps, lay under umbrellas
Of the tumid shade; they told colours
In every story. When the pelican glided,
They overcame light, where the daisy unpeeled
They saw graveclothes. There were many
With eyelashes like Veronese's fans,
Others sat solitary as meat on a plate
Waiting for heaven to happen. Change,
Said some, was the way of their world,
Animals answering the call of light
Under Hyperion's crag. But, said several,
It is the unchanging we celebrate,
Sirocco afternoons, gods hard-pressed
By their abstract eyes. Dangerous modes
In all weather when obsessionals walk
To a favourite spur above the land –
Below them kingdoms boil and they find
Twisting paths through middle space.
This is the sumptuous gallery of those
Who have eaten the world. Oh the ochre,
Burnt siena, the pulverising red
Which rocks have earned from the sun –
In little spaghetti-making towns,
The dead artificers' creations burn
All sophistry from pilgrim's eyes.

It was a wonderful party to be at.
We write our thank-you letters
In the world's far-reaching galleries.

264

Who will clean up now? All the water
In the reservoirs won't remove the stain
From Golgotha. We think back instead:
Little Andrea has drawn a sheep
With a bright stone upon a smooth-faced rock.
Lucky for him a Medici is passing.
Soon the banquet will be set again.

'Talking Shop' Tanka

Looking at six books
of poems, painfully and
        yet so slovenly
produced over thirty years,
I notice one well-wrought phrase.

My friends are subtle,
their insights into colonels,
        keys and plasticine
shame my generalisations
and Horatian pleasantries.

After toothache or
sexual rejection, the
        epics are supposed
to come: instead, sexual
rejection and toothache recur.

Why are Catullus,
Baudelaire and Neruda
        so much translated?
the task is impossible,
the intention praiseworthy!

On the steps after
the Memorial Service
        for Auden, five men
talking – the legendary
Establishment in full view!

265

Loss or gain, the change
in Western self-consciousness
                may be measured by
the distance between Rameau's
Nephew and Beethoven's.

                We are too many
is also what the Muses
                said to Apollo.
The only domain with room
for everyone is Limbo.

                The Church, the Army
and the Law are all too hard –
                nowhere to pack off
a useless son but the Arts,
preferably Poetry.

                All those brainy girls
editing Meredith – no
                wonder the Muses
come to us as sex pots, and
Hermes wears a mackintosh.

                Lope de Vega's
daughter, prop of his old age,
                was carried off by
a hidalgo. The plots of
his plays had long schemed revenge.

                Goethe pleases all
Germans and Wystan Auden,
                but Schiller via
Schubert touches our hearts with
his 'Schöne Welt, wo bist du?'

                'Since she whom I loved
hath paid her last debt to Nature
                and to hers, and my
good is dead . . . ' I can't go on,
I share death not faith with Donne.

Schumann Sings Schubert

An old woman,
so the record sleeve denotes,
is singing of death
in a young world –
the glow of a wedding dress,
the shine on a coffin.

German Art,
how it penetrated
our dull afternoons!
Vienna's sons
journeying across carpets
of millstreams and graveyards.

'So lasst mich scheinen . . . '
One day Mignon will get
over the Alps
to America or Australia
and offer them death
to sweeten their late songs.

Non Piangere, Liù

A card comes to tell you
you should report
to have your eyes tested.

But your eyes melted in the fire
and the only tears, which soon dried,
fell in the chapel.

Other things still come –
invoices, subscription renewals,
shiny plastic cards promising credit –
not much for a life spent
in the service of reality.

You need answer none of them.
Nor my asking you for one drop
of succour in my own hell.

267

Do not cry, I tell myself,
the whole thing is a comedy
and comedies end happily.

The fire will come out of the sun
and I shall look in the heart of it.

A Brahms Intermezzo

The heart is a minor artist
hiding behind a beard.
In middle age
the bloodstream becomes a hammock
slowing down for silence –
till then, this lullaby,
arpeggiated thunder
and the streams running
through Arcadia. I, too,
says the black-browed creature
am in this vale of sweetness,
my notes are added to eternity.

A Scarlatti Sonata

When I see her hand on an envelope
my own hand shakes. While I am explaining
the ritual to my heart, she is writing
to the stars. As plain rules add to richness,
our rare arrival covers manuscripts.
These are clothes to wear before our father.

I stare at my own hand and at the marks
it makes on paper. Untrained fingers
shape the cursive style of love. Her hands
are fitting out the gods as well as
writing letters. Fewer notes than usual
from the harpsichord, each one a sun.
Her voice will speak of love
but her hands must prove it in the world.

L'Incoronazione di Poppea

To have known personally the demon
he who sits singing in the fire
('the occupational disease of poets is frivolity')
to experience suffering real as a colour
and hear it praised (green, green, O green)
to wait at the hospice for death
one hand searching for another
a continuous melody, a story
this was worth being born for
the world's unfairness still playing
we have invented love, it licks us
(*pur ti miro, pur ti godo*)
the great bridges bow, the streets appear
the marriage of never to now
against any justice or reason
unfaithful, steadfast, forever
(Bacchus in his barge, an end to ending)
the golden eyes of the phoenix
the coronation of fire

Roman Incident

The two of us, tired after a night
of quarrelling and making love
to make up quarrels and not quite
succeeding, first found the airline
in a Roman street and made our bookings,
then moved in a slightly drunken way
through the boring Via Veneto
to the Borghese Gardens. So far, so much.
An ice-cream eaten, a path adopted –
she must simply lie down and sleep
in the grass and I who couldn't sleep
stay there beside her. A woman sleeping
makes me lonely: I saw love in her face
and I had seen love die before,
so I left her and walked across other lovers
to the Gallery. All that awful
Carravagiesque paint and Cardinal Scipio
straight from the movies. At last,

a marvellous Carpaccio of a whore,
a quick look at my watch, thinking of
her lying there in the grass,
resolved to make one circuit and then leave –
but here I came upon a picture,
Dosso Dossi's *Melissa*, apotheosis
of the watching female and her autumn shades.
Left hand lower corner a labrador
ready to nuzzle to his master
in stockbroker Surrey and in the woods,
russet with the ferns of terra firma,
the enclosed bodies of men reassuming
their uncanted shapes. Garrulous
as a Fabian hostess, the lady ties
your looking with her colours –
the painter has borrowed Titian's later dyes
for pure frivolity. Armorial death
enchants when this Melissa looks:
frozen jibes from long-running
civil epics out of Italy, Ariosto's suspense,
Tasso's cracks on the head – Dossi warms them
in his hand. Life is a spell
and when we wake from it
the animals of our senses stand
with us in play-power paradise.
Visit Melissa's extra-mural zoo,
you'll find yourself hiding in shrubbery
when a truthful woman summons you.
Standing frozen before her on a plinth
of grief and awkwardness, I tried to cry,
to force water from my eyes, so that
Melissa might turn me back to manhood –
that, I said, is what I want. Magic, fortune, love:
the luck to be kissed and smiled on
no matter what ridiculous wizard
corks up my heart. To mother,
wife and all the sultry dead I prayed,
lead me to the enchantress whose one kiss
undoes the tactless misery of self.
      When I got back
to our flattened patch of grass, she'd gone
and I was desperate. Of a sudden
I heard her call my name and saw her body

approaching on the path. Her sleep had eased her
so we walked to lunch and an afternoon's
sightseeing via Pantheon and Forum,
ahead of us the night and our hotel.

Under New Management

After a discipleship of plain days,
The first born of the bourgeoisie,
It is disturbing to be offered this coast
For one's training as Messiah,
Albeit (as the careful programme says)
The faithful will be few and the heathen
Prominent – the change is quite important,
There is to be a seascape out of dreams
And a city founded where tears fell.

Congratulations have filtered down through fear:
It might have been finished, all the words
Laid on that coffin for the fire. Not that
Reports show any alteration yet – capering
Creatures dance undisturbed, the Natural Histories
Keep their gods. No, in this ministry
Expect to find insurance and small print,
Miracles being where a higher syntax reigns,
Masters of the dormitory of graves.

But, as in a chorus by Euripides,
We speak of other instances – the nightingale
Among the lines of village washing,
The idiot with his windmill arms –
These are a species of true fiction
Which cities burned for or a river turned –
Give them to Helen for her civic rape
Or a Baptist figure scrambling ashore
To be Athens, Florence and the cliffs of mind.

The world, not just a section of the bowel,
Is under new management. Call it
A time of hope, that will not be wrong,
But say of it that the sleeper finds
A daytime dream: strangeness persists,

271

As when hibiscus wavers on the path
And shows a face of love and several words
To mask it. Poets and warriors seek the supreme
But we have here the very quotidian.

The occasion for a sermon is at hand
(Other than love letters which speak
Into a mirror) – the place, a landscape
Under Winter Hill. I saw the river
A ribbon of death and the willows weeping
To the grass – now it's a bland decalogue,
Music for a while. Time ends amazingly
Among the notes, sinopia of Eden,
And worms are for forever in the Campo Santo.

This long way round, this garrulous hopefulness
Is how we veterans speak. Younger callings
Assume the pulpit, making love by harangue.
Our gospel (I must not call it mine)
Is to praise the seconds into minutes,
Making the minutes hours, and to let them all
Dance while the light lasts – trite under
Its poetry, hardly a philosophy,
But a change of programme in the blood.

I dedicate my years in the field to one
Body only, she of the catalytic eyes.
Whether Dionysus or some other hard man
Of the hills will lead us, we shall be
Caught up in the evening's enterprises.
As god of this place, my own savannas,
I praise her and I lead her forth
Into a published garden. She'll be silver
By mine and by the stars' true light.

ENGLISH SUBTITLES

English Subtitles

How much we need these annotations
When every frame prepared by the exacting eyes
Is a tableau from a famous series!
I can gaze from the eighth floor of the tower
Quite unconcernedly, but cannot avoid
Registering a fresco; then think of the intensity
When our looking is done within, the promontory
Of dreaming. It's all foreign languages,
Unfamiliar feelings, yet absolutely known
So that the craziest, most autonomous
Bulb-grower or Christmas fantasist
Is an unattainable part of the plot
Helping things make sense; or if rats
Coming ashore bring history with them
It will be hung round the necks of plants
In our well-cued crystal palaces.
And all the magazines I read,
Those articles which make me reach for
My spectacles spotting the word pluralism,
Their substance is our beautiful Northern tongue,
So useful for asking for fasteners in
As well as for caning professors:
I suppose my feeling foreign is just because
I have never got used to ambition
In my friends – how can they think it worthwhile
Dazzling and adoring so persistently,
Waking up to find themselves half-famous?
Although I feel I am becoming extinct,
A sort of adaptation to unloveableness,
I also have my calling, the quest for
Freedom wide enough to die in. Thus spake the words,
Just as I was swearing to abjure them all:
'Perhaps you should say something
A bit more interesting than what you mean.'
O bold deliverance! I can face my books

273

And the well-lit feast of journals,
I am anthropology itself. The used-up world
Becomes my kindly uncle: we are going
To that fascinating film which is always showing
To the cognoscenti. As we sit in the dark,
I turn the more uncomfortable passions
Into slim sentences, such old words
As I know you know. This is language
I would go into the jungle with,
English of the Rider Haggard sort
Reversed-out on the glare of consequence.

The Winter Capital

Sinking with distracted plumage now
Venus' doves decline towards the hospice
Of the West. The corrupted sea looks up
At keels furnished for eager roads
And tall economies. Blazon us
Upon the air, sigh defeated magistrates,
We should have stayed with princes
Among flat keys, a lengthy footage
Of worn wars and unimpressive foreheads.

Tread on the earth with the sweet
Misura of a perfect instep – it is not
Too late to be free of history:
Sisters of the quail in broad sun hats,
You have the Cart of Venus under you
And plural cities waiting. No one
May break the dance and changing partners
Is called love. Not just Winter
But the genius of the world has turned.

The Need for Foreplay

Is felt by these trees
accepting the wind along
their winter arms.

By dogs sniffing species
upon the thawing path
or stalled at fashionable ankles.

Even by the sun itself
greeting and then retreating
behind cloud for further teasing.

Earth with its motor defect
lurches suddenly to Spring,
over-explaining, under-achieving.

We are out early too,
unrepentantly interpreting
natural by learned responses.

Amazed sophistication
to love the mechanics of love,
go backwards into mystery.

My Old Cat Dances

He has conceived of a Republic of Mice
and a door through the fire,
parables of the reinstatement
of his balls. But not this night.
Isn't there a storm in the light bulb,
condors circling the kittens' meals
on the television screen?
He heard once that people wearied of
each other to escape unhappiness.
In his lovely sufficiency
he will string up endless garlands
for the moon's deaf guardians.
Moving one paw out and yawning,
he closes his eyes. Everywhere
people are in despair. And he is dancing.

275

Visiting Cornish Churches

Folded in lush combe
Or sentinelling the land,
The wide-naved churches stand,
Like platitudes of doom.

Lanteglos with Polruan,
Lansallos by Lantivet –
Paths of the stormy privet
Where leaves soundlessly are strewn –

Hoarders of forgotten saints,
Sites for moral doggerel,
Lit by the improbable
Gold of restorers' paints,

Sancturies of afternoon
When the sun lies in the wheat
And flower-arrangers meet
To make comfortable God's room.

Past Celtic Cross and over
Graves at a hundred angles,
Through grass and nettle tangles,
The tourist breaks from cover.

The air he breathes is clean
And roseate with death,
Pevsner-listed souls beneath
Share with pew and screen

Small absolutes of fame:
Nothing remarkable here
But men's and women's fear
Of losing even a name,

And when he comes to quiz it
No monument will keep
Him long. He hopes they sleep
The better for his visit.

How Important is Sex?

Not very. Even if it plays a not
Inconsiderable part in misery,
You can be unhappy without reference
To its intervention or its absence.

Our researchers have discovered even
Species whose reproductive processes
Are quite unsexual – and usually these
Are the more efficient and uncomplicated.

But, says the man waiting for a letter
And trying to read an article in a liberated
Magazine, I haven't been able to keep
My mind off sex since I was seven.

Others' minds go further back. Perhaps
Our evolution took the one track
(As the mind has it) into love and found
That those innovatory machines

The genitals, once in place, wouldn't
Be denied their significance. The sight
Of mummy's hair puts us on the spot,
A cave more mysterious than the mouth.

Now flow from it plays and operas
And the horrible spoutings of rancid
Kitchens: a world of novels awaits
The boy taught things by his jokey schoolmates.

But you are talking about love, you'll say.
Yes, and I know the difference,
Taking down a wank magazine,
Then a note more fingered than any photo.

Nevertheless, I am a respecter
Of power, having seen a skinny girl
Screaming in the playground, oblivious
Of boys, wake to her hormonal clock

As Juliana or as Mélisande –
Even the great gods and captains
Might relax with a plaything
As bold and changeable as this.

The American Articulate

The opening-up,
audacity of
thinking what terrifies
with its demands
on heroics,
on the here and now –

Could it be voices
filling a new demesne,
gossip in the stockade
till the spirits stop ringing,
chirp, chirp of species
soon to be extinct?

Novelist by day,
chucker-out in a brothel by night,
the stoicism of prose
and the garrulity,
paradigms
of the making of money.

Knowing it will spread,
that unconscious fondness
for being first,
until the grieved globe
shrinks to Tennessee –

Far from aristocrats
keeping ahead of taste,
their meringue of gods
and cavalry lieutenants,
ready to follow
a trail to
the other ocean,
the big one of loneliness.

She wouldn't come downstairs,
he walked to the office
as if it were Königsberg,
their talking done on paper.

And now the flowers appear
on the earth. Nobody can be heard
above the shouting land.
What would they say?
What could they leave unsaid?

A Philosopher of Captions

The knowledge anyway is worth something,
That no person from this liner-browed brain
Will reach the height of those grave captains
Whose Dantesque walk and Homeric facing
Still flare on our desolate concrete plain
So late; that I am a philosopher of captions.

This special authenticity must grow on one
After baffled if dutiful years putting down
Some orders of words towards definition –
Here space a fear and there placate a pun,
Or adjudicate through childhood, one noun
Up and another down, with everything a fiction.

And the shouters, the ones met at stations by crowds,
One can only admire them, join the acclamation
And worry at their simplifying stance. The text,
After all, belongs to its explainers; those clouds
Are felt only as rain; an acceleration
In the speed of madness, harder saving from the wreck.

But the power is still somewhere in us, hovering
In the forehead auditorium of sounds:
Those who were with us and have changed their shape
Come back, like old ladies with parcels moving
To the chair beside us; embarrassment abounds
That pain is the one immortal gift of our stewardship.

Occam's Razor

Never take the more unlikely explanation
of any event in preference to the likely –
just so, I say to myself, as I consider
my life and conclude that this long haul
to a sort of maturity is nothing more
than a persistence of arriving in someone
with nowhere to go, rather than, as I once thought,
an inveterate but soon to be vindicated
earnest restlessness at the port of life,
a magic resistance to time, enough to
keep me the youngest person in the room
as well as the most ironically serious.

But then reflect that if one is to tease
out feelings from razors, one might prefer
to think of Ibsen's madman sharpening himself
or, in grateful suddenness, Haydn offering
his English visitor that marvellous quartet
in F Minor – what the gods mean by words
goes the long way round or takes on flesh
in dreams for the far vistas of nicknames.

Returning

Nobody feels well after his fortieth birthday
But the convalescence is touched by glory
So that history's truculent deeds of hate
Are lived through in dreams, the story
Followed to the investigator's hut, pain seen
Through a window on its knees, late
Help lost over marram dunes or never
Felt at the deliverance on a screen.

Marvellous means of escaping time and time's
Chosen people: sleep on the knowledge of
God's monsters! The school of love and crimes
Is open every night and the sedentary
Heir of men of action dashes off
A sonnet before execution. What you see
Is coiled in an uneventful past, rough
Justice of the body's failures, a commentary.

Yet never daring enough, even those hours
When the timid rule of truth relents
And every written word is without sense
As in some ultimate avant-gardish shape –
The apostle of plain dullness has powers
Of arrest and will use them; nightmares
Are prized categories too, a southern rape
Modelled in blood but with a classic tense.

It is time to recompose the face
Into a serious map, the children now
Envied creatures across a room, the case
Being settled for the present. Home is
The veteran of the adjectival run,
His images intact. He has learned how
To live another day and wakes, ringed
By the golden wallpaper of the sun.

Good Ghost, Gaunt Ghost

She is coming towards me,
looking at me to turn me to stone,
saying my name and turning herself
into territories I know from books,
into the damned who are behind blinds,
the peaceful madmen of the parish.

She has walked through an invisible screen
into the fire of every change,
a certificate of final adaptability –
she will dress in a novel
and loiter, as is usual, in a dream,
but that is accountability.

Her clothes are syntax, so that I read
someone else's poem and I am there
on the banks of salvation
or crying in a furnace. Why has thou
held talent above my head
and let me see it, O my God?

Her shadow is rational, rationed of
tears and nocturnal commissions
saying the ego is always sublime,
the sublime always anticipatory,
and shadows our sisters under the skin:
each time we return to earth we die.

Words importing the masculine gender
include the feminine gender. Exactly,
and I see her as my hero-coward
who has dared to be myself, erasing
caution and suspicion. Soon I will be her
and we shall keep creation to ourselves.

Bei Einer Trauung

Off to the slaughterhouse
Of his or someone's imagination,
She has dipped in white
And orange blossom the tongue
Of her trust; a gambler
Raising the stakes, a cause
Of tension in the falling stockings
Of all old bags, she spools
Ordinary days from tangles
Of hope: whoever heard of
Liking at first sight?

O love, it must be love!
The face, careless of mirrors,
Will buzz about the house
Outraging cynic dust.
The organ hangs with glances
Which often raised her legs
In occasional beds,
But now she's comet-struck
By under-gods. Bury the father,
Snub the mother, club the lover.
Afternoon enters in its morning dress.

Sonata Form: The Australian Magpie

It makes a preliminary statement
with its head to one side and an eye
far too large to be seemly.

It is no relation to the English magpie
yet is decently black and white,
upstaging its cousin the currawong.

Its opening theme is predation.
What it scavenges is old cake
soaked in dew, but might be eyes.

Such alighting and strutting
across the mown grass of the Ladies' College!
Siege machines are rolling near.

Bustle in a baking tin,
a feast of burnt porridge –
the children are growing on their way to school.

You can upbraid the magpie,
saying, 'What do you know of Kant?'
It might shift a claw an inch or two.

It can tell when an overlord is unhappy.
When one sweeps out in tears to clatter
the petrol mower, magpie flies off.

But never flies far. Big feet
are moving to their place in dreams –
a little delay in the sun won't count.

We have certainly heard this theme before,
the sound of homecoming. Anticipation
needs a roof, plus a verandah for magpies.

Are these the cries of love or of magpies
sighting food? Some things about desire
call for explicit modern novels.

Magpie talk: Nation, National, Nationalist!
In this tongue its name is legion.
We speak English ourselves, with a glossary.

The coda, alas. It can be Brucknerian.
We say the end is coming. The magpie
has found its picture in an encyclopaedia.

Where can there be nature enough
to do without art? In despair, the poet
flies to the top of a camphor laurel.

Girl and magpie leave him in the tree.
Tomorrow a trip down the coast for her
and spaghetti rings left out for the bird.

All the Difference in the World

Between the sun beyond the window
and the black Latomia of despair
where her picture lives and where
sexual spasm jets into the ear of Dionysus.

Between those friends on the stairs
bringing wine and praises and the one voice
at midnight reminding me that reparations
are exacted of the talentless.

Between the memories of floral sheets
exuding the smell of us in bed
and the hospital ending in
a vapour of morphia and cocoa.

Between the Heavenly Philharmonic
and a sea raging at an inner port
whose veins spell death by pressure,
a stroke on the tympanum.

Between the arrival of letters,
neither long enough nor sufficiently tender,
and the platitudes of dreams
stalled on their evolutionary ladder.

Between wounds made by words
and the enduring silence of those
who can talk of love
only in the cadences of memory.

284

Between the soul as silkworm,
spinning out its time for a new house,
and the soul as a blackened Strozzi
churched in death and unawakenable.

Between poems which make litanies
of our being born and dying
and oracles which mislead us
about the differences between.

Myopia

It is to see things as God sees them,
up close, thread on thread,
but in the distance
an envious generality.

And not seeing what one doesn't want to see –
the contemporary leer and haircut
of the banjo player in the 'Shawm
and Sequence Band', a shadow
along the lip of someone axed
from memory by guilt,
a world which appears to have learned nothing.

Distortion by halation
as if we were afloat on music –
twenty/twenty vision is a myth
of the lost leader, the Emperor
asleep in the mountains.

And on to and up to death,
not believed in until
established by a unison of facts –
she has proved mortal
and you have observed an angel
in the cemetery rain.

Change your glasses
and you can't find the pavement
under your feet. Another change
and there are things in the prayerbook
will shock your pagan heart.

Making love and looking down
on a beautiful face,
the lips just pulling away
in absolute truth
from the apostolic teeth,
and know chillingly
there is no closer approach possible
than approximate ecstasy.

In seventy years one may learn to live
with defective vision. Take up art!
If your eyes meet Christ's eyes
they will never need to count
the limbs of the sleeping soldiers
in Piero's *Resurrection*.

Believing is not seeing
but a theology of doubt.
In dreams the exaggerations of language
become shapes and outlines
and at last the rower
thrusting the damned back into the sooty water
with his paddle is not just Charon
or the quacking guide a Virgil
nor yourself someone with a pen,
but all the creatures of a smalltime childhood
crowd to the boat and are classic
in the clearness, and of all greetings
none is so sharply sounded
from such known features
as the Mother's, out of sight of her son,
looking for the love which she was promised.

What I Have Written I Have Written

It is the little stone of unhappiness
which I keep with me. I had it as a child
and put it in a drawer. There came
a heap of paper to put beside it,
letters, poems, a brittle dust
of affection, sallowed by memory.

Aphorisms came. Not evil, but
the competition of two goods
brings you to the darkened room.
I gave the stone to a woman
and it glowed. I set my mind
to hydraulic work, lifting words
from their swamp. In the light from the stone
her face was bloated. When she died
the stone returned to me, a present
from reality. The two goods
were still contending. From wading pools
the children grew to darken
gardens with their shadows. Duty
is better than love, it suffers no betrayal.

Beginning again, I notice
I have less breath but the joining
is more golden. There is a long way to go,
among gardens and alarms,
after-dinner sleeps peopled by toads
and all the cries of childhood.
Someone comes to say my name
has been removed from the Honourable
Company of Scribes. Books in the room
turn their backs on me.

Old age will be the stone and me together.
I have become used to its weight
in my pocket and my brain.
To move it from lining to lining
like Beckett's tramp,
to modulate it to the major
or throw it at the public –
all is of no avail. But I'll add
to the songs of the stone. These words
I take from my religious instruction,
complete responsibility –
let them be entered in the record,
What I have written I have written.

The Killing Ground

Who comes in this disputed territory?
Just now the bored cat prowling
stops for a minute by the milk bowl
on the yellow, watching mat –
the kings of the earth rise up
and the rulers take breakfast together.
Our great men grant us equality,
they pardon us our lack of power
once they have considered
that we too die like them.

But this not yet. The air is lined
with demarcations of despair.
Each burly mote can tell
how she sat there at last breakfast,
night fumes in her dressing-gown,
and how she said the sun upon the square
was a massacre if only we would see
the bodies. Then the cats walked straight to her
with authority from the tomb,
debating exits with their excellent tails.

Ever since that day there have been parties
of chomping sightseers to show round:
we want to know our nation's starting point.
Such pharaonic air, kippered happiness
which makes the postcards curl –
nobody believes the screaming guest
who says he sees a coopered figure
still at home. This cursed spot
brings thunder to the calm keyboard.

Be welcome then you cats who pass unscathed
through danger. You see me come to greet
friendship with apologies, knowing
I have never shifted from the killing ground.

The Imperfection of the World

It was after the idea of perfection
that the idea of reconciliation came –
nothing could mollify the one
and a sense of homecoming
justified the other.

Yet I foresee a new quadrangle,
ivy covering glazed brick,
and a man standing on a grille
while his colleagues decide
whether to stone him.

Or, to look less far, someone
in an apron discovering that love
is not what she wanted from life
but the name of the discontent
she feels in herself.

That the dreams which the gods bring
in their plural jackets are to show us
our ends cannot be disputed,
nor is the shape we make bearable
entering silence.

Yet we are haunted by our memory
of perfection, of setting out among ferns
for our father, the birds of the air
moderating painful noon
with their clamant cries.

Not even regret may stay in Eden.
Bellini's melodies are spoiled
by scratches on a record's surface
and a baby wakes to light fleeing
the face of nothing.

'A bee is a device invented by a gene
to make more genes like itself.'
Therefore in the night when I cry
that I have been deserted, I am
once more made perfect.

The Future

It is always morning in the big room
but the inhabitants are very old.
Crooking her finger on a watering-can,
a precise figure of regret, no wisp
of her silver hair disturbed, drips succour
on a cat-predated plant. Words here
are shredded like its silver leaves,
they are epitomes of chanciness,
none will get you through the day.
When the sun fills the windows with its
misleading call to truth, the old woman
changes to a young girl, then to a man
from a novel looking up to ask
why things have gone so very wrong.
I am allowed, as if this were a dream,
to join them on their tableau.
We do not die, they say, but harden
into frescoes. This is what the future means,
her seeking me on her knees, poignant
as a phrase from a Victorian novel
or farewell spoken beyond a watercourse,
lyrical erotica I have no talent for –
Just the one room brightening, to which
hasten all the relatives of insecurity,
talking of my brief Bohemian days:
To be poised as the long-necked swan
or collared badger while the work
of worldliness is done, to stay the same
after the sun has gone, waiting merely
for light to show us up; the future
is to stand still with one gesture held,
a white glove entering a confluence.

The Story of Jason

As with all good stories, one cannot tell
If it is an allegory. If it is,
What should we do tomorrow,
In another week with a Thursday
To redeem our ordinariness or find

Some virtue to take the place of courage?
But it is a quest with pictures
And we can set a ship like a barque
Out of literature or an Adriatic liner
Somewhere in the immanent foreground,
A view of the Symplegades behind;
Caparisoned horses, gods and kings
And a great deal of that burning saffron
Which came in with the fifteenth century –
This will suffice to identify
Jason and help him steal the fleece.

But then the sadness of pictures hits us:
We are far into the twentieth century
And must sit in innocence
Admitting that hell is possible.
We see the hero setting out
From an impoverished quay, his
Companions smiling conquistadores.
What we need are stories. Regard this
Poem up to now as preparation.
A certain loquacity is natural,
Long and high visions have prevailed.
Someone is alighting on the mole
And asking for the magic gardens.
He seeks old age and academies,
Wife and amanuensis ready,
Twilight around him and a bell
Ringing in the Palazzo Vendramin.

Garden of Earthly Delights

It has its corner shops, no dogs allowed,
Its tireless, unenfranchised natives of Mauritius;
Here too are city beehives, well endowed
By walks of public flowers; it knows ambitious
Men with calm rosettes, ignorant of history,
Their world a new place to be conquered
Because they have arrived in it; the sea
Far off is sobbing with its cargoes, word
Made flesh in geodesic domes, lithe coils
Of dog turd smoking in autumnal streets.

Its many mad show dream-syntax rules.
Not to live in the real world and other defeats
Are topics for the kebab clique. The city regards itself
In terror as in harmony. I invented Man,
It says, I named him Ghibelline and Guelf
And let his blood dry on my open plan.
There were far worse terrors to be fleeing from –
Moonscapes of imagining, plains where faces
Cut diamonds, a mirror is a bomb,
Pelting pastoral of nomadic races.
Our bourgeois duty is to make gods,
Expensive ghosts to act for sex; our cranes
Outsoar the trees for flowering rods,
We publish Nature with the trails of planes.
This turmoil is to fund a sense of loss:
Look up the legs of the garden-sunning nymph,
An angel sleeping with sword across –
It is the city-building goddess on her plinth.
Into this concrete garden come rumours of streams,
Gothic forests unexplored, the dales of death.
Better to be here than be forced to dream
Back the delta world which gives us breath,
Fonder for humans to tell the upper globe
They will not be intimidated, though
They know their end, wires to each lobe
Fixed by God's technicians. Now go
Forward to the formal park, fanfares of
Hedges and the sparrow-eaved rotundas filled
With music. Pavilions of self-love
Adorn the grass: and here you must build.

Alcestis and the Poet

As the little blue-tongued lizard runs across
The floor and clambers on the cushions, so I
Have spent my life in your service. I have
Risen from beds of my own melancholy to grant
Your distress an audience, heard the chorus of self
Desert its lord to swell your tragedy. It wasn't
Self-effacement but a bonding-up of time. We
Start with bodies from our wounded parents, not knowing
That the early flesh is useless, that its greyness

Towards death is what we love in it. So,
As young Shakespearean gestures, we glow among our feelings
And are pointless. Then, as the shades of madness
Intervene, we become important. Voices singing German ask
'Watchman, what of the night?'; geniuses ever upward tell
Of willing death, of lining tombs for study, Chattertons
Who persist in books. The soft arrival counts. Now,
When the rake of afternoon has laid the shadows,
We are ready to do each other service. Can
I march tongue-tied to the end; will you
Find the inexplicable, the out-of-reach-of-art
Intensity you mourn for outside Hades? I took
Your place and watched the stories grow. But it
Was no more than giving up a good position
In the queue – we are all for darkness. Death
Is in the small print, as Stevie Smith showed,
Ringing the word in galleys on her final bed –
Thus the loving woman does her duty and is
Woven into legend. The king sits in his kitchen,
Not certain if the world knows of her sacrifice,
Though don't his cats despise him? Are you there
Where each new disappointment makes you think that life
Is geared to reparation? And this time who is
Hercules? The joy of giving up, of saying sweetly,
'It could never have worked – real love must be
Thrown away or it will burn us.' The rest
Is timing. On the moon, they say, we find
The things we've sacrificed, pristine and waxing. Such dreams
Are cheats. Sited in great art, but tearful still,
The creatures that we are make little gestures, then
Go to nothing. The wind urges the trees to sigh
For us: it is not a small thing to die,
But looking back I see only the disappointed man
Casting words upon the page. Was it for this
I stepped out upon the stairs of death obediently?

Addio Senza Rancor

'Such past and reticence!' – George Macbeth

Two girls in their last year at school,
in the back row since they are taller,
stay young in the autograph album
which has slipped into sight from among
the fallen contents of the bookcase. Here are
the ingredients of sorrow, forever renewing
itself by generations – one was to die
at forty-one and the other at forty-four.

Not young by the standards of the world's unfairness,
only by those of our spoiled corner of it.
Why do we go on manufacturing misery,
waking when it cries, cleaning it for school,
clapping at the prize giving? The new girls
are in their mothers' clothes and the new fathers
stripping for the shining theatre instruments –
Unhappiness lives on, depression dies early.

Friends and lovers, kept apart by photographs,
we have made so much life to give away,
our generous faces must outlast us!
The shadows of that richness look over
my shoulder as I pick up a postcard
with a bent pin through it. Earliest yellow leaves
are appearing on the plane trees in the square –
the playground of maturity shall bury them.

Two friends high on death – what can I say to you,
not having experienced the mystery
which choked you? Nothing of the ordinariness
which lives in words and pictures trained you
for such priesthood. You are nowhere
in the evening light: what I see instead
are two white presences, playing with life,
smiling and letting it go without reproach.

Talking to You Afterwards

Does my voice sound strange? I am sitting
On a flat-roofed beach house watching lorikeets
Flip among the scribble-gums and banksias.

When I sat here last I was writing my *Exequy*,
Yet your death seems hardly further off. The wards
Of the world have none of the authority of an end.

If I wish to speak to you I shouldn't use verse:
Instead, our quarrel-words, those blisters between
Silences in the kitchen – your plainly brave

Assertion that life is improperly poisoned where
It should be hale: love, choice, the lasting
Of pleasure in days composed of chosen company,

Or, candidly, shitty luck in the people we cling to.
Bad luck lasts. I have it now as I suppose I had it
All along. I can make words baroque but not here.

Last evening I saw from the top of Mount Tinbeerwah
(How you would have hated that name if you'd heard it)
A plain of lakes and clearances and blue-green rinses,

Which spoke to me of Rubens in the National Gallery
Or even Patinir. The eyes that see into Australia
Are, after all, European eyes, even those Nationalist

Firing slits, or the big mooey pools of subsidized
Painters. It's odd that my desire to talk to you
Should be so heart-rending in this gratuitous exile.

You believed in my talent – at least, that I had as much
As anyone of a commodity you thought puerile
Beside the pain of prose. We exchanged so few letters

Being together so much. We both knew Chekhov on marriage.
The unforgivable words are somewhere in a frozen space
Of limbo. I will swallow all of them in penance.

That's a grovel. Better to entertain your lover with sketches
And gossip in a letter and be ever-ripe for death.
You loved Carrington as you could never love yourself.

I think I am coming within earshot. Each night
I dream comic improvements on death – 'Still alive
In Catatonia', but that's no laughing matter!

Perhaps I had Australia in me and you thought
Its dreadful health was your appointed accuser –
The Adversary assumes strange shapes and accents.

And I know, squinting at a meat-eating bird
Attempting an approach to a tit-bit close to me,
That our predatoriness is shut down only by death,

And that there are no second chances in a universe
Which must get on with the business of living,
With only children for friends and memories of love.

But you are luckier than me, not having to shine
When you are called to the party of the world. The betrayals
Are garrulous and here comes death as talkative as ever.

The Werther Level

Then he must wear his suffering like a sailor-suit,
something his mother found at a jumble sale
when she was being careful about money
and spending even more of it than usual,
what I mean is you can't do anything about clothes
unless you've got style – that is
flair which goes with feeling this is your world,
it fits you and there is certainly a lot
to be grateful for among the origins of love,
the trays of satisfactions.
                                        I suggest that the mystery
is what is so daunting eventually. Over lunch,
an old friend tells you all the philosophies
or what they come down to, that another girl
will become available when this one's hysterics
have been outfaced, that you don't even look so bad,
in fact she'd go so far as to say that your body
at fifty is a better prospect than it was
in its tied-up, fitful twenties, and loneliness
is a sort of relief beside the obligatory togetherness

of parenthood – oh and so much more
and sincerely meant. But it won't work;
that rather well-dressed figure from the world's
most famous novel of self-pity hovers in sight,
so unlike today's casual narcissists, a pure
cavalier of auto-angst.
                    He has a message for you
which he puts with deliberate tactful insistence
as if through his speaking the pale certitude
of letter-writing in the great age could be reborn
and morning desks might once more
shine behind every window whose debates
consume the course of unkind love
as surely as the sun its own ascent.
'Do not think to escape responsibility
for living. Though the crime is not gazetted
punishment is palpable and that's the same
as law. Why have you never grown up,
grown out of that childish whimper brought back
from school, "it's so unfair." Try to think
of this flesh as clothing, not as envelope;
now we must do what is required of us,
write death into our Briefe, a discipline
of being garrulous for burghers. I light the lamp,
the room is dark in fits, as I sit to a piece
of paper white with wonderment. These
are the right clothes to welcome love in,
blood from a pistol wound or some trimming
from the newer Germany, a serious sight
among creatures light enough to miss the net of death.'

The Unlucky Christ

Wherever they put down roots
he will be there, the Master-Haunter
who is our sample and our
would-be deliverer. Argue this –
there were men before him,
as there were dreams before events,
as there is (or perhaps is not)
conservation of energy. So he
is out of time but once stopped here

297

in time. What I am thinking
may be blasphemy, that I
am like him, one who cannot
let go of unhappiness, who has
come closer to him through suffering
and loathes the idea. The ego now,
that must be like a ministry,
the sense of being chosen among men
to be acquainted with grief !
Why not celebrate instead
the wayside cactus which enriches
the air with a small pink flower,
a lovely gift to formalists?
Some people can take straight off
from everyday selfishness to
the mystical, but the vague shape
of the Professional Sorrower
seems to interpose when I try
such transport. The stone had to roll
and the cerements sit up
because he would have poisoned
the world. It has been almost possible
to get through this poem without writing
the word death. The smallest
of our horrors. When they saw him
again upon the road, at least they knew
that the task of misery would be
explained, the evangelical duty
properly underlined. Tell them
about bad luck, he said,
how people who get close to you
want to walk out on you,
tell them they may meet one person
even more shrouded than themselves.
Jesus's message at Pentecost
sounded as our news always does,
that there is eloquence and decency,
but as for happiness,
it is involuntary like hell.

Two for the Price of One

But the gift total is the gift in small
and before a structural horror of white paper
the maker finds a phrase which grows into
a power of everything. He cannot call back death,
he has licensed disappointment and regret,
his stay must be all imagination
and the working-out of time. Planes circling
the sky's rotunda may come down anywhere,
the Carmine frescoes crack before the eyes
of light machines. Magnificent and terrestrial things
are with the Spinners: some they leave in uncleaned
cupboards, some rise resistless like the sun.

*

That many of the Ark's denizens could not now report
to a new Deucalion is not the nastiest story.

Some living their lives in sulphuretted half-light
or slatted over shit might prefer extinction,

might watch enviously the passenger-pigeon
practise its lack of adaptation to the gun.

Survival can kill. Not just of cat and mouse and dog
but the million-faceted virus. Inventive Man

breeds a more economical red-meat quadruped
or white-fleshed avian source of protein

for his Nursing Homes, and hears above his hi-fi'd Bach
a cry from the drawing-board, the Unicorn's love laugh.

Lip Service

Game, set and match to the blubbering king.
What you do with lips is amazing
But you may prefer to eat, win points or sing.

They go over the side of the rubber raft,
All those losers, those words like *bereft*.
To come out of our warm books would be daft.

Heart Failure! The lower lip has whitened
With a blue pump-line like the back-end
Of our fattest silkworm. So rich, so frightened!

These mouth the rituals which we say the eyes
Are the home of, soul-cities. An old wheeze
Of the invisible, not to know truth from lies.

Two armies meet and recoil, they roll up their fronts
On a smile: gravestones wettened like fonts.
Fafner skulks here who was a giant once.

Thus the tongue which must tell the old old story
Of those who lie on each other long and warmly
Is betrayed and discovered. The chorus: 'Orrore! Orrore!'

Pope's Carnations Knew Him

But they knew they were on duty, replacing
the Rose of Sharon and the lilies of the field
for a gardener who never put a foot wrong.

It was their duty to rhyme in colour,
to repeat their reds and pinks and shield
the English rose with their Italianate chiming.

He had such a way with the symmetry
of petals, he could make a flower yield
an epic from its one-day siege. His rows

of blooms had their grotesques but they
took the place of music. They bowed, they kneeled,
they curtseyed, and so stood up for prosody.

No wonder Smart learned from their expansive
hearts that they loved the ordered, the well-heeled
and ornate, the little poet with the giant stride.

Each gossipy morning he sniffed their centres
and they saw him: the lines of paradise revealed.
God make gardeners better nomenclators.

Nights at the Opera

Sympathy for Scarpia

If she should have all the beauty, passion, honour,
Her lover the artistic temperament and courage,
Then why not Scarpia the will, the lust, the power –
All three are to get the crude justice of death.

Lucia in the Sky with Diamonds

Mad as she is, this girl
can't have the last word.
Her lover, equipped by the Scottish
Tourist Board, is going to bring
Italian opera into church. While she
encroaches on the constellations,
he extols a carnal love
or sepulchre of kisses wearing kilts.
The same contrivances evading death
honour a tone-deaf poet's end.

Waiting for Isolde

Love's wounds are transformation scenes.
The seagull over unarriving waters
swoops on the darkness of tumescence.
A relative named Amfortas elsewhere
moans in sympathy. If she never comes
he will grow old adoring Haydn.

How would you like to be called Wurm?

Villains are pillars of the ancien régime:
They have met innocence in a bad dream.

Papageno's Panti-hose

While Tamino learns philosophy
and how to play the trombone,
our good Viennese works to keep
his partner pregnant. Must it
come down to café society? Will

Papagena sympathize with all
Pamina's plaints? The opera
is forever fresh but the world
takes the waters out at Baden
and only half-reads letters.

If you can't join them, beat them

With that 'dumme knab' Siegfried around
Fafner had to be a sluggish dragon,
Wotan a quenchless ancient
and Brünnhilde in the Red Brigades.
Such things happen when fate comes between
two peerless lovers in their self-absorption –
the universe ends up a noisy joke.

O.K., Nerone

No opera ends less morally,
not even *Turandot*. The ruthlessness
of the young composer, which went with idealism,
now in old age becomes visionary:
only power lives on equal terms with beauty.

Audience at La Scala

Taught to suck from capitalist sores their venom,
Marxist First Nighters dress in well-cut denim.

Es sucht der Bruder seine Brüder

Faithful love has shown what it can do,
The syncopation gets more complex,
A cyclorama of celestial blue
Lifts our minds forever above sex.

About the New

Then this is the name
whispered in the street of horror,
(forgetting that we live just one time),
to try to bring to a point
the lines before your face at waking.

Yet it dirties the same paper
and cries out similarly
when oxygen is denied:
insipid over-achievers
worship it: it makes them profound.

There is Mr M
who has a spit problem,
grilling all writing but his own.
He has his generosity too,
he serves the cottage industry of words.

And think of the incomparable S,
putting away for Stratford,
for 'the dark house and the detested wife',
and afterwards through love
turning a sonnet into slippers.

A frivolous essay in aesthetics!
When they found themselves
in sordid cities where armless
pregnant girls begged for bread,
they cried 'Behold Neopolis!'

Do not confuse this with despair.
At any moment someone is born
wishing to forget everything
the world has ever known,
to found a university of starting.

I prefer the vision of Walter Pater
who didn't know much art
but looked at pictures to save them
from the scholars. God too
glances at our biros enthusiastically.

What an amazing thing, the confidence
of the world! It might be
'an accompaniment to a film scene',
'a systematically deployed semantic tic',
or just a dead sheep on the Downs.

Here at the end I must admit
that some things are definitely new
though undoubtedly made up
of bits of old things. To those in heaven
I shall say in greeting, 'Hello, you two.'

Which makes this a short essay
if rather a long poem by today's standards.
It took a few risks with syntax
but isn't innovatory. I expect to find
what's new beyond the encroaching fire.

About on the Serchio
for Ronald Ewart

Shelley's unfinished poem
must have been written near the mouth
on the flat dull stretch to Pisa.

Here, by the Devil's Bridge,
a glint on water is pollution,
though the heaped-up stones hide anglers
and hang-gliders float
impenitently down.

I am used to Tuscany
but not to the Garfagnana,
to the Beatles from a top piazza,
to SKYLAB and the high green figs.

There is no cure for the eye
and its pronouns
unless unhappiness be starved
like saints out of their country
of memory among the chestnut groves.

For Sophonisba Anguisciola

So much going for you,
a woman painter of the sixteenth century,
dying at ninety-seven
if the reference books are right,
and with such an elegantly
unpronounceable name.

It seems an attainment of grace
just to honour you and to forget
some undistinguished pictures,
almost as if the procession of geniuses
with their 'Triumphs of Time'
and their 'Feasts of the Gods'
passed right through the town
and out into the countryside
leaving you, me, my typewriter
and an honoured calling
to represent the human race.

Pienza Seen by Prudes

There is so much which poetry turns its back on,
The Rout of the Past, the you and you and you
For whom I don't exist, the crossing
Of these hills in our over-powerful car,
Up and down the fawn of Tuscany
To the Pope's town: clouds sail to worlds
Beyond us as we motor into visions
Harder than paint. Scattered by tyres,
Angels disperse to fresco-bearing trees.

The mind is made of Guide Books, factitious
Chapters of a biased history. Where local boy
Made good, things stay looking good, dust sheets
Over faction, and deracinated ankles
Swell on the way to Calvary. A little
Renaissance is put in the palm of hand
To keep the wonder venial. Today
Our poets are not fit to be provincial
Governors, nor will they fruit like olives.

The town has made a sculpture of the sky.
Pale prudes of their own blood approach
This vine-upholding vale looking for
Simplicities of everything too difficult.
Why, when the grandest of us little men
Is whisked away to Heaven, should survivors
Flounce to the parapet explaining things?
Sausages and wine are placed before us,
The wheel of work rolls past the perfect town.

At Lake Massaciuccoli

*'Ecco il lago Massaciuccoli
tanto ricco di cacciagione
quanto misero d'ispirazione'*
— d'Annunzio

A huge bombardment on the lake's long plain
As green worlds collide and skim above
The oily surface – visible to us only
As a dust of spume and green confetti
Where small frogs jack-knife on to lily-pads –
Tall rushes begin beyond the rotting jetty
And over their grave heads an oriental bridge
Leads nowhere. Toffee-coloured heat
Holds the outdoor café and the pampered villas,
A stain of rice-fields in the middle distance –
Indiscreet lemons lean across the road
To naturalise the noonday tide of cars:
Italy still fights its history
With engines. Where, though, I ask myself
Are the descendants of those ducks Puccini shot
With all the skill of a Ferrari engineer,
Where the ghost of that armed man wading
'To terrorize the palmipeds of his adoration?'
Boom. Boom. Fall of the executioner's axe,
The cancer surgeon's scalpel, the gong
Which announces that death's challenge
Has been taken up. Eighty cigarettes a day –
Pilgrims waiting at the gates observe
The lung-coloured lake. *L'homme armé*
Goes too far back and yet walled Lucca
Has a league of high composers no less

Pungent than Castruccio. Putting on his waders,
He might think of art, of facing the public
Armed with the visible part of dreams. Disappointment,
For all his calculation to a quaver's whisper,
Leaves him no resort but slaughtering ducks.
No one produces the art he wants to,
Everything that he makes is code,
To be read for its immaculate intention.
Then in death he finds the final disappointment,
That no clarity comes anywhere, the perfect
Vision has gone into the mist, as when dawn
Wakens the wet-winged skimmers on the lake
And every hazy lineament lures the hunter
Into a picture-postcard world. *O mors inevitabilis*,
Not to be held back by more than function,
A pot of Stephens' Blue Black Ink, a gale
All night among the pines and yet no air
Upon our planet – nothing so well observed
As pain, apotheosis of things out of place.
To return then after some small adultery
To the mystery of fiction; to write letters
To the world's four corners while mosquitoes
Shake like stage scrim across the door:
There must be a vision, perhaps of cruelty
In Venetian Peking (better at least
Than the sort of thing d'Annunzio would offer) –
It hardly matters, since the big tunes
Wait in the desk for him to pick them up
And a wife can keep one's view of sorrow fresh.
He should think himself most fortunate
Never having needed to be autobiographical.
At the lake's side, I too, maker of this
Near dramatic monologue, honour him truly
Yet could not bear an enlargement of
The world these frogs and teeming spawn inhabit.
He was not so soft: what he saw
Was this lake made into the world – not to be
Changed or pitied but crying through the night
Abandoning life for love. The dark will come
To every average denizen the same,
Sounds upon the shore staying for waftage.

The Unfortunate Isles

From the gunwale the dazzle is like spray,
yet past the low reefs and their morning surge
gloriettes of cacti wait, summer houses
flensed from trees, a palimpsest
of childhood books and hardihood
of castaways. An hour ashore
and you forget your face, a week later
your colonists are raising ghosts
of the great world. Can all these
have swum in from the wreck – dreamers
stung by lexicons, lackland dowsers
imposing on the dark, sorters of bird droppings
granting interviews by gravesides?
Open the dictionary of discontinuity
and read about these islands. 'Over the swell
of everyday begins that archipelago
where the irreligious may taste ecstasy.
This is at balanced armslength from
the Heroes' Home, and at any time a battlefield
is fulcrum. Follow your face here
among the scone-and-strawberry pantiles,
see a dream identity turn a corner,
aunts and uncles of the might-have-been
distributing their malaise. All currents swing
us to these shoals and as we pass
we note imagination is bureaucratized,
each island so characteristic of itself
we are no more than sorted as we float
like seeds to a soft imprisoning.
Here collects the melancholy
of deep coincidence, an airborne spored
unhappiness which centuries have used
to establish hallmarks. Europe, Asia,
lost Atlantis are hardly continents
seen beside the wreck of self – there stands
the Principality of Childhood reduced
to a crumpled letter, there a rain tank
rusting into canna flowers which marks
the courtliness of love. Nobody weeps here
for what he's lost, since everything is home.
Each is a creature calming himself

with more anxiety. The prevailing wind
blows memory in your face, and up the beach
the harmonies of death return to breed.'

Landscape with Orpheus

'Man lebt nur einmal, dies sei dir genug.'

It was as if the film had stuck, he was always
Back at the point where he moved up the latch
And stood facing down the street, aware of
The cicadas turning themselves on in both tall
And dumpy trees: what he saw was limited
But included lakes of dirt-in-asphalt
Before his feet, the unfortunate slug about
To cross the pavement with no more instinctive
Knowledge of its danger than he had of the sun
Perhaps on his neck, and of course always
The Dutchman's Pipe flowers he never failed
To notice, their purple mouthpieces like Disney
Saxophones, edible, sexual and howling for the dead.

It would take a lifetime to make it to the ferry,
A sunstroke's distance amid pavilioned leaves
And so desirable an ending. Well, there was a life
To spend and this was time, the softest element,
Like sap from poinsettia leaves, the milky pus
Of dreams – Eyes stood on tiptoes in those hedges,
So perhaps he should begin. It was late and it was early
In his sorrow and he had the world's tunes to play
And a landscape of peace and obsession there –
To see it all stretched out and hardly a step taken,
Such was the gift of time, walking down to the ferry
With love to come and snake-bite and the bitches flying
As calm as tapestry, in light-soaked Poussin shades.

Praise of his bloodstream flowed on then in sounds.
That this untrained imagination out of mercantile
Forebears should be Emperor of Cadences didn't surprise,
Don't we all know we are immaculate in our dress
Of self, and the twenty billion succinct souls
Hanging on God are just light in the distance
By which pilgrim feet find tracks to follow,

309

And that this fold of fact would undo and show
A hidden nothing if we blinked? The place of the ordinary
Is on the throne: save afternoons for judgement
And every morning for our table music. Could he have
Passed the big house with the haunted windows
And nipple-pointed fence, he had hardly moved?

But the stickiness underfoot was disquieting,
Perhaps the land was Avernus, with those
Bamboo raggednesses above the fence and the pale smell
Of warm tar on the air. Through fur of sugar-grass
He saw the river and all remote existence
Sculling across the darkened tide. What blew in his face
Were words, those he would speak in love and those
Which fattened on betrayal. The words for death
Were still unknown and yet he knew they sought him
On the street. A wind of big mothers mixing drinks
Caught him suddenly with laughter. What if he got
To the wharf, what if the ferry with a Lady's Name
Were there? He sang, in case, 'Goodnight, deceiving world!'

The cicadas stopped. Silence grew into a theatre
With everybody watching. According to the small print,
When love has failed to come you choose your end
By divination. Child or old man, now is the hour
And memory's prevarication cannot last.
With final breath whisper us your Eins, Zwei, Drei.
The sun in intervention breaks the sky,
The camera is rewound and there is the old latch,
The gate, the pepperina tree, the ferry rounding
Onions Point. The future must be crowded into now,
Paradise and hell on deck. Viewed through the telescope,
The Town Hall clock shows Orpheus looking back.

AFTER MARTIAL

I. xliii

What a host you are, Mancinus;
there we were, all sixty of us,
last night, decently invited guests
and this was the order of dishes
you pampered us with:
    NO late-gathered grapes
    NO apples sweet as honeycomb
    NO ponderous ripe pears lashed to the branch
    NO pomegranates the colour of blowing roses
    NO baskets of best Sassina cheese
    NO Picenian jars of olives

Only a miserable boar so small
a dwarf could have throttled it
one-handed. And nothing to follow,
no dessert, no sweet, no pudding, nothing . . .

    We were the spectres, this was the feast,
    a boar fit for the arena, duly
    masticated by us –

    I don't want to see you struggle
    in your turn for a share of the crackling –
    no, imitate instead
    that poor devil Charidemus
    who was shredded in the ring –
    rather than miser eats boar
    let's have boar eats miser:
    bon appétit, my host of nothings,
    I can almost feel the tushes in your throat.

I. lxxi

Here's a toast to the ladies –
six tiltings of the jug
to Laevia, seven for Justina,
five for Lycas, four Lyde
and three for Ida: one for
each letter of our mistress' names –
too bad the bitches never come,
so five up-endings of
Falernian more – that'll be enough
to call the girl who never fails,
warm-tailed and celerious sleep!

II. xvii

At the entrance to the dark Subura
    where you catch a glimpse of
the executioners' masterpieces,
    blood-stained bodies hanging
in their beaten racks; where many a cobbler
    knocks out the rhythms of the Potters'
Field – there, Ammianus, sits a famous
    female barber. I said a female barber
but she shears no heads – not for her
    the basin cut, the pudding crop.
What does she do, this female barber,
    if she doesn't clip into a dish?
And why do men flock to her? She won't
    carve or slice you but she'll plate you.

II. lii

Dasius, chucker-out
at the Turkish Baths,
is a shrewd assessor;
when he saw big-titted
Spatale coming, he decided
to charge her entry for three
persons. What did she do?
Paid with pride of course.

312

II. lix

Small and select, the restaurant called *The Mouthful*
    Overlooks Caesar's tomb and you may view
The sacred domes with garlic on your breath.
    Wine and dine there if you've got the pull,
See and be seen, for even as you chew,
    The God Augustus welcomes you to death.

II. lxx

Our fastidious friend Cotilus is not fond
    of the public baths. You've no idea,
my dear, who's been in before you,
    he says, and lets his face wrinkle up
at the prospect of unnamed pollution.
    I don't mind, if I can be sure
I'm the first, he admits, scraping
    a toe along the water's skin.
To make your prophylaxis certain, Cotilus,
    don't wade in, take a running dive
and get your head under before your prick.

II. lxxxvi

Because I don't attempt those modern poems
like lost papyri or Black Mountain Lyrics
stuffed with Court House Records, *non sequiturs*,
and advice on fishing; and since my lines
don't pun with mild obscenities in
the *Sunday Times*; nor yet ape Ezra's men
in spavined epics of the Scythian Marsh,
The Florentine Banking Scene, or hip-baths
in Northumberland; nor am I well-fledged
in the East European Translation Market,
whose bloody fables tickle liberal tongues;
despite this I make my claim to be a poet.
I'm even serious – you don't ask a runner
to try the high-jump, and if my trade is words
I'd be a misfit in the People Show.

From Liverpool to San Francisco, poets
are tuning to the Underground, a pop-
ulous place where laurels pale. My pleasure
is to please myself and if the Muses listen
I may find an ear or two to echo in.

III. xi & III. viii

I was silly enough to use your name
    in a recent epigram, Quintus,
and I spoke of your Thais (perhaps as
    a change from Lais) – after all,
I could have chosen Hermione or any
    other name. To make amends,
I've revised the epigram: Book 3, No. 8:
    'Sextus loves Hermione.' 'Which Hermione?'
'Hermione, the one-eyed.' 'Hermione lacks
    one eye, but Sextus both!' Now the names
are changed, you won't see any similarities.
    Didn't a satirist say that satire
is a sort of glass, wherein beholders do
    generally discover everybody's face
but their own? Names are another matter!

III. xii

At dinner yesterday the smell was heaven
As we sat down to dine at seven;
Fabullus, our host, splashed the place with perfume,
More like a boudoir than a dining room,
But when it came to time to carve
He just sniffed the air and let us starve.
Fabullus, I said, please mind my seat,
I'm off to buy a winding sheet –
To be anointed but unable to ingest
Is the fate of a corpse, not of a guest.

314

III. xxii

Twice thirty million sesterces spent
In the service of his famous stomach
Apicius followed where his money went
Under a wide and grassy hummock.

He'd counted his wealth and found there were
Ten million left. Mere hunger and thirst!
Soon life would be more than he could bear
So he drank a beaker of poison first.

Romans are noble in everything – yes,
Even Apicius, the notorious glutton.
He died for his principles – to eat the best
And deny the very existence of mutton.

III. xxxv

Instant Fish
by Phidias!
Add water
and they swim.

IV. xviii

Near the Vipsanian columns where the aqueduct
    drips down the side of its dark arch,
the stone is a green and pulsing velvet
    and the air is powdered with sweat
from the invisible faucet: there winter
    shaped a dagger of ice, waited till
a boy looked up at the quondam stalactites,
    threw it like a gimlet through his throat
and as in a murder in a paperback the clever
    weapon melted away in its own hole. Where
have blood and water flowed before from one wound?
    The story is trivial and the instance holy –
what portion of power has violent fortune
    ever surrendered, what degraded circumstance
will she refuse? Death is everywhere
    if water, the life-giving element,
will descend to cutting throats.

IV. xxi

'The skies are empty
     and the gods are dead',
says Segius, the proof of which
is that he sees himself made rich.

IV. xliv

Hear the testament of death:
yesterday beneath Vesuvius' side
the grape ripened in green shade,
the dripping vats with their viny tide
squatted on hill turf: Bacchus
loved this land more than fertile Nysa:
here the satyrs ran, this was Venus' home,
sweeter to her than Lacaedemon
or the rocks of foam-framed Cyprus.
One city now in ashes the great name
of Hercules once blessed, one other
to the salty sea was manacled.
All is cold silver, all fused in death
murdered by the fire of Heaven. Even
the Gods repent this faculty,
that power of death which may not be recalled.

IV. xlix

Believe me, Flaccus, the epigram is more
than just a cracker-motto or an inch
of frivolous joking to fill up a column.
Really, he's more frivolous who thinks poetry
demands portentousness, that some subjects
are proper to the Muse and others aren't.
It depends, my friend, which Muse you honour –
you won't get all the usual stuff from me:
Tereus the Terrible eating filial pie,
Thyestes choking over knucklebone soup,
Daedalus fitting out his son with Wool-
worth wings, nor those old scenes from the Odyssey,

especially Brobdingnagian Polyphemus
and his silly sheep. Some call this grandeur
and some tradition; I think it's merely *wind*.
It's tragic only that the Tragic Muse
has to put up with such stilted nonsense.
'What's that you say, everybody likes it,
buys it, praises it. That's what poetry's about,
solemn Horror Stories from the Ancient Greek.'
No doubt, but don't set store by what men praise
nor what they proudly put upon their shelves –
surprise them reading, it'll be something
true and scabrous from my kind of book.

V. x

As you know, Regulus, men are pharisaical,
They're always whoring after the classical;
They read but never praise our living writers
(Though the classics hit them like St Vitus).
For them the time's always out of joint
And the past, being past, can't disappoint.
How they claim they miss those shady halls
Of Pompey's; or despite the balls-
Up Catulus made of the restoration
Of Jupiter's temple for a grateful nation,
How the fogies praise it because it was done
Back sometime around the year One;
Remember what Rome read in Virgil's time,
Old Ennius and the primitive sublime;
Go further down in the collective past,
Who thought Homer was going to last
And in that fashionable sump, the theatre,
Who fancied Menander a world beater?
Recall, if you can without apoplexy,
The lifetime of Ovid, so smooth and sexy,
The greatest Roman stylist only read
By Corinna, his mistress, and then in bed.
Such Injustice! but hang on a second,
Is that Fame, that creature that beckoned,
With slatted sides and a charnel breath
And a club badge saying *Kiss Me Death*?

Then wait a while, my books, I'll stay
Alive and unknown another day —
If I can't be famous till I'm dead
I'm in no great hurry to be read.

V. xviii

Comes December and the giving season, when
every shop is stocked with gadgets — hand-
kerchiefs with Aunts' initials, silly spoons
to lock away forever, candles sculptured
like ten castles, personalized mauve paper
with embossed addresses, and amazing plums
that only Fortnum's would import; why have I
sent nothing better than my own new poems
(home-made nourishment indeed) — am I
self-satisfied or merely stingy? My thoughts
aren't pendulums to swing back all my way —
Great gifts are guiles and look for gifts again;
My trifles come as treasures from my mind.
I quote. To catch the greedy bream you cast
the glittering fly. Which of us hasn't ex-
pectations of his benefactors as
his gods? In truth, the poor man, Quintianus,
is generous to his well-heeled friend when he
looks him out a keepsake, writes a card,
and leaves him off his Christmas Shopping List!

V. xxxiv

To you, the shades of my begetters, Fronto
and Flaccilla, where you lie in sweet
decay, I commend with love the body
of my darling child Erotion.
                              A home-
bred slave yet tender as a golden dormouse,
rarer than the Phoenix, whiter than
an unsmudged lily —
                        guide her spirit home
so she may look for lights in Tartarus

and miss the snapping jaws of hell-hound
Cerberus. She'd have lived six shivering winters
if she hadn't died that many days before
the anniversary.
                    Now let her play
light-heartedly in the ever-darkened house
beside such sure protectors.
                              May my name
be burbling on her tongue, the childish gift
of sorrow spent on age.
                        And monumental earth,
draw back eternal weight from her
small bones;
             don't be severe and tread
on her with gravity: she never did on you.

V. lviii

Tomorrow is the time to live; tomorrow
    the tide will turn, says Postumus,
the golden days begin. Where's that tomorrow,
    Postumus, when will it arrive?
When it comes, won't it come as today,
    or is it hidden and must we search for it?
Perhaps the Parthians and Armenians
    have it locked in a sacred Ark;
maybe it's already as old as Priam
    or Nestor, and we'll meet it
coming round the other way. Perhaps it can
    be bought; how much then will it cost?
Tomorrow you will live, is that your
    firm intention? To live today
is already too late: *living*, Postumus,
    is what the wise man did yesterday.

VI. xix

I've got the best counsel in the land,
the trouble is I'm not on a States Secrets Case
but in a civil action over three nanny-goats
stolen by my neighbour, and the judge

319

has already ruled the case is proven!
Yet my barrister's in full cry; he's
already modulated to the Punic Wars,
the massacre at Cannae, Mithridates
and the poison cup, the Age of Sulla
and Mariuses and Muciuses various
as sea shells. Stop a minute please,
just mention *once* my three nanny-goats!

VI. xxiii

Send your husbands to me, wives, says Lesbia,
    I'll recharge their batteries,
And addresses me jokingly, 'Eveready'.
    Really, Lesbia, it's a disease
With you. One's prick isn't an opera singer
    Following the conductor's finger.

You're willing, I must admit, to play your part;
    What hand may do and lip
Is sweetened with the most unusual words
    But it's just bad generalship
To boast our fight will make the bedsprings rattle
    When your face has already lost the battle.

VI. xxvi

Sotades' head is in the noose.
How come? Who would accuse
so upright and so straight a man?
He's under a different sort of ban –
a pity a chap who's so well-hung
has to rely upon his tongue.

It's good to have a quiver-full of kids, Cinna,
        even these days –
    to hell with the population explosion,
    your little woman's done a great job.
        There's just one matter I'd mention,
        none of them is yours!
Nor your neighbours', nor your friend's,
nor the Elks', nor the Buffaloes', nor the Rotarians',
nor even an overnight hippy's in the sleep-out!
        You can tell this lot were mapped
        on unmade morning beds or sliding mats.
        Here's one with steel-wool hair;
        a gift from Santra the Cook;
        that other with the joke-shop lips
    and nostrils like cut-up avocadoes
is the spitting image of Pannichus the Wrestler
    (I'll bet he was never late for rehearsals);
    If you've ever seen Dama, the Baker's Son,
the original idle apprentice, knobbly, cataracted,
        with the expression of a frozen cod,
then you'll recognize your own third son;
        Number Four's the worst –
    his forehead slopes like a loading chute,
his face is as white as a maggot, he's from an unlikely
        source – your bed-mate Lygdus – so you can
        use him the way you do his father,
        it's a hallowed practice!
    Consider the one with the coconut head
and ears lie Eeyore, he's a perfect Identikit
of Cyrta the Cretin: two daughters, one dark,
one red-headed, you owe to Crotus the musician,
(some Ball he fluted at!) and Carpus the Bailiff
(it took him quite a time to deliver his injunction!).
        If it weren't that
        your other two servants, Coresus, and Dindymus,
        are eunuchs,
you'd be the Niobe of the Age. That's good luck, anyway,
Cinna. The gods won't punish, they'll only pity you.

VI. xl

Lycóris darling, once I burned for you.
Today Glýcera heats me like a stew.
She's what you were then but are not now –
a change of name requires no change of vow.

VI. xlvii

In sickness the world has double purity;
with death so close a cold transparency
descends upon the skin of life; the stream
that snakes as quickly as a dream
beneath the house of Stella and concurs
with jewelled halls and chalcedony doors,
this is no local freshet, for it springs
from Aricia, sipping place of kings;
solemn Egeria set it flowing, Numa
was often there when troubled by a tumour,
Diana of the Crossways' Water-Course,
sacred to the Ninth Italian Muse.
So, pale-boned nymph, your Marcus here complies
with his sickness-vow to offer sacrifice –
a sucking pig that sniffs your garden borders –
I drank your water against doctor's orders
and I'm much better: pardon me my fault,
may dam or upland never give you halt,
instead your crystal waters always slake
my living thirst. The world is warm, opaque,
but death sees through, so one transparent slave
begs of his nymph her light and curing wave –
I watch the crust of earth returning to
its salutary self and drink to you!

VI. xlix

I am not made of fragile elm
and though I wear a fluted helm
I always stand with rigid shaft
however deep or fierce the draught!

My sappy life is given dress
in carvings of long-lived cypress –
a thousand days within my sight
are one tired moon and one bright night,
and like the rose that roots in clay
I live to shoot another day.
Then all who come here out of bounds,
be warned that these are sacred grounds,
just lay a hand on plant or house
and I who guard as well as rouse
will punish the offender where
my kingdom stops by half a hair.
Take note, I am Priapus who
engenders love and virtue too;
my punishments in clusters come,
I plant ripe figs inside your bum
and every thief who jail avoids
shall bear my crop of haemorrhoids.

VI. lxvi

Black, I'll grant you the times we live in. Here's an example,
not even the Government Market where the slaves of nubile years
are auctioned off at a rattle is free of the huckster's ginger:
it's Gellienus I'm speaking of, the People's Auctioneer;
he had a girl whom most knew was not of wholesome savour,
a sort of famished Bunny, too often topped and tailed, but
still a bit of a sizzler, sitting demure and cross-legged
in the heat of the Subura. The bidding was going slowly,
too slowly for his comfort, and though the girl looked decent,
Gellienus fancied the customers might be proving reluctant
for fear she was clapped or dirty, so like the Jew in the story,
he grabbed her and kissed her with more than an uncle's slobber,
this bit, that bit, a veritable ordnance survey –
'By God, I've been all over', he shouted to the bidders,
'She's as sound as the National Grid.' Disgusting, of course,
but she had to put up with it, all in the way of business.
These auctioneers! But this was a case of the biter bitten
(or the kisser clipped), all he achieved by the pawing
was a bidder of six hundred sesterces immediately
withdrew his bid. Be warned, you impudent tricksters,
sometimes the proof of the pudding isn't in the eating!

VII. xvii

How bucolic a bibliothèque
where the charmed reader looks out
over raspberry canes
on the encroaching city! If
in these rural stacks there's room
among the heavyweight authors
for the sort of poem which delights
sophisticated Thalia (say a shelf
between the national epics
and the medical encyclopaedias),
then receive these seven modest
books, with the author's latest
emendations (these alone
will enable your heirs to sell them
to a North African University) –
take them, friendly space of
truth and learning, and guard
them well, for by these inconsequential
gifts the world will come
to honour the country library
of Julius Martialis, man
of taste and friend to genius.

VII. xix

This fragment of mere driftwood is holy:
it's part of the first keel to slice
through undiscovered waters. What the sliding doors
of Bosphorus could not crack nor the inky
storms of that Black and well-named sea
subdue lies in the hands of time.
You are worth more to me, piece of wood,
than a ship at anchor. The sea worm
has pitted you, but you have been beyond
the world's edge and yet come home to me.

VIII. xxix

To I.H.

The short poem signals
much suffering suppressed –
like the German Fleet at Scapa Flow,
only the flying pennants show!

Such terseness shames all us
chapter-and-versifiers –
but what's the point, since Fabers took
enough to make another book?

VIII. lxviii

You are king of gentleman-farmers, Entellus,
 Alcinous's orchards pale by yours;
you have destroyed the very Seasons. Your grapes
 sway through brutal Winter in
corybantic clusters: you hold Bacchus himself
 under glass as an ant in amber –
a woman's limbs are outlined thus in silk,
 so shines a sunken pebble in a stream –
you have bent Nature itself to your mind,
 my Lord of Greenhouses, yet I fear
that, when it comes to factory-farming, death
 has the best of ever-bearing crops.

IX. xxxiii

Outside the Baths you hear applause –
Flaccus, you know the likely cause.
Connoisseurs love fine workmanship,
Maron has let his towel slip.

IX. liv

If I had hillside olives to fatten fieldfares
    or Sabine woods strung with gins
to cruelly carry hot bodies from the sky
    or could conduct like lightning
small morsels down on a stick, to walk
    grand garnerer of their flutterings,
crop on crop in my meadows of death:
    then I would send you these in token
of love, that you might bite their flesh
    as it were mine. Alas, my fields are asphalt
and listen only to the songs of starlings,
    the fidgeting of finches. The green
of tapered hedges hides the shrill sparrow,
    here the magpie suffers an air-change
to death's bird, while the banished kite
    haunts open fields, the only free man
in a heritage of dependence. Instead,
    I offer you the imagination of birds
whose hard eye drops on the brown earth
    without pardon: come to the start
of the world, we will deal with things cruelly
    as we have love and an inclination to.

X. xlvi

Matho wants all he says thought smart.
I gave him these hints for a start.

Sometimes to shock them, say what's good.
It won't be easily understood.

Then say what seems an in-between.
They'll wonder what you really mean.

Now say the bad, your gamut's run.
They want a talker and you're one.

X. xlvii

Friend and namesake, genial Martial, life's
happier when you know what happiness is:
money inherited, with no need to work,
property run by experts (yours or your wife's),
Town House properly kitchened and no bus-
iness worries, family watchdogs, legal quirks.
Hardly ever required to wear a suit,
mind relaxed and body exercised
(nothing done that's just seen to be done),
candour matched by tact; friends by repute
won and all guests good-natured – wise
leavers and warm stayers like the sun;
food that isn't smart or finicky,
not too often drunk or shaking off
dolorous dreams; your appetite for sex
moderate but inventive, nights like sea-
scapes under moonlight, never rough;
don't scare yourself with formulae, like x
equals nought, the schizophrenic quest!
What else is there? Well, two points at least –
wishing change wastes both time and breath,
life's unfair and nothing's for the best,
but having started finish off the feast –
neither dread your last day, nor long for death.

X. lxvi

It's a piece of Theophrastian cheek
        assigning my Theopompos to
the kitchen seven days a week –
        to lean that face above the stew
which launched a thousand kisses is
        as wasteful as the Trojan War –
those sumptuous curls all scorched and frizzed –
        the gods are pushing things too far!
I fancy you in see-through shirt
        sorting a vintage from the rack;
you simper, 'Under all this dirt
        (the poor thing's been upon its back)

lurks a Falernian True Blue,
    just have a sip and be convinced.'
I'd make a Ganymede of you,
    no mere Custodian of Mince,
we'd romp on the Cytherean shore!
    But, frightful thought, what if instead
my instinct's wrong and my little whore
    from the kitchen prove a cook in bed?

XI. xxx

It's just pathetic fallacy, says Doctor Zoilus,
that the most practised liars, lawyers and poets,
should so frequently have bad breath.

Nerves affect us all, old chap, they play hell
with our digestion, and who is more
open to taint than a veteran cocksucker?

XI. xlvii

Why does Lattara keep away from the Baths
where all the pretty women congregate?

So he won't be tempted to fuck them!

Why won't he go where all the high class tarts are –
outside Pompey's Porch or the Temple of Isis?

So he won't be tempted to fuck them!

Why does he cover himself with yellow linament
like an athlete and take cold baths apart from the girls?

So he won't be tempted to fuck them!

Why, when he appears to avoid the whole generation
of women like the plague, is he a known licker of cunts!

So he won't be tempted to fuck them!

XI. xcix

Yours is a classic dilemma, Lesbia;
whenever you get up from your chair
your clothes treat you most indecently.
Tugging and talking, with right hand and left
you try to free the yards of cloth swept
up your fundament. Tears and groans
are raised to Heaven as the imperilled
threads are pulled to safety from
those deadly straits: the huge Symplegades
of your buttocks grip all that pass.
What should you do to avoid such
terrible embarrassment? Ask Uncle Val –
don't get up girl, and don't sit down!

XI. civ

You're my wife and you must fit my ways
Or leave the house: I don't keep fastdays,
Nor do I care how Tatius, Curius, Numa
Acted – founding fathers and consumer
Research heroes don't make me repent –
Sex is sex whichever way it's bent!
I prefer it served up elegantly:
A bladder full of wine's no enemy
To what we want to do (if it lies longer
At the point it makes the pleasure stronger),
But keep to water as you always choose,
Not caring to make love on top of booze,
And see what happens – half-way through your stint
You feel the urge, you disengage and sprint
To the loo, sad-eyed water-spiller, and then
You're back berating the appetites of men.
Another thing, I set no limit to
Love's duration: if before I'm through
Daylight's screaming in the floral pane
I say it's night-time still, so once again!
What's night to you? No night is dark enough
To get a head of steam up, no rough stuff
Keeps away the dragomans of sleep
Nor touch upon your haunches gets love's bleep!

It's bad enough, god knows, that you're inclined
To go to bed at half-past-bloody-nine
In opaque winceyette and cummerbund –
I like a girl that's naked, with her sun
Blazing its circuit for my solar lips
Or playing lost in space to fingertips;
For kissing I make doves my paradigm,
Beak to beak to dribble out the time;
Your sort of kissing is a woolly smother
Offered at breakfast to your old grandmother
And nothing will persuade you, neither words
Nor noises like those Kama Sutra birds,
To use a hand upon my other altar
Or try that *reservatus* style from Malta.
Consider the tradition of the service:
Andromache rode Hector like a war horse
While posted at the bedroom door the Phrygian
Slaves were masturbating (that's religion
For you), and in legendary days,
When heroes lived on earth and not in plays,
On Ithaca the while the Master slept
Penelope's well-instructed fingers kept
Their own appointment. You say that your arsehole
Is not for use, though good Cornelia, soul
Of Rome and glory of our past, reversed
Herself to Gracchus, Julia reimbursed
Her Pompey at the northern postern, and
Brutus's Portia served him contraband,
While long before the gods had Ganymede
To mix their drinks, proud Juno had agreed
To play the pretty boy to Jupiter –
Then why can't I with you, if Him with Her?
The gods and heroes gave all sex its due
But only abstinence will do for you:
I tolerate Lucretia by daylight
But I want Lais in my bed at night.

XII. xvi

Labienus sells three smallholdings
and buys three houseboys –
Labienus still has three smallholdings.

330

XII. xvii

Here comes Dives, full tilt from the quack,
  hot as curry but won't keep his bed.
He thinks he'd miss something on his back,
  won't trust doctors, treats himself instead.

'Health, friend, what a gift! Listen to my groans,
  each a pedal note of pain. Fever pulls
the stops out – breathing booms in 8ft tone.
  I let the experts fossick in my stools.

I get into my litter, leave the fever up
  with the carriers, still it hots my face.
It dines on mushrooms, loves to sup
  on oysters from Ostia (that little race

of varicose bi-valves which seem to slip
  past your uvula like silk); it dotes on sow's paps
(see Apicius, his tour-de-force), it will sip
  my Setine while I'm measuring up the laps

of dinner guests, it gulps Falernian
  but refuses Caecuban unless
strained through snow water, gentian-
  tinted. Siesta-sung-to or moon-witnessed

by a serenade, wrapped in roses,
  quilted dark with balsam, stretched out
at banquets breathing what patrician noses
  have expelled, darkened under gout

on purple bedding, simmering its sleep,
  each duck's feather like a fluke of lead,
my fever will not leave me, I must keep
  an omen reader, pools of leeches to be bled

by, Galen's textbooks, a hair of death
  to change the shape of living. O friend,
Sickness is ungrateful, I give it breath
  but still it chases me to worms' end.'

My sympathy, poor Dives, I said, but since
   your fever lives so comfortably,
is so well-off, how could you convince
   it to migrate? Over what black sea

should it fly if used to breath of musk?
   Can wine-washed pain fraternize with pus?
Would you have it root in bins, chew husks
   or make a home of sores with Lazarus?

XII. xviii

Friend to friend, though from so far away,
greetings and happiness dear Juvenal
(malice aforethought, because we need
sharp natural spurs to our communication,
this prognostication), you're likely
at this moment to be tramping round
that speculator's mile, the loud Subura,
where Empire ticks are sucking blood (called rental)
from families and young provincials slink
home at evening clutching half a kipper;
or perhaps feeling the gravel of Diana's
hill under your thin-soled sandals; or then
fording the thresholds of the newly great,
aware of the sweaty draughts convected by
your toga – the big and little Caelian,
the sixpenny rides to newly elevated
broiler kings brooding on Palatine
penthouses: think of me and how you laughed
when I set off for Spain. I'm all right,
I'm a big frog in Bilbilis: many Decembers
spent in Rome find me back among
these unsophisticated craftsmen
of the heights, kneaders of gold and iron,
great auricular nomens if unable
to do much with the subjunctive. I'm lazy
here, a toff, I raise a spade just
to let it fall (the Government stroke we say);
I make friends in Boterdus and Platea
(I give you two whole pentameters
to laugh at these our Celtiberian names).

When I go to sleep, it's not just pausing,
getting back my strength to tackle tough-guy
patrons and insurgent tradesmen, it's real
long, self indulgent dreaming: huge un-
conscionable sleeps which even ten
o'clock can't founder. It's my post-war credit
for everything that Rome did; when I hear
some simple corporal at our feeble barracks
playing the Last Post on a wooden bugle
I think of all those stupid pushers listening
to bucinas in the Forum, girls on heat
and clever dicks from Thessaly touching
them up, wiping thumbs on blazers.
They can have it. I don't even have
a toga. If Aunt Lucy turns up at the door
with a basket full of cucumbers and lettuce
come to be useful at a lying-in,
I snatch a yard of ticking from the chair,
wrap it round me and play Jugurtha
or Caractacus upright at a Triumph.
They can't tell the difference, so why bother,
it's the man that makes the toga. Here they spend
hours just helping you, they really care
if you can stand the smell of oakwood smoke,
the savour of mosquito repellents.
My bailiff's wife crowns the dying fire
with my breakfast pot; I see her do it
opening half an eye to let the violet
air in, streaming from the upland plain.
My huntsman follows her, such a youth
as would set a dozen pens free-wheeling
in your bugger's land – one of our sycophants
would have him even if it cost as much
as an actor's villa in oiliest Misenum.
This man would be charmed if I
ventured as far as half-way to his rump;
in a grove of holy pines near Rome meeting him
you'd spend every waiting minute tearing
at your nails, and if he didn't come you'd
make from this fermata half a dozen
sub-Horatian odes. Here he's mine and so
I choose to close him only with my eyes.
He feeds my slaves, gathers up my acorns,
carries from snow-swollen Salo

all my washing water and then asks me
whether he should crop his hair. Here Juvenal
we see the seasons swing as never saw
Romans where the Tiber carries bodies:
this is how I live, friend, this is how
I love to live and am prepared to die.

XII. xxxi

This phalanx of pines, these demi-fountains,
this subtle pleaching, this irrigation system
ductile as a vein (water meadows under mountains),
and my twice-blooming roses richer than Paestum's,
the rare herb-garden – even in January, green –
my tame eel that snakes about its pond,
white dovecote outshone by its birds – I've been
a long time coming home and you, my fond
benefactress, dear Marcella, gave all this
to me. A miniature kingdom to do
with as I please. If Nausicaa with a kiss
should offer me her Father's gardens, you
need not worry: to everything that's grown
I give one answer, *I prefer my own.*

XII. xxxiv

I've counted it up and it's thirty-four years
since our friendship began, old comrade Julius!
The sweet and the bitter came swanning together
but pleasure prevailed. If we took from God's bottle
the pebbles dropped in for each day we've been friends,
the black and the white in two piles neatly sorted,
the white would outnumber the black five times over.
It wasn't perfection. To escape all unpleasantness,
all quarrels and heartbreak – have no one for friend,
be a dusty recluse who can sniff out a motive,
a *tabula rasa* no trust ever wrote on!
You wouldn't be let down as I must unwittingly
have let you down often, you wouldn't get fed up
nor bored stiff nor borrowed from. But what of those years when

the heart leaves its harbour and there's no warmth
in any acquaintance? What comfort can caution bring,
what words for despair? Only past happiness fans into fire,
only old friendship will solace old sorrow.

XII. lxxxv

Orthodox to the last, Fabullus,
you make a moral metaphor
to play up your virility:
*The flavour of sodomy comes out
the other end as halitosis.*

This has a heterodox side,
what do you say to another aphorism
for your medical table talk?
*The uxorious man doesn't get his fishy
smell from licking postage stamps.*

XIV. xxxix
A Bedside Light

I show but do not countenance what you do.
Douse me. The only record is in you.